Aviation

The Hulton Getty Picture Collection

Aviation

The Early Years

Die Anfänge der Luftfahrt

Les Premières Années de l'Aéronautique

Peter Almond

KÖNEMANN

German boys playing with a toy
Zeppelin, October 1928.

Deutsche Jungen spielen mit einem
Spielzeugzeppelin, Oktober 1928.

Des petits Allemands jouent avec
un Zeppelin en octobre 1928.

First published in 1997 by Könemann Verlagsgesellschaft mbH, Bonner Str. 126, D-50968 Köln

©1997 Könemann Verlagsgesellschaft mbH. Photographs ©1997 Hulton Getty Picture Collection Limited

All photographs from the Hulton Getty Picture Collection, London, with grateful acknowledgment to TRH Pictures.

This book was produced by The Hulton Getty Picture Collection Limited, Unique House, 21–31 Woodfield Road, London W9 2BA

For Könemann:
Production manager: Detlev Schaper
Managing editor: Sally Bald
Assistant editor: Susanne Hergarden
German translation by Manfred Allié
French translation by Arnaud Dupin de Beyssat

For Hulton Getty:
Art director: Michael Rand
Design: Ian Denning
Managing editor: Annabel Else
Picture editor: Leon Meyer
Research: Roger Syring, Ali Khoja, Alex Linghorn
Darkroom: Brian Doherty, Steve Eason,
Kevin Gleeson, Donald O'Connor.
Editor: Elisabeth Ingles
Production coordinator: Elisabeth Ihre

Typesetting by Greiner & Reichel Fotosatz. Colour separation by Jade Reprographics Ltd
Printed and bound by Sing Cheong Printing Co. Ltd., Hong Kong, China

ISBN 3-89508-682-7

Frontispiece: Dapper M. Guillon attempts to demonstrate his Guillon and Clouzy aeroplane
on Epsom Downs, England, in April 1907. Only the front wheel left the ground.

Frontispiz: April 1907: Der schmucke Monsieur Guillon müht sich in den Epson Downs, England, seine Guillon
und Clouzy-Maschine vom Boden zu bekommen. Das Vorderrad blieb jedoch der einzige Teil, der sich hob.

Frontispice: Tout fringant, Monsieur Guillon tente de faire décoller son aéroplane Guillon et Clouzy de la
prairie des Epsom Downs (Angleterre), en avril 1907. Seule la roue avant réussit à quitter le sol.

Contents

Inhalt

Sommaire

Introduction

Of all the great steps in mankind's progress, from the wheel to the printing press, the sailing ship to the computer, few have had such an enormous impact as aviation. Aircraft have shrunk the world, ended the isolation of cultures, invigorated trade and human communication; they have also created a terrible new dimension to warfare. Within the first 30 years of the 20th century – a blink of an eye in the magnitude of human existence – man mastered movement through the one basic element hitherto denied him – the air.

Aviation has developed so dramatically from its beginnings that it is hard to imagine that people alive today can still remember the very first flying machines, so fragile that death was only a gust of wind or broken wing spar away.

But the dawn of aviation is one major human achievement that does not require imagination. Running parallel with it was the science of photography, which recorded aviation almost from the start. With the exception of balloonists such as the Montgolfier brothers in 1783, photographers have captured every aspect of aviation's progress. Indeed, photography and aviation have often justified each other. Without seeing photographs of Otto Lilienthal flying a glider in *McClure's Magazine* in 1894, for instance, the Wright brothers might never have taken to the air.

Seeing from the air what cannot be seen from the ground has always been one of the best reasons for aviation. The military possibilities were identified as early as 26 June 1794, when a Revolutionary French captain helped General Jourdan's Army of the Meuse defeat the Austrians by observing their deployments from a balloon. When Gaspard-Félix Tournachon (Nadar) took a series of photographs from a balloon high above the Arc de Triomphe in Paris in 1858, the value of aerial observation was proved to all. It was hard work, however: Nadar produced his somewhat murky image on a collodion wet plate, stripped naked to save weight, concealed behind a dark curtain in the basket of the tethered balloon.

But photography progressed much faster than aviation. By 1903, the date of the Wright brothers' first controlled powered flight, Julius Neubronner in Germany had built an automatic camera so small it could fit onto the chest of a pigeon, anticipating remote-controlled spy planes by almost 75 years. The same year, also in Germany, Alfred Maul fitted a camera into the nose-cone of a rocket that rose to 2,600 feet in eight seconds and – on its way down by parachute – exposed the glass plate by timing device.

Then it was aviation's turn to catch up. By 1914 all combatants of World War I knew the value of aerial photography, which recorded enemy trenches, gun positions and troop movements far beyond any possible ground reconnaissance. It is estimated that by war's end in 1918 two thirds of all military intelligence came from, or was verified by, aerial photography. At Verdun the French had photo-processing points at each corps headquarters, each day churning out 5,000 prints of German targets for distribution to forward units. Significantly, of the 80 aircraft shot down by Baron von Richthofen, the legendary German air ace, 47 were on photo reconnaissance missions.

By 1921 the newly independent Royal Air Force was so confident of its ability that it took over the policing of Mesopotamia (Iraq) from the army. Remarkably clear aerial photographs taken near Baghdad in 1918 show Turkish trenches, ammunition depots and gun pits in a way that would look familiar to allied planners preparing air strikes on almost the same sites in the Gulf War of 1991.

Who were the aviation photographers, the aerial equivalents of the war photographers Robert Capa and Larry Burrows? In many cases we just don't know. For all its great achievements, early aviation attracted very few dedicated, skilled, artistic photographers. The cameraman who photographed the first aircraft to take off from the deck of a warship in 1910 is unknown. John Daniels, the man who took the famous picture of the Wright brothers' first powered flight, was just a local resident at Kitty Hawk who was told to squeeze the bulb of a pre-set camera at a certain moment. Jacques-Henri Lartigue, one of the few French photographers to take pictures at the earliest air shows, took his first photo of a Voisin glider in 1904 as an unskilled ten-year-old child. Edward Steichen, born in Luxembourg and naturalized American, was director of aerial photography for the allies during World War I (and director of US naval combat photography in World War II), but considered himself primarily a painter. In Britain only a few names emerge: one was Charles Brown, who started with a small folding camera in 1910, aged 14, and spent 50 years as an aviation photographer. No great photographers came out of World War I because the military of all sides took tight control of photography.

It was as if the public in those early years still didn't fully

Previous page
Louis Blériot flying over a field near Dambron, France, in the first city-to-city monoplane flight, November 1908.

Vorherige Seite
Louis Blériot über einem Acker bei Dambron, Frankreich – der erste Eindeckerflug zwischen zwei Städten, November 1908.

Page précédente
Louis Blériot survole en monoplan les champs près de Dambron (France) lors du premier vol de «ville à ville», effectué en novembre 1908.

understand the point of flying. William Preston Mayfield, having taken America's first-ever aerial photograph from a Wright Flyer in 1910, rushed back to Dayton, Ohio, only to have his boss at the *Daily News* refuse to print the picture. 'That's nothing but a big empty field,' Mayfield was told. 'There are no people.' In California, Fred Wiseman enthusiastically built a Wright brothers plane from a photograph, then carried the world's first airmail in 1911, but gave up two years later when people realized they could watch him fly at fairgrounds without having to pay. Wiseman went into the automobile business, saying he didn't see much future in aeroplanes.

Aviation was not easy to capture on film. Aircraft zoomed from close-up to distant dot in seconds, but cameras did not. Skies varied from bright sun to dark cloud, presenting photographers with tough exposure problems. On the ground aircraft shapes struggled against awkward backgrounds. And how was a photographer chasing a Bleriot, a Lindbergh or a Farman to keep up with them? At the beginning of their flight or at the end? It was difficult to do both. Until the advent of passenger-carrying airliners in the 1920s photographers could only rarely get into the air themselves, and then had to contend with wind, vibration and cramped conditions.

What survives, then, may not be great art but, rather, snapshots of an age. Unconsciously, the photographs of the early years often depict contrasts: society struggling to catch up with technology, or sometimes what we now regard as its infantile faith in its new machines. We look with amazement at Santos-Dumont standing up in his tail-first box-kite plane making Europe's first powered flight in 1906 as if he were in a balloon; at the World War I pilots who had no escape if they were shot down, even though parachutes did then exist; at passengers being served lunch in a panelled, curtained dining room in the *Graf Zeppelin* airship.

By the 1920s and 30s aircraft had a firm hold on the public imagination. World War I took aviation out of the hands of pioneers into those of 'ordinary' young men. Somebody knew somebody else who was a flyer. Everyone, it seemed, wanted to be part of the thrill of aviation. Those who could afford it went up as pilots or passengers, those who couldn't went to air shows, or watched barnstormers and record-breakers. Newspapers vied to offer big prize money and involved their readers in the great adventure of flight.

There was Alan Cobham, his engineer already dead from a

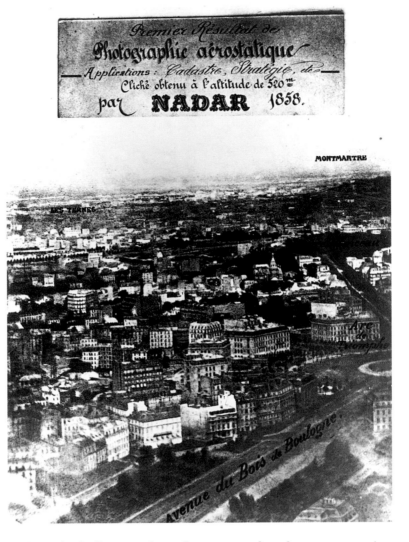

The first aerial photograph, showing the Place de l'Étoile looking towards Montmartre, Paris, taken by Nadar from a tethered balloon in 1858.

Place de l'Étoile, Paris, Blick zum Montmartre: Das erste Luftbild aller Zeiten, aufgenommen von Nadar im Jahre 1858 von einem Fesselballon aus.

La première photographie aérienne – la place de l'Étoile en direction de Montmartre – fut prise par Nadar en 1858 depuis un ballon captif.

Bedouin's bullet as they flew over the desert, returning exhausted from Australia, landing his seaplane outside the Houses of Parliament in London. Or Charles Lindbergh, landing in Paris after his record-breaking flight from New York. Who, even today, does not shrink with horror from the slaughter that was the Western Front, but thrill to the chivalrous knights of the air of World War I – Adolphe Pégoud of France, Manfred von Richthofen of Germany, George Lanoe Hawker of Britain and Eddie Rickenbacker of America?

As we prepare to enter the 21st century, with each fly-by-wire fighter, each 550-seat airliner costing many years of work and many millions of pounds, it seems inconceivable that it all began with a few lengths of wood and sailcloth, an engine, and incredible bravery or naïveté so few years ago.

But it did, and the following photographs tell the story.

Einleitung

U nter all den großen Fortschritten der Menschheit, von der Erfindung des Rades über den Buchdruck und das Segelschiff bis hin zum Computer, hat kaum einer die Welt so sehr verändert wie die Eroberung der Lüfte. Distanzen sind kleiner geworden, ganze Kulturen aus ihrer Isolation herausgekommen, das Flugzeug hat Handel und Kommunikation belebt und gleichzeitig wurde mit ihm eine furchterregende neue Dimension des Krieges geschaffen. In den ersten drei Jahrzehnten des 20. Jahrhunderts – kaum mehr als ein Augenblick in einer langen Entwicklungsgeschichte – hat der Mensch das letzte der vier Elemente beherrschen gelernt, das sich ihm bis dahin entzogen hatte.

Die Entwicklung der Luftfahrt war so dramatisch, daß man kaum glauben mag, daß es noch Menschen gibt, die mit eigenen Augen die allerersten Flugmaschinen gesehen haben – Maschinen, die so empfindlich waren, daß schon ein Windstoß oder ein gebrochener Holm für den Flieger den Tod bedeuten konnte.

Doch sind wir, wenn wir uns vorstellen wollen, wie es in den Kindertagen der Luftfahrt aussah, nicht wie bei anderen großen Errungenschaften der Menschheit auf unsere Phantasie angewiesen, denn zur gleichen Zeit entwickelte sich die Kunst der Fotografie, die fast vom ersten Tag an die Geschichte der Flugpioniere begleitet hat. Von frühen Ballonfahrern wie den Brüdern Montgolfier im Jahre 1783 einmal abgesehen, haben Fotografen die Entwicklung in allen Einzelheiten festgehalten. Flug- und Fotokunst regten sich sogar oft gegenseitig an. Hätten zum Beispiel die Brüder Wright nicht 1894 in *McClure's Magazine* Aufnahmen von Otto Lilienthals Gleitflugexperimenten gesehen, so hätten sie sich vielleicht nie mit der Fliegerei beschäftigt.

Von oben zu sehen, was vom Boden aus nicht zu sehen ist, war von Anfang an einer der besten Gründe, sich in die Lüfte zu wagen. Das militärische Potential wurde schon 1794 erkannt, als ein Hauptmann der französischen Revolutionsarmee am 26. Juni mit der Beobachtung des feindlichen Aufmarsches vom Ballon aus seinen Beitrag zum Sieg über General Jourdans Moselarmee leistete. Die Aufnahmen, die Gaspard-Félix Tournachon (Nadar) 1858 in Paris von einem Ballon hoch über dem Triumphbogen aus machte, führten den Wert der Luftbeobachtung auch der breiteren Öffentlichkeit vor Augen. Obwohl es Schwerstarbeit war: Nadar produzierte seine ein wenig verschwommenen Bilder nach dem nassen Kollodiumverfahren, und der Korb des Fesselballons war mit einem schwarzen Dunkelkammer-Vorhang verhüllt, hinter dem er nackt agierte, um Gewicht zu sparen.

Zunächst machte die Fotografie weitaus schnellere Fortschritte als die Luftfahrt. Als den Gebrüdern Wright 1903 der erste gesteuerte Motorflug gelang, hatte Julius Neubronner in Deutschland schon eine Kamera entwickelt, die so klein war, daß man sie einer Taube vor die Brust binden konnte; er nahm damit das ferngelenkte Spionageflugzeug um beinahe 75 Jahre vorweg. Im selben Jahr montierte, ebenfalls in Deutschland, Alfred Maul eine Kamera in die Spitze einer Rakete, die binnen 8 Sekunden 800 Meter hoch aufstieg; während sie am Fallschirm wieder herunterschwebte, wurde mittels Selbstauslöser eine fotografische Platte belichtet.

Doch dann holte die Luftfahrt auf. 1914 hatten alle Beteiligten des Ersten Weltkriegs den Stellenwert von Luftaufnahmen bereits klar erkannt, mit deren Hilfe sich feindliche Gräben, Geschützstellungen und Truppenbewegungen weitaus besser lokalisieren ließen, als mit einer Aufklärung am Boden je möglich gewesen wäre. Nach Schätzungen stammten bei Kriegsende im Jahr 1918 zwei Drittel aller militärischen Informationen aus der Luftfotografie oder wurden durch diese bestätigt. In Verdun hatten die Franzosen Fotolabors in allen Truppenhauptquartieren und stellten Tag für Tag 5.000 Abzüge von Aufnahmen deutscher Stellungen her, die an die Fronteinheiten verteilt wurden. Es ist aufschlußreich, daß von den 80 Maschinen, die das deutsche Jagdflieger-As Baron von Richthofen abschoß, 47 auf Fotoaufklärungsmissionen unterwegs waren.

1921 hatte die eben erst selbständig gewordene Royal Air Force schon soviel Selbstvertrauen, daß sie die Überwachung Mesopotamiens (Irak) von der Armee übernahm. Bemerkenswert präzise Luftaufnahmen, die 1918 bei Bagdad entstanden, zeigen türkische Gräben, Munitionsdepots und Maschinengewehrnester – Bilder, die den alliierten Strategen, die 1991 im Golfkrieg an fast den gleichen Stellen Luftangriffe planten, vertraut vorgekommen wären.

Wer waren die Fotografen, die für die Luftfahrt das sind, was später Robert Capa und Larry Burrows für den Krieg zu Lande wurden? In vielen Fällen wissen wir es nicht. Trotz ihrer großen Leistungen zogen die Flugpioniere nur selten engagierte, professionelle, künstlerische Fotografen an. Wer die Aufnahme des Flugzeuges gemacht hat, das im Jahr 1910 als erstes vom Deck eines Kriegsschiffs startete, ist nicht überliefert. John Daniels, der Mann, von dem das berühmte Foto vom ersten Motorflug der Gebrüder Wright stammt, war einfach nur ein Einheimischer aus Kitty Hawk, der zu einem vorher verabredeten Zeitpunkt den Auslöser einer fertig präparierten Kamera drück-

An automatic camera is prepared for flight under a captive balloon in 1908. Aerial photography would rapidly become of vital national importance.

Eine automatische Kamera, an einem Fesselballon befestigt, wird im Jahre 1908 für den Flug vorbereitet. Schon bald würde die Luftfotografie von entscheidender militärischer Bedeutung sein.

Installation d'un appareil-photo automatique sur un ballon captif, en 1908. La photographie aérienne sera, depuis cette date, d'une importance vitale pour les nations du monde.

te. Jacques-Henri Lartigue, einer der wenigen französischen Fotografen, die bei den frühen Luftfahrtschauen Aufnahmen machten, knipste sein erstes Bild von einem Voisin-Gleitflugzeug 1904 als zehnjähriger Knabe ohne jede Fachkenntnisse. Edward Steichen, in Luxemburg geboren, doch amerikanischer Staatsbürger, leitete die alliierte Luftaufklärung im Ersten Weltkrieg (und organisierte im Zweiten Weltkrieg die Schlachtenfotografie der U.S.-Marine), verstand sich jedoch in erster Linie als Maler. In Großbritannien sind nur einige wenige Namen überliefert – einer davon Charles Brown, der im Jahr 1910 mit einer kleinen Klappkamera anfing und für die nächsten 50 Jahre Flugfotograf blieb. Der Erste Weltkrieg hat keine bedeutenden Fotokünstler hervorgebracht, weil das Militär die Fotografie auf allen Seiten unter strenger Kontrolle hielt.

Es war, als habe die Öffentlichkeit damals noch gar nicht verstanden, was das Fliegen wirklich bedeutete. Als William Preston Mayfield 1910 von einem Wright-Flyer aus die erste Luftaufnahme Amerikas geschossen hatte, eilte er damit zurück nach Dayton, Ohio, nur um zu erfahren, daß sein Chef bei der *Daily News* nicht bereit war, es zu veröffentlichen. »Da ist doch nur ein leerer Acker drauf«, bekam Mayfield zu hören. »Überhaupt keine Leute.« In Kalifornien baute Fred Wiseman voller Begeisterung nach einer Fotografie eine Wright-Maschine und war 1911 der erste Luftpostpilot der Welt, doch zwei Jahre darauf gab er das Fliegen auf, weil das Publikum inzwischen dahintergekommen war, daß man seine Kunststücke auf Rummelplätzen auch von außerhalb und ohne zu zahlen sehen konnte. Er ging ins Automobilgeschäft, denn für seine Begriffe hatte die Fliegerei keine Zukunft.

Es war nicht leicht, das Fliegen im Bild festzuhalten. Ein Flugzeug war im einen Augenblick direkt vor der Linse, im nächsten schon nur noch ein Fleck am Horizont, und die Fotoapparate konnten ihm nicht folgen. Der Himmel wechselte von greller Sonne zur finstersten Wolke, und die korrekte Belichtung stellte hohe Anforderungen. Maschinen am Erdboden waren oft vor den verschiedensten Hintergründen schwer auszumachen. Und wie sollte ein Fotograf, der einem Blériot, einem Lindbergh oder Farman auf den Fersen war, mit ihm mithalten? Er hatte nur die Wahl, beim Abflug oder bei der Ankunft dabei zu sein – beides zugleich war kaum möglich. Bis zur Gründung der Passagierlinien in den zwanziger Jahren hatten die Fotografen kaum Gelegenheit, selbst in die Luft zu kommen, und wenn es ihnen gelang, dann mußten sie mit Wind, Vibration und der Enge im Flugzeug zurechtkommen.

Was sich erhalten hat, ist also in der Regel keine große Kunst – es sind die Schnappschüsse einer Epoche. Unbewußt stellen diese Bilder der frühen Jahre oft Gegensätze heraus: eine Gesellschaft, die Mühe hat, mit der technischen Entwicklung schrittzuhalten, und bisweilen auch das, was uns heute als kindischer Glaube an die neuen Maschinen vorkommt. Ungläubig sehen wir Santos-Dumont, wie er beim ersten Motorflug Europas im Jahre 1906 in seiner Kastendrachen-Maschine, Leitwerk voran, in einem Korb steht, als sei es ein Ballon; ungläubig hören wir, daß die Piloten des Ersten Weltkriegs, wenn ihre Maschine abgeschossen wurde, umkamen, obwohl es damals längst Fallschirme gab; und ungläubig betrachten wir den getäfelten, mit Vorhängen drapierten Speisesaal des Luftschiffs *Graf Zeppelin*, wo den Passagieren erlesene Mahlzeiten serviert wurden.

In den zwanziger und dreißiger Jahren waren Flugzeuge aus der Öffentlichkeit bereits nicht mehr fortzudenken. Der Erste Weltkrieg sorgte dafür, daß das Fliegen zur Sache »normaler« junger Männer wurde – man hatte nun Familien in der Bekanntschaft, deren Sohn Pilot war. Offenbar wollte nun jeder am aufregenden Fliegerleben teilhaben: Wer es sich leisten konnte, stieg als Pilot oder Passagier in die Lüfte, die anderen gingen zu den Luftfahrtschauen oder ließen sich vom Spektakel der Kunst- und Rekordflieger anlocken. Zeitungen setzten immer größere Preisgelder aus und steckten ihre Leser mit dem Flugfieber an.

Es gab Leute wie Alan Cobham zu sehen (dessen Kopilot beim Flug über die Wüste von der Kugel eines Beduinen getötet wurde), als er, erschöpft vom Australienflug zurück, mit seinem Wasserflugzeug vor dem Londoner Parlamentsgebäude landet. Oder Charles Lindbergh, der am Ende seines Atlantik-Rekordfluges in Paris anlangt. Selbst heute wird es niemanden geben, der nicht mit Entsetzen an das Blutvergießen der Westfront denkt, doch faszinieren nicht die Fliegerasse des Ersten Weltkriegs – Ritter der Lüfte wie Adolphe Pégoud aus Frankreich, der Deutsche Manfred von Richthofen, der Brite George Lanoe Hawker und Eddie Rickenbacker aus Amerika – noch immer?

An der Schwelle zum 21. Jahrhundert, wo die Entwicklung jedes mit Elektronik vollgestopften Kampfflugzeugs und jedes 550-sitzigen Linienjets Millionen an Kosten und Arbeitsstunden verschlingt, kann man sich kaum noch vorstellen, daß alles erst vor wenigen Jahren mit ein paar Holzstangen, einem großen Stück Leinentuch, einem Motor und einer unglaublichen Portion Mut oder Naivität begann.

Doch so war es, und die Fotografien der folgenden Seiten erzählen die Geschichte.

De toutes les grandes inventions de l'homme, de la roue à l'imprimerie et du bateau à voiles à l'ordinateur, peu ont eu sur l'humanité un impact aussi fort que l'aviation. Les avions ont réduit les dimensions de la Terre, supprimé l'isolement des cultures, fortifié le commerce et amélioré les relations humaines ; ils ont également donné une nouvelle et terrible dimension à la guerre. Au cours des 30 premières années du XXe siècle – une goutte d'eau dans l'histoire de l'humanité –, l'homme est parvenu à maîtriser les déplacements dans l'un des quatre éléments – l'air – qui lui était resté jusque-là inaccessible.

L'aviation a connu un développement si rapide qu'il est difficile d'imaginer qu'il existe encore aujourd'hui des gens qui peuvent se souvenir des toutes premières machines volantes, si fragiles qu'un brusque souffle de vent ou la rupture d'un hauban d'aile pouvaient entraîner la mort de leur occupant.

L'aviation est, par chance et contrairement à beaucoup d'autres, l'une des réalisations de l'homme pour laquelle point n'est besoin de faire assaut d'imagination car c'est à la même époque que se développait parallèlement la science de la photographie. En effet, à l'exception des exploits d'aérostiers comme les frères Montgolfier en 1783, la photographie nous offre des images de l'aviation pratiquement depuis ses premiers débuts et tout au long de son évolution technologique, à tel point que photographie et aviation se sont souvent justifiées mutuellement. On peut même se demander si les frères Wright auraient jamais pris décollé s'ils n'avaient découvert des photographies des «glissades» en planeur d'Otto Lilienthal dans le *McClure's Magazine* de 1894.

Voir depuis le ciel ce qu'on ne peut pas voir du sol a toujours été l'un des meilleurs alibis de l'aviation. Ses potentialités dans le domaine militaire avaient été reconnues dès le 26 juin 1794, lorsqu'un capitaine français de la Révolution aida l'Armée de la Moselle du général Jourdan à vaincre les Autrichiens en espionnant leurs mouvements depuis un ballon. Tout l'intérêt de l'observation aérienne se révèle en 1858 lorsque Gaspard-Félix Tournachon (Nadar) publie une série de photographies prises en ballon captif au-dessus de l'Arc de Triomphe de Paris. L'entreprise était pourtant difficile : Nadar avait en effet réalisé cette image un peu sombre sur une plaque au collodion, dissimulé derrière un rideau noir dans sa nacelle et complètement nu par souci du poids.

La photographie fit toutefois des progrès plus rapides que l'aviation. En 1903, l'année même du premier vol motorisé et contrôlé des frères Wright, l'Allemand Julius Neubronner avait déjà construit un appareil-photo automatique si petit qu'il pouvait être fixé au cou d'un pigeon – anticipant ainsi de près de 75 ans les avions-espions télécommandés. La même année, toujours en Allemagne, Alfred Maul fixa un appareil sur le cône d'une fusée qui l'éleva à 800 m d'altitude en huit secondes et exposa une plaque de verre lors de sa descente en parachute.

L'aviation combla bientôt son retard. En 1914, tous les combattants de la Première Guerre mondiale connaissaient la valeur de la photographie aérienne, permettant de filmer les tranchées ennemies, les emplacements des canons et les mouvements de troupes de manière bien plus efficace que les reconnaissances au sol. On a estimé qu'à la fin de la guerre, en 1918, les deux tiers des renseignements militaires provenaient de la photographie aérienne ou avaient été confirmés par elle. À Verdun, chaque corps d'armée français disposait de laboratoires de développement où étaient tirées chaque jour 5 000 photos des cibles allemandes pour être ensuite distribuées aux unités du front. Il est significatif que, des 80 appareils abattus par le baron von Richthofen, l'as légendaire de l'aviation allemande, 47 l'aient été au cours d'une mission de reconnaissance.

En 1921, la Royal Air Force, unité récemment indépendante, était si confiante dans ses capacités qu'elle prit la relève de l'armée de terre pour assurer le maintien de l'ordre en Mésopotamie (Irak). Des photographies aériennes d'une remarquable netteté prises près de Bagdad en 1918 montrent les tranchées, les dépôts de munitions et les positions des canons turcs sous un aspect qui semblerait sans doute familier à tous les stratèges alliés préparant les frappes aériennes – presque sur les mêmes sites – lors de la Guerre du Golfe de 1991.

Nous ignorons, pour la plupart d'entre eux, qui sont ces photographes de l'aviation, alter ego anonymes des photographes de guerre Robert Capa et Larry Burrows ? Il est vrai que, malgré les vastes horizons qu'elle leur ouvrait, l'aviation attira peu de photographes artistiques passionnés et talentueux. L'homme qui, en 1910, photographia le premier décollage d'un avion depuis le pont d'un navire de guerre est demeuré inconnu, et John Daniels, à qui l'on doit d'avoir immortalisé le premier vol motorisé des frères Wright, n'était qu'un simple habitant de Kitty Hawk chargé d'appuyer à un moment précis sur le déclencheur d'un appareil-photo préréglé. Quelques noms pourtant surgissent : Jacques-Henri Lartigue, l'un des rares Français à avoir photographié les premiers meetings d'aviation, il n'a que dix ans lorsqu'il prend sa première photo en 1904, celle d'un planeur Voisin; Edward Steichen, originaire du Luxembourg et naturalisé américain, s'il fut le directeur des opérations de photographie aérienne pour les Alliés au cours de la Première Guerre mondiale, et le chef du service photographique naval américain pendant la Seconde Guerre mondiale, se considérait d'abord comme un peintre. Pour la Grande-Bretagne, seuls quelques noms sont sortis de l'anonymat, parmi lesquels celui de Charles Brown, dont la longue carrière de 50 années au bénéfice de la photographie d'aviation débuta en 1910, à l'âge de 14 ans, avec un petit appareil pliable. En revanche, aucun des grands photographes de la Première Guerre mondiale ne s'est révélé, les militaires des deux camps conservant un contrôle étroit de la photographie.

On a parfois l'impression que le public de ces années de genèse de l'aviation n'a pas compris l'intérêt de voler. Ainsi, en 1910, lorsque William Preston Mayfield se précipite à Dayton (Ohio) après avoir pris la première photographie aérienne de l'Amérique à bord d'un Flyer Wright, son patron du *Daily News* refuse de publier son cliché en disant: «Il n'y a rien qu'un champ vide. On ne voit personne!». En Californie, après avoir construit avec enthousiasme – d'après photo – un Wright, puis effectué le premier vol postal en 1911, Fred Wiseman abandonne deux ans plus tard en comprenant que les gens s'étaient rendu compte qu'ils pouvaient le voir voler sur les champs de foire sans payer; Wiseman se reconvertit dans l'automobile en assurant qu'il ne voyait pas beaucoup d'avenir à l'avion.

La photographie d'aviation n'était pas une activité très facile. Les limites techniques des appareils de prise de vue les empêchaient de suivre le mouvement des avions s'approchant puis s'éloignant de l'opérateur en quelques secondes, de s'adapter aux variations d'exposition d'un ciel changeant, de plein soleil à sombre et nuageux, tandis que les silhouettes «filaires» des avions au sol se distinguaient mal de l'arrière-plan. Et comment un photographe traquant les moments importants de la vie de Blériot, de Lindbergh ou de Farman aurait-il dû travailler? Lui fallait-il être présent au début ou à la fin du vol puisqu'il était en tous cas impossible de faire les deux. Jusqu'à l'avènement des avions de ligne dans les années 1920, les photographes eurent rarement l'occasion de voler eux-mêmes; et lorsqu'ils le pouvaient, il leur fallait s'arranger du vent, des vibrations et d'une position inconfortable.

Les photos que nous offrent ces photographes des origines de l'aviation sont des instantanés d'une époque qui illustrent,

inconsciemment sans doute, les contradictions d'une société s'efforçant de combler son retard technologique tout en montrant une foi parfois infantile dans ces nouvelles machines. Et nous nous étonnons de voir Santos-Dumont dans son aéroplane cellulaire «canard» effectuer debout, comme s'il était installé dans la nacelle d'un ballon, le premier vol motorisé d'Europe en 1906; ou encore, pendant la Première Guerre mondiale, de découvrir que les pilotes n'avaient d'autres ressources que de s'abattre avec leur appareil s'ils étaient touchés, alors que le parachute salvateur existait déjà; sans parler aussi des passagers du dirigeable *Graf Zeppelin* se faisant servir à dîner dans une salle à manger lambrissée ornée de rideaux.

Dans les années 1920 et 1930, l'avion commençait d'enflammer l'imagination et le goût du public. La Première Guerre mondiale avait permis à l'aviation d'échapper à l'emprise des pionniers pour devenir la passion de jeunes gens «ordinaires». Il y avait toujours quelqu'un qui connaissait quelqu'un qui était pilote. Tout le monde voulait éprouver le frisson de l'aviation. Ceux qui pouvaient se le permettre étaient pilotes ou passagers, les autres assistaient aux meetings aériens, regardaient les «cirques» aériens ambulants ou suivaient les exploits des briseurs de records. Les journaux, qui se faisaient alors une âpre concurrence pour offrir des prix aux vainqueurs, faisaient participer leurs lecteurs à la grande aventure du ciel.

Ces héros étaient Alan Cobham, revenant seul d'un épuisant périple depuis l'Australie, son mécanicien tué par la balle d'un Bédouin tandis qu'ils survolaient le désert, et faisant amerrir son hydravion devant le Parlement de Londres; ou Charles Lindbergh, atterrissant à Paris après avoir effectué un vol transatlantique historique. Et puis, au-delà de la boucherie et de l'horreur, comment ne pas acclamer ces chevaliers du ciel de la Première Guerre mondiale que furent le Français Adolphe Pégoud, l'Allemand Manfred von Richthofen, l'Anglais George Lanoe Hawker et l'Américain Eddie Rickenbacker?

Alors que nous nous préparons à entrer dans le XXIe siècle, à une époque où le moindre chasseur à réaction ou avion de ligne nécessite des années de travail et coûte plusieurs millions de francs, il semble encore quelque peu inconcevable que ces monstrueux «plus lourds que l'air» soit issus de ces quelques bouts de bois et de tissu à voile assemblés autour d'un moteur et pilotés avec une incroyable bravoure – ou naïveté – il y a si peu d'années par une poignée d'hommes.

Cette épopée fut réelle et ces hommes ont existé. Les photographies de ce livre en racontent l'histoire.

Exotic aviation pioneer Samuel F. 'Colonel' Cody taking photographs at the Aero Club exhibition at Britain's Alexandra Palace in 1907.

Der Abenteurer und Flugpionier Samuel F. »Colonel« Cody macht Aufnahmen bei den Vorführungen des Aero-Clubs im Alexandra-Palast, England 1907.

Le «colonel» Samuel F. Cody, un des pionniers de l'aviation, s'adonne à la photographie lors du salon anglais de l'Aero Club à l'Alexandra Palace, en 1907.

—— 1 ——
The Dream Unfolds

'Of what use is a balloon?' asked the bystander to the excited American observer.
'Sir,' responded Benjamin Franklin, 'of what use is a new-born baby?'

On 27 August 1783, two months after the French chemist Antoine-Laurent Lavoisier named a newly-discovered gas 'hydrogen', Professor Jacques Charles of the French Academy of Sciences filled a 12-foot diameter unmanned balloon with the gas, launched it from the Champ-de-Mars in Paris and watched it disappear into the clouds. When it landed 11 miles away, near the village of Gonesse, frightened villagers thought it was an evil-smelling monster and hacked it to death.

The villagers' fear was understandable. Large, man-made objects floating through the air just didn't happen. Despite centuries of effort, the closest man had come to flight were ill-fated attempts to flap like birds or to hang on to Chinese-designed kites. But this was something quite different – a machine that could float through the air – and it attracted French interest at the highest level. Within a month King Louis XVI and Queen Marie Antoinette watched the Montgolfier brothers loose their first full-sized hot-air balloon, and two months after that François Pilâtre de Rozier and the Marquis d'Arlandes made the first free-flight balloon ride, quickly followed by Professor Charles in his hydrogen balloon. Within two years the first rudimentary hand-cranked airscrew propelled a balloon through the air, and Jean-Pierre Blanchard and the American John Jeffries crossed the English Channel in a hydrogen balloon. Jacques Garnerin made the first parachute descent from a balloon in 1797.

It was not until the 1860s that balloons really came into their own. The American Civil War encouraged the Union Army to form a five-balloon, 50-man Balloon Corps to observe Confederate troop movements. In 1870, during the Franco-Prussian War, such balloons became the only lifeline to the outside world for besieged Parisians. Before the city fell in 1871, hydrogen balloons made a total of 66 one-way flights over the heads of Prussian troops, carrying 110 people and almost three million pieces of mail. It was an uncertain airline, however. Some of the flights landed in Holland, one in Norway, and one was shot at by a British ship over the North Sea. One poor balloonist was last seen dropping his dispatches over Cornwall before disappearing forever over the Atlantic.

If ballooning was to have a future then clearly it had to be with much greater aerial control, as Gaston Tissandier, one of the pilots who had flown out of Paris during the Siege, knew all too well; in 1875 he had been the only one of his three-man crew to survive a disastrous attempt to beat the 29,000-foot British altitude record. In 1883 he built a 'dirigible', a steerable balloon powered by a Siemens electric motor. A year later another, more powerful dirigible, *La France*, built by C. Renard and A. Krebs, became the first fully controllable airship to fly.

In Germany, the cavalry officer Count Ferdinand von Zeppelin heard about *La France* with alarm. The airship had been flown by two French army officers, and von Zeppelin feared the military implications for the Fatherland. He determined that Germany should have its own fleet of battle airships, and he used his own fortune to build the gigantic Luftschiff-Zeppelin 1 (LZ1). People gasped with amazement when they saw it emerge from its hangar on Lake Constance on 2 July 1900, even more so when its twin Daimler engines flew it for 20 minutes. The airship was barely under control, and it was not until 1906 that von Zeppelin solved his problems with his second dirigible, LZ2.

Perhaps he had learned from Alberto Santos-Dumont. A Brazilian living in Paris, Santos-Dumont had built a series of small airships and in 1901 attempted to win a prize for being the first to travel a seven-mile route to the Eiffel Tower and back in under 30 minutes. In two dramatic attempts, he won his prize and proved that airships could be made to travel distances and be manoeuvrable.

And yet control was the key. Were airships really the answer? The wing-flapping 'Ornithopter' – driven by steam, gunpowder, rubber bands and clockwork – had largely had its day. And, until hang-gliding many years later, so had the ancient concept of man-carrying kites, although the Australian Lawrence Hargrave's 1893 box-kites proved to be very important for the first European aeroplane builders. Helicopters, a toy since the 14th century, had been tried but with even less success at control.

Could the air then be *used*, as a bird learns to glide? In 1799 Sir George Cayley, a Briton now regarded as the 'Father of Aeronautics', had established the principles of flight in a design for an aeroplane that involved fixed wings, a pilot sitting in a fuselage and a tail unit comprising a combined tailplane, vertical fin and rudder. Ten years later he built history's first full-sized glider, which lifted him up for a few yards.

But few paid attention to him. It was up to a handful of inventive tinkerers to take on his ideas. One of them, Samuel Henson, an English engineer, in 1843 designed the Aerial Steam Carriage, the first real-looking aeroplane. The Russian Alexander Mozhaiski and the Frenchman Félix du Temple made brief, steam-powered hops in the 1880s. In 1890 Clément Ader made a sustained steam-powered 'flight' of 160 feet in his bat-winged *Éole* plane at Armainvilliers in France, but it did not have effective controls.

Control was still the great goal. By the late 1880s Cayley's ideas had been greatly refined and widely published, and yet, curiously, it was a German believer in ornithopters who turned out to be the last and greatest link to manned powered flight before the Wright Brothers.

Otto Lilienthal took up Cayley's studies in an 1889 book, *Bird Flight as the Basis of Aviation*, and over the next few years put his theories into practice with 2,500 hang-gliding flights near his home in Berlin. The wings of his lightweight monoplane gliders built between 1893 and 1896 were sparred and the fabric of their wings waxed and stressed, combining to create heavier air pressure underneath than above. By launching himself from a small hill he was able to make long glides of up to 750 feet with remarkable ease, controlling his craft by shifting his body in his straps. He died in a glider crash in 1896, unaware that the new petrol engines could have taken him infinitely further.

Lilienthal was a true aviator, a man who carefully studied and recorded all his findings and had long experience of flying. His reports, together with photographs of him flying, were translated and reproduced all over the world, directly influencing his natural successors, Percy Pilcher of England, the Wrights in America and the French pioneer Captain Ferdinand Ferber, and proving to the public that manned flight in a heavier-than-air machine was possible. In America, the French-born civil engineer Octave Chanute picked up Lilienthal's ideas and produced a series of gliders; the key example, the biplane kite structure, ultimately evolved into the Wright Flyer.

It was from Lilienthal that Orville and Wilbur Wright hit on the central idea of 'wing warping' to control a glider in flight. But rather than shifting their bodies from side to side to achieve lateral stability, the Wrights pulled wires to warp or twist the wing surfaces, making them go up or down. The concept would develop into ailerons. Wing warping was a feature of the brothers' first glider, built in 1900 and tested at Kill Devil Hills, North Carolina, at a site meteorologists told them would have steady, stiff winds, low hills and soft landing areas. Glider No. 2, built in 1901, turned out to be too big and uncontrollable and the Wrights dumped Lilienthal's investigations to conduct their own, including the use of a wind tunnel to test model wings. Glider No. 3 was built in September 1902. The brothers knew they had a winner and applied for a patent. Then, switching their attention to a power source, they built their own four-cylinder, water-cooled engine and did their own research into propeller design.

They spent all the next summer rebuilding Glider No. 3 at Kitty Hawk. On 17 December 1903, Orville Wright lay at the controls of the machine, launched himself down a rail into the air and became the first human to achieve sustained, controlled flight in an aeroplane.

*»Und wozu soll ein Ballon gut sein?« fragte ein Schaulustiger
den Amerikaner, der voller Begeisterung zusah.
»Sir«, antwortete Benjamin Franklin, »wozu ist ein neugebore-
nes Kind gut?«*

Am 27. August 1783, zwei Monate nachdem der französische Chemiker Antoine-Laurent Lavoisier ein von ihm entdecktes Gas »Wasserstoff« genannt hatte, befüllte Professor Jacques Charles von der Académie des Sciences damit einen unbemannten Ballon von 3,65 Metern Durchmesser, ließ ihn vom Pariser Marsfeld aufsteigen und sah ihm nach, bis er in den Wolken verschwand. Als der Ballon 18 Kilometer weiter beim Dorf Gonesse niederging, hielten die verängstigten Bauern ihn für ein stinkendes Ungeheuer und hackten ihn in Stücke.

Die Furcht der Dorfbewohner war verständlich. Große, von Menschen gemachte Objekte, die durch die Luft schwebten, gab es einfach nicht. Trotz jahrhundertelangem Bemühen waren ein paar erfolglose Versuche mit vogelartigen Schwingen und die Möglichkeit, sich an einen Drachen nach chinesischem Vorbild zu hängen, das Äußerste, was die Menschheit in puncto Fliegen bis dahin zustandegebracht hatte. Doch dies war etwas ganz anderes – eine Maschine, die schweben konnte – und erregte in Frankreich Interesse in den höchsten Kreisen. Noch nicht einmal einen Monat später sahen Ludwig XVI. und Marie Antoinette den Brüdern Montgolfier zu, die ihren ersten großen Heißluftballon steigen ließen, und zwei Monate darauf unternahmen François Pilâtre de Rozier und der Marquis d'Arlandes die erste Freiballonfahrt; Professor Charles folgte mit seinem Wasserstoffballon bald darauf. Schon zwei Jahre später wurde ein Ballon von einer ersten handbetriebenen Luftschraube bewegt, und Jean-Pierre Blanchard und der Amerikaner John Jeffries überquerten in einem Wasserstoffballon den Ärmelkanal. 1797 unternahm Jacques Garnerin von einem Ballon aus den ersten Fallschirmsprung.

In größerem Maße flogen Ballons jedoch erst seit den 1860er Jahren. Im Amerikanischen Bürgerkrieg gründete die Südstaatenarmee ein Ballonkorps (5 Ballons, 50 Mann), das die Bewegungen der Nordstaatentruppen beobachtete. 1870 waren im Deutsch-Französischen Krieg Ballons die einzige Verbindung des eingeschlossenen Paris zur Außenwelt. Bevor die Stadt 1871 fiel, entkamen 66 Wasserstoffballons über die Köpfe der preußischen Truppen hinweg und brachten 110 Personen und beinahe 3 Millionen Poststücke heraus. Allerdings

fuhren sie in ein unsicheres Schicksal. Einige dieser Ballons landeten in Holland, einer in Norwegen, einer wurde auf der Nordsee von einem britischen Schiff beschossen. Ein unglücklicher Ballonfahrer konnte noch seine Postsäcke in Cornwall abwerfen, bevor er für immer über dem Atlantik verschwand.

Wenn die Ballonfahrt eine Zukunft haben sollte, dann mußte eine Möglichkeit der Steuerung gefunden werden – das war Gaston Tissandier, als er den Flug aus dem besetzten Paris wagte, klargeworden, und der katastrophale Ausgang eines Unternehmens, mit dem er 1875 den von Briten gehaltenen Höhenrekord von 8.840 Metern überbieten wollte, bekräftigte es noch; er war der einzige einer dreiköpfigen Mannschaft, der überlebte. 1883 stellte er sein »dirigible« vor, ein von einem Siemens-Elektromotor angetriebenes lenkbares Luftschiff, und im Jahr darauf bauten Charles Renard und Arthur Krebs eine größere Variante und nannten sie *La France* – das erste wirklich steuerbare Luftschiff der Welt.

In Deutschland vernahm der Kavallerieoffizier Ferdinand Graf von Zeppelin die Nachricht mit Sorge. Die beiden Luftschiffer bei der ersten Fahrt der *France* waren Armeeoffiziere gewesen, und Zeppelin erkannte die militärische Bedrohung für das Reich. Er beschloß, daß Deutschland seine eigene Flotte von Kriegsluftschiffen haben sollte, und baute auf eigene Rechnung das gigantische Luftschiff Zeppelin 1 (LZ1). Die Zuschauer hielten den Atem an, als sie es am 2. Juli 1900 aus seiner schwimmenden Halle auf dem Bodensee hervorkommen sahen, und mehr noch, als es sich mit seinen zwei Daimler-Motoren in die Lüfte erhob. Steuern ließ sich das Schiff allerdings kaum, und erst 1906 mit seinem zweiten starren Luftschiff, der LZ2, bekam Zeppelin diese Schwierigkeiten in den Griff.

Vielleicht hatte er von Alberto Santos-Dumont gelernt. Der in Paris lebende Brasilianer hatte eine Reihe von kleinen Luftschiffen gebaut und trat 1901 an, um einen Preis zu gewinnen, der für einen Sieben-Meilen-Rundflug um den Eiffelturm in weniger als 30 Minuten ausgesetzt war. In zwei dramatischen Anläufen gewann er die Prämie und bewies damit, daß Luftschiffe auch längere Strecken bewältigen konnten und daß sie lenkbar waren.

Steuerbarkeit blieb jedoch das Hauptproblem. Waren Luftschiffe wirklich die beste Lösung? Der mit den Flügeln schlagende »Ornithopter« – ob nun mit Dampf, Schießpulver, Gummibändern oder Uhrwerk betrieben – war schon weitgehend aufgegeben. Und auch die alte Vorstellung vom bemannten

Nadar photographed Jules Duruof's balloon *Neptune* about to depart from Montmartre on an observation mission during the Siege of Paris in September 1870.

Nadar hielt Jules Duruofs Ballon *Neptune* im Bild fest, wie er während der Belagerung von Paris im September 1870 vom Montmartre zu einem Beobachtungsflug aufsteigt.

Photographie par Nadar du *Neptune*, ballon de Jules Duruof, au moment de son départ de Montmartre pour une mission d'observation au cours du siège de Paris en septembre 1870.

Drachen wurde, bis viele Jahre später der Sport des Drachenfliegens aufkam, ad acta gelegt, obwohl die 1893 von dem Australier Lawrence Hargrave vorgestellten Kastendrachen eine wichtige Inspirationsquelle für die ersten europäischen Flugzeugbauer waren. Mit Hubschraubern, als Spielzeug schon seit dem 14. Jahrhundert bekannt, wurden Versuche unternommen, doch ließen sie sich noch weniger steuern.

Konnte man denn vielleicht die Luft selbst nutzen und wie ein Vogel im Gleitflug fliegen? 1799 hatte der Engländer Sir George Cayley, der heute als »Vater der Luftfahrt« gilt, die Grundprinzipien des Fluges bereits erkannt und ein Flugzeug mit starren Tragflächen entworfen, mit einem Rumpf, in dem der Flieger saß, und einem Heckleitwerk, das Stabilisator, Seiten- und Höhenruder vereinte. Zehn Jahre darauf baute er das erste bemannte Gleitflugzeug und flog auch einige Meter damit.

Doch kaum jemand beachtete ihn. Nur eine Handvoll phantasievoller Bastler griff seine Ideen auf. Einer davon, der englische Ingenieur Samuel Henson, baute 1843 seine »Aerial Steam Carriage« – der erste Entwurf, der die späteren Motorflugzeuge ahnen ließ. Dem Russen Alexander Mozhaiski und dem Franzosen Félix du Temple glückten in den 1880er Jahren mit Dampfkraft einige Hüpfer. 1890 gelang Clément Ader im französischen Armainvilliers mit seinem fledermausflügligen, mit Dampfkraft betriebenen *Éole* der erste »Flug« von 50 Metern, doch sein Apparat hatte keine brauchbare Steuerung.

Steuerung war und blieb die entscheidende Frage. Ende der 1880er Jahre waren Cayleys Ideen wesentlich weiterentwickelt und vielfach publiziert worden, und doch war es ein deutscher Verfechter der Ornithopter, der zum letzten und wichtigsten Glied in der Kette werden sollte, die zum ersten bemannten Motorflug der Gebrüder Wright führte.

Otto Lilienthal griff Cayleys Studien in seinem 1889 erschienenen Buch *Der Vogelflug als Grundlage der Fliegekunst* auf, und in den folgenden Jahren setzte er in 2.500 Flügen mit dem Hängegleiter nahe seiner Heimat Berlin diese Ideen in die Praxis um. Die Tragflächen der leichten, einflügeligen Gleiter, die er zwischen 1893 und 1896 baute, bestanden aus Holmen, die mit gewachstem Segeltuch bespannt waren, was dafür sorgte, daß der Luftdruck unter dem Flügel größer war als darüber. Lilienthal sprang von einem kleinen Hügel ab und legte dann mit bemerkenswerter Leichtigkeit Gleitflüge von bis zu 250 Metern zurück; in den Riemen, mit denen er unter seine Flügel geschnallt war, konnte er sich bewegen und so mit dem ganzen Körper den Gleiter steuern. Er kam 1896 bei einem Absturz ums Leben, ohne daß er je die neuen Verbrennungsmotoren erwogen hatte, die ihn unendlich weiter hätten fliegen lassen.

Lilienthal war ein echter Flieger, der seine Experimente sorgfältig dokumentierte und vielfältige Erfahrungen sammelte. Seine Berichte wurden in zahlreiche Sprachen übersetzt und zusammen mit den Aufnahmen von seinen Flügen überall auf der Welt publiziert; sie waren von unmittelbarem Einfluß auf Nachfolger wie Percy Pilcher in England, die Gebrüder Wright in Amerika und Capitaine Ferdinand Ferber in Frankreich, und sie bewiesen aller Welt, daß der bemannte Flug mit Maschinen, die schwerer waren als Luft, möglich war. In Amerika griff der aus Frankreich stammende Bauingenieur Octave Chanute Lilienthals Ideen auf und baute selbst eine Reihe von Gleitern; aus dem wichtigsten davon, dem Doppeldecker in Kastendrachenform, sollte der Wright-Flyer hervorgehen.

Lilienthal gab Orville und Wilbur Wright die zentrale Idee der Steuerung eines Gleitflugzeuges durch Verwinden der Tragflächen ein. Statt jedoch zur Wahrung der Querstabilität ihren Körper hin- und herzubewegen, zogen die Wrights an Drähten die Tragflügelenden gegenläufig auf- bzw. abwärts und glichen so die Rollbewegung aus. Daraus entwickelte sich das Querruder. Verwindbare Tragflächen zeichneten den ersten Gleiter der Brüder aus, der im Jahre 1900 entstand und den sie in den Kill Devil Hills in North Carolina erprobten – einer Gegend mit gleichmäßigen steifen Winden, sanften Hügeln und weichen Landeflächen. Gleiter Nr. 2 aus dem Jahre 1901 erwies sich als zu groß und zu schwer zu beherrschen, und von da an verließen die Wrights sich nicht mehr auf Lilienthals Studien, sondern führten eigene Untersuchungen durch, bei denen sie auch Modelle von Flügelformen im Windkanal testeten. Gleiter Nr. 3 entstand im September 1902. Die beiden erkannten sofort, daß sie diesmal einen sicheren Gewinner hatten, und meldeten ihn zum Patent an. Als nächstes wandten sie sich der Frage des Antriebs zu und bauten ihren eigenen wassergekühlten Vierzylindermotor, und auch der Propeller entstand nach eigenen Experimenten.

Den Sommer des folgenden Jahres verbrachten sie damit, Gleiter Nr. 3 in Kitty Hawk zum Motorflugzeug umzubauen. Am 17. Dezember 1903 legte Orville Wright sich hinter die Steuerhebel, startete von einer Schiene, die als Anflughilfe diente, und hob sich in die Luft – der erste längere, gesteuerte Motorflug in der Geschichte der Menschheit.

«À quoi peut donc servir un ballon?», demanda un specta-teur à son voisin, un Américain passionné.

«Monsieur, répondit Benjamin Franklin, à quoi sert un bébé nouveau-né?»

L e 27 août 1783, deux mois après que le chimiste français Antoine-Laurent Lavoisier ait baptisé «hy-drogène» le gaz qu'il venait de découvrir, le profes-seur Jacques Charles, de l'Académie des sciences, remplit de ce même gaz un ballon (sans équipage) de 3,50 m de diamètre qu'il lâche au Champ-de-Mars, à Paris. Lorsque l'aérostat s'abat près du village de Gonesse, à 20 km de son point de départ, les habitants apeurés, pensant qu'il s'agit d'un monstre diabolique, le lacéreront sans pitié.

La peur de ces villageois était compréhensible. Il était im-possible qu'existent des objets de grandes dimensions cons-truits par l'homme qui puissent flotter dans les airs. Malgré des siècles de persévérance, les quelques malheureuses tenta-tives faites par l'homme pour voler, soit en battant des ailes comme un oiseau soit en s'accrochant à un cerf-volant chi-nois, s'étaient soldées par un échec. L'expérience de Charles était toutefois très différente, puisqu'il s'agissait d'une machi-ne se déplaçant dans les airs, et elle éveilla aussitôt l'intérêt du roi Louis XVI et de Marie-Antoinette qui, le même mois de 1783, assistèrent au lancement par les frères Montgolfier de leur premier ballon à air chaud. Deux mois plus tard, François Pilâtre de Rozier et le marquis d'Arlandes effectuaient leur premier vol en ballon libre, rapidement suivis par le profes-seur Charles à bord de son ballon à hydrogène. Au cours des deux années suivantes apparaissaient les premières hélices rudimentaires qui, actionnées à la main, permettaient de pro-pulser un ballon, et dont se servirent le Français Jean-Pierre Blanchard et l'Américain John Jeffries pour traverser la Man-che dans un ballon à hydrogène. En 1797, André-Jacques Gar-nerin effectuait la première expérience de saut en parachute à partir d'un ballon.

Toutefois, le ballon ne trouva réellement sa justification qu'après 1860. Pendant la guerre de Sécession américaine, l'Armée de l'Union eut ainsi l'idée de former un Corps d'Aéro-stiers – composé de 50 hommes pour 5 ballons – afin d'obser-ver les mouvements de troupe des Confédérés. En France, lors de la guerre de 1870, ces ballons furent le seul moyen de liai-son entre Paris assiégé et le monde extérieur. Avant que la ca-pitale ne tombe aux mains ennemies, en 1871, les ballons à hy-

drogène avaient effectué un total de 66 voyages en passant par-dessus les lignes prussiennes, ils avaient emporté 110 per-sonnes et presque trois millions de lettres. L'entreprise était cependant risquée et la destination aléatoire : plusieurs vols aboutirent en Belgique et aux Pays-Bas, un ballon atterrit en Norvège et un autre fut abattu par un navire britannique au-dessus de la mer du Nord ; on vit même un de ces malheureux aérostiers en train de larguer ses sacs postaux au-dessus de la Cornouailles avant de disparaître au-dessus de l'Atlantique.

Si l'aérostation devait avoir quelque avenir, il faudrait alors pouvoir mieux contrôler le vol de ces ballons. Gaston Tissan-dier, l'un des aérostiers qui avaient échappé au siège de Paris et le seul des trois membres de l'équipage à avoir survécu en 1875 à une désastreuse tentative de battre le record d'altitude établi précédemment par les Britanniques (8838 m), en est pleinement conscient et construit en 1883 un «dirigeable», c'est-à-dire un ballon propulsé par un moteur électrique Sie-mens. Un an plus tard, un autre dirigeable plus puissant, *La France*, devient le premier aérostat véritablement gouvernable.

En Allemagne, un officier de cavalerie, le comte Ferdinand von Zeppelin, s'émeut d'autant plus du succès de *La France* qu'il avait été piloté par deux officiers de l'armée française. Voyant sa patrie menacée, il s'engage à ce que l'Allemagne possède sa propre flotte de dirigeables militaires et consacre sa fortune à la réussite de l'entreprise. Les quelques specta-teurs présents sur le lac de Constance le 2 juillet 1900 assis-tèrent alors avec stupéfaction à la sortie des hangars du gigan-tesque Luftschiff-Zeppelin 1 (ou LZ1) et furent encore plus étonnés lorsque le dirigeable évolua pendant 20 minutes au-dessus d'eux, propulsé par ses deux moteurs Daimler. Ce bal-lon étant encore peu maniable, il fallut attendre 1906 pour que von Zeppelin résolve ce problème avec un deuxième dirigea-ble, le LZ2.

Zeppelin avait peut-être tiré des enseignements des expé-riences réalisées par Alberto Santos-Dumont. Ce Brésilien de-meurant à Paris avait en effet construit une série de petits aé-rostats et tenté, en 1901, de remporter le prix attribué au pre-mier homme qui effectuerait un circuit de 8 km aller-retour jusqu'à la tour Eiffel en moins de 30 minutes. Il remporta la ré-compense après deux tentatives infructueuses et dramatiques, prouvant ainsi que les dirigeables pouvaient réaliser de longs parcours et être manœuvrables.

Si la maîtrise de l'air demeurait effectivement la clé du vol, les dirigeables offraient-ils vraiment une réponse adaptée ? Si

Alberto Santos-Dumont included breathing apparatus and an altitude meter in his prize-winning balloon in 1910.

Alberto Santos-Dumont hatte ein Sauerstoffgerät und einen Höhenmesser in dem Ballon, mit dem er 1910 im Wettbewerb erfolgreich war.

En 1910, Alberto Santos-Dumont avait installé un masque à oxygène et un altimètre dans son ballon.

l'« ornithoptère » à ailes battantes, actionnées par un « moteur » à vapeur, à poudre, à caoutchoucs ou mécaniquement, était largement dépassé, il en était de même du vieux concept de cerf-volant – au moins jusqu'à l'arrivée des planeurs, plusieurs années plus tard et bien que les expériences de l'Australien Lawrence Hargrave en 1893 aient eu un intérêt indéniable pour les premiers constructeurs d'aéroplanes. Quant à l'hélicoptère, un rêve depuis le XIVe siècle, il avait été essayé mais on réussissait encore moins à le maîtriser.

L'homme pourrait-il alors utiliser l'air tout comme l'oiseau s'en sert pour planer ? En 1799, l'Anglais Sir George Cayley, aujourd'hui considéré comme le « père de l'aéronautique », établit les principes du vol dans le projet d'un aéroplane disposant d'ailes fixes, d'une nacelle pour un pilote assis et d'un empennage équipé d'un stabilisateur et d'un gouvernail de direction et de profondeur. Dix ans après, il construisait le premier planeur habité de l'histoire, sur lequel il aurait décollé sur quelques mètres.

Ses idées eurent cependant peu d'écho véritable, sinon auprès d'une poignée de bricoleurs inventifs parmi lesquels on peut compter l'ingénieur anglais Samuel Henson, qui conçoit en 1843 l'« Aerial Steam Carriage » (ou « char à vapeur volant ») – premier modèle d'un aéroplane digne de ce nom –, mais aussi le Russe Alexander Mozhaiski et le Français Félix du Temple qui, dans les années 1880, font quelques bonds propulsés par un moteur à vapeur. En 1890, à Armainvilliers (France), un autre émule de Cayley, Clément Ader, effectue sur l'*Éole*, un appareil à ailes de chauve-souris équipé d'un moteur à vapeur, un « vol » de 50 m soutenu et propulsé mais pas encore véritablement contrôlé.

La maîtrise du vol demeure l'objectif essentiel. Vers la fin des années 1880, si les idées de Cayley ont été grandement améliorées et largement diffusées, c'est curieusement un adepte de l'ornithoptère, l'Allemand Otto Lilienthal, qui fut – avant les frères Wright – le dernier et le plus important maillon de la chaîne conduisant au vol humain propulsé.

Lilienthal reprend les idées de Cayley dans un ouvrage publié en 1889, *Der Vogelflug als Grundlage der Fliegekunst* (*Le Vol des oiseaux considéré comme base de l'aviation*) puis met ses théories en pratique en effectuant quelque 2500 « glissades » près de son domicile à Berlin. Construits entre 1893 et 1896, ses planeurs monoplans ultra-légers disposent d'ailes haubanées et tendues d'une toile cirée afin d'accroître la pression de l'air sur la surface inférieure de la voilure. S'élançant

du sommet d'une petite colline, il effectua avec une remarquable facilité de longs vols planés sur plus de 200 m, équilibrant son appareil par des mouvements du corps. Il mourut en 1896 des suites d'un accident de planeur sans savoir si les nouveaux moteurs à essence auraient pu l'emmener plus loin.

Lilienthal était un véritable aviateur, qui analysa et nota soigneusement toutes les découvertes réalisées au cours de ses nombreuses expérimentations. Traduits et publiés dans le monde entier, ces comptes rendus qu'accompagnaient des photographies prises lors de ses vols influencèrent directement ses successeurs – Percy Pilcher en Angleterre, les Wright aux États-Unis et le capitaine français Ferdinand Ferber – et révélèrent au public que le vol contrôlé dans un « plus lourd que l'air » était possible. Aux États-Unis, reprenant les travaux de Lilienthal, l'ingénieur d'origine française Octave Chanute créera une série de planeurs, dont un biplan à structure cellulaire qui inspirera le Flyer des Wright.

C'est à Lilienthal qu'Orville et Wilbur Wright doivent le principe fondamental du gauchissement par torsion des extrémités des ailes permettant de contrôler le planeur en vol. Mais, au lieu de déplacer latéralement leur corps pour équilibrer l'appareil, les Wright actionnaient un câble permettant d'exercer une torsion sur l'une ou l'autre des extrémités de la voilure, assurant ainsi le contrôle de l'assiette et du tangage (concept primitif de l'aileron). Ce système de gauchissement d'aile par câbles équipe le premier planeur des Wright, construit en 1900 et testé à Kill Devil Hills (Caroline du Nord) dans une région de collines basses où les météorologues leur avaient annoncé un régime de vents forts et réguliers. Après l'échec du Glider N° 2, construit en 1901 et qui se révéla trop grand et incontrôlable, les Wright abandonnèrent la voie de Lilienthal pour entreprendre leurs propres recherches, utilisant notamment un tunnel de soufflerie pour tester les modèles de voilure. Les Wright terminèrent le Glider N° 3 en septembre 1902 et, après des essais réussis, déposèrent un premier brevet. Désireux de passer à l'étape de la propulsion, ils fabriquèrent eux-mêmes un moteur à quatre cylindres et refroidissement par eau et étudièrent la conception d'une hélice.

Après avoir passé tout l'été à reconstruire le Glider N° 3 à Kitty Hawk, Orville Wright s'installa aux commandes de l'appareil le 17 décembre 1903 et, s'élançant depuis le rail de décollage, devint le premier homme à accomplir un vol soutenu et contrôlé à bord d'un aéroplane.

French aviation pioneers Albert Tissandier (on left) and his brother Gaston, founders of the Paris Balloon Post in 1870.

Die französischen Flugpioniere Albert (links) und sein Bruder Gaston Tissandier, die im Jahr 1870 die Pariser Ballonpost begründeten.

Albert Tissandier (à gauche) et son frère Gaston, pionniers de l'aviation française et fondateurs de la Poste aérienne de Paris en 1870.

The beginning

Balloons were first popularized by the Montgolfier brothers' hot-air machines in the 1780s. Later hydrogen balloons appeared, such as this one (**1**), ready for departure with Louis and Jules Godard at St-Cloud, Paris, in 1866. Since balloon construction was expensive, flights in them were often grand occasions, as here marked by photographer and band.

Die Anfänge

In den 1780er Jahren machten die Brüder Montgolfier ihre ersten Flüge mit dem Heißluftballon. Bald darauf folgten die Wasserstoffballons, von denen wir einen hier (**1**) im Jahre 1866 in St. Cloud, Paris, sehen; Louis und Jules Godard machen sich bereit für den Flug. Der Bau eines solchen Ballons war teuer, und ein Aufstieg war ein großes Ereignis, bei dem Fotograf und Blaskapelle nicht fehlen durften.

Au commencement

Les aérostats à air chaud des frères Montgolfier rendirent populaire le vol en ballon à partir des années 1780. Quelques années plus tard apparaissaient les premiers ballons à hydrogène comme celui-ci (**1**), prêt à s'envoler en 1866 depuis Saint-Cloud, près de Paris, avec Louis et Jules Godard à son bord. La construction des ballons étant onéreuse, les vols en aérostat avec passager sont souvent l'occasion de grandes manifestations, avec orchestre et photographe.

An explosive end

By 1902 hydrogen balloons were more sophisticated, aerodynamically superior and more colourfully marked. But that didn't stop *Pax* (**3**), an airship designed by the Brazilian Augusto Severo (**2**, on left), from ending in a fiery wreck on the Avenue du Maine in Paris on 12 May. Watched by thousands on its maiden flight, *Pax* rose suddenly, and Severo and his engineer threw out ballast rather than release gas. The airship climbed higher, the gas expanded and the balloon exploded. Both men were killed.

Am Ende geht er in die Luft

Bis 1902 waren die Wasserstoffballons nicht nur bunter geworden, sondern auch aerodynamischer und technisch anspruchsvoller. Doch auch das konnte nicht verhindern, daß das von dem Brasilianer Augusto Severo (**2**, links) konstruierte Luftschiff *Pax* (**3**) am 12. Mai jenes Jahres als brennendes Wrack in der Pariser Avenue du Maine endete. Tausende, die zum Jungfernflug gekommen waren, sahen, wie die *Pax* sich schlagartig in die Lüfte hob; Severo und sein Ingenieur warfen Ballast ab, statt Gas abzulassen – das Luftschiff stieg immer höher, das Gas dehnte sich aus und explodierte. Beide Männer kamen ums Leben.

Un fin explosive

En 1902, les ballons à hydrogène sont plus aboutis techniquement, ont de meilleures qualités aérodynamiques et ont une enveloppe bien plus colorée. Rien de tout cela n'empêcha le *Pax* (**3**), un dirigeable conçu par le Brésilien Augusto Severo (**2**, à gauche), de s'écraser dans l'avenue du Maine, à Paris, sous les yeux de milliers de spectateurs venus assister à son vol inaugural, le 12 mai 1902. En effet, Severo et son mécanicien ayant jeté du lest au lieu de libérer le gaz lorsque le *Pax* s'éleva brusquement dans les airs, l'aérostat poursuivit son ascension rapide, provoquant une dilatation du gaz ; l'enveloppe explosa les deux aéronautes furent tués.

A thing of beauty

In 1909 the new excitement was heavier-than-air flying machines which projected man ever higher, faster and longer through the air. But there was no mistaking the gentle appeal of balloons. These hydrogen balloons, assembled for a race meeting at Hurlingham sports ground near London, ignored the new technologies of aeroplanes and generated a public appeal which has never faded.

Die reine Schönheit

1909 redeten schon alle von Flugmaschinen, die schwerer als Luft waren und die Menschen länger, höher und schneller denn je durch die Lüfte befördern konnten – doch daß Ballons ungleich sanfter waren, war keine Frage. Die Wasserstoffballons, die sich hier auf dem Sport-platz von Hurlingham bei London zu einem Wettflug versammelt haben, scheren sich nicht um die neuartigen Flugzeuge, und das Publikum locken die Ballons bis heute an.

Un bel objet

En 1909, on se passionne pour les aérodynes – les «plus lourds que l'air» –, ces nouvelles machines volantes qui emmènent l'homme toujours plus haut, plus vite et plus longtemps dans le ciel. Les ballons conservent toutefois tout leur charme et leur attrait. Ces ballons à hydrogène, réunis à l'occasion d'une compétition sur le terrain de sport de Hurlingham, près de Londres, n'utilisent guère les nouvelles techniques mises en œuvre pour les aéroplanes et s'attirent un engouement qui ne s'est jamais complètement démenti de la part du public.

Complementing nature

Ballooning, as always, was man against wind, final destination uncertain. A crowd at the Andrea Doria velodrome, Genoa, cheered and a band played the "Marseillaise" when the aeronaut Dartois from the Aéro-Club de France set off for a brief trip to the River Po in May 1903 (**1**).

Im Einklang mit der Natur

Bei einer Ballonfahrt liefert der Mensch sich den Elementen aus, und wo er landet, weiß er nie. Hier hat sich eine Menschenmenge auf dem Andrea-Doria-Velodrom in Genua versammelt, um den Aeronauten Dartois vom Aéro-Club de France zu verabschieden, der im Mai 1903 zu einem kurzen Flug über die Poebene aufbricht. Eine Kapelle spielt die »Marseillaise« dazu (**1**).

S'allier la nature

La pratique de l'aérostation, aujourd'hui comme hier, fait se confronter l'homme et le vent, pour une destination finale incertaine. Tandis qu'un orchestre joue la «Marseillaise», la foule rassemblée salue, en mai 1903, l'envol de l'aéronaute Dartois, de l'Aéro-Club de France, parti du vélodrome Andrea Doria de Gênes en direction de la vallée du Pô (**1**).

Aerial sport

Ballooning and motoring were the exciting new sports of the early 1900s, and remained popular well after the introduction of sport aeroplanes. Sir Claude de Crespigny and his lady were passengers on an outing from Hurlingham, London, in 1909 (2), while ladies watched an earlier lift-off at the same place (3), and in 1913 a photographer prepared to record the view from above (4).

Der Flugsport

Ballon- und Autorennen waren die aufregenden neuen Sportarten des frühen 20. Jahrhunderts, und Ballons blieben populär, als es längst auch schon Sportflugzeuge gab. Von Hurlingham, London, steigen im Jahre 1909 Sir Claude de Crespigny und Gattin zu einem Flug auf (2), und die Damen verfolgen am selben Ort einen früheren Start (3); 1913 schickt sich ein Fotograf an, den Blick aus den Lüften festzuhalten (4).

Un sport aérien

Les deux nouvelles aventures sportives du début des années 1900, l'aérostation et l'automobile, restèrent populaires bien après l'arrivée des aéroplanes. En 1909, Sir Claude de Crespigny et son épouse (2) sont les passagers d'un vol en ballon effectué à partir de Hurlingham, près de Londres, d'où un groupe de femmes avait assisté un peu plus tôt à un autre départ (3); en 1913, c'est un appareil-photo que l'on installe dans un ballon pour photographier la terre depuis les airs (4).

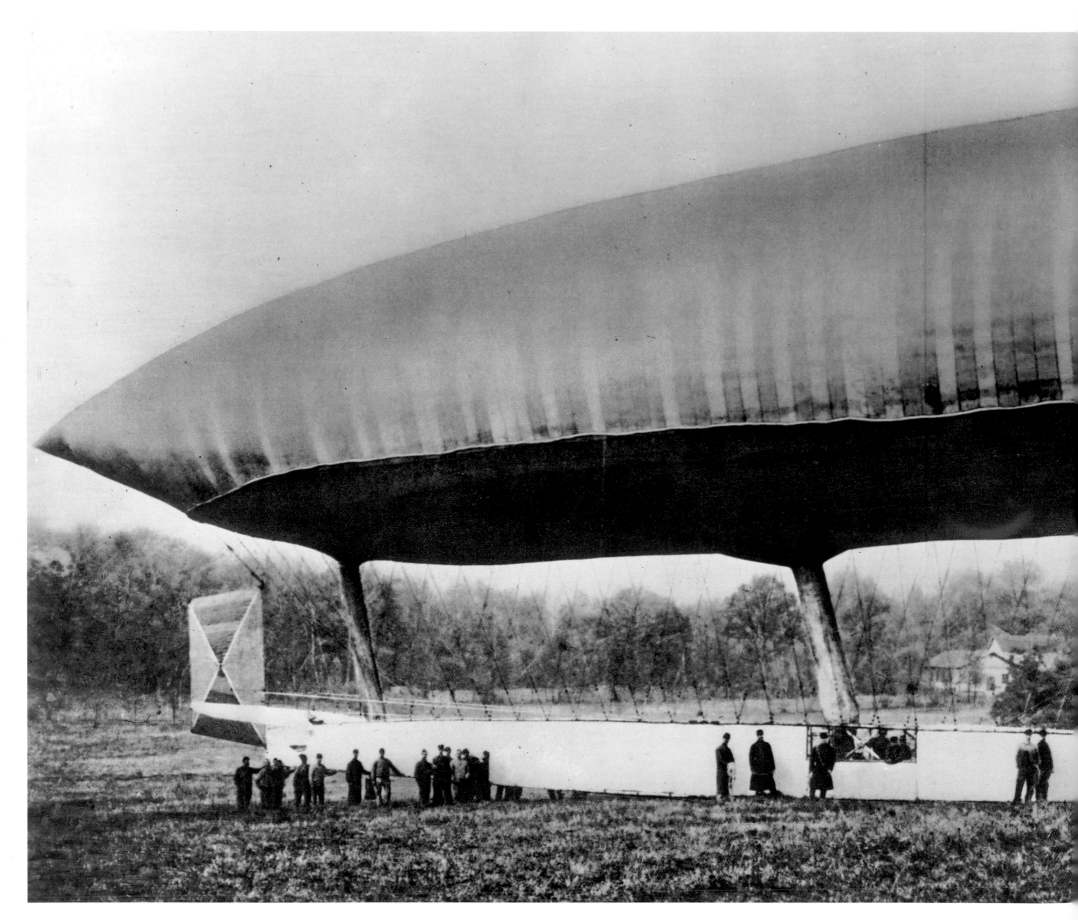

Vive *La France*

Like some giant insect larva, the dirigible (steerable airship) *La France* prepared for its five-mile round-trip maiden flight from the French town of Chalais-Meudon in August 1884. Built and flown by Captain Charles Renard and Lieutenant Arthur Krebs, it was powered by a 9hp electric motor. Although it lacked the supporting framework of later airships and could be flown only in the lightest of winds, *La France* was the first fully controllable airship.

Vive *La France*

Wie eine gewaltige Insektenlarve wirkt das lenkbare Luftschiff *La France*, das hier im August 1884 bei der französischen Stadt Chalais-Meudon für seinen Fünf-Meilen-Jungfernflug vorbereitet wird. Das von Hauptmann Charles Renard und Leutnant Arthur Krebs gebaute und geflogene Schiff wurde von einem 9-PS-Elektromotor angetrieben. Zwar fehlte ihm noch das verstärkende Gitterwerk späterer Modelle, und bei stärkerem Wind konnte es nicht aufsteigen, doch war die *France* das erste wirklich steuerbare Luftschiff.

Vive *La France*

Ressemblant étrangement à quelque larve d'insecte géante, *La France* se prépare, en août 1884, à effectuer son premier vol en circuit fermé (7 km) au départ de Chalais-Mcudon. Construit et piloté par le capitaine Charles Renard et le lieutenant Arthur Krebs, cet aérostat était mû par un moteur électrique de 9 ch. Bien que ne disposant pas de l'armature rigide des aérostats ultérieurs et ne pouvant voler que par vents très faibles, *La France* est le premier véritable dirigeable, c'est-à-dire un aérostat gouvernable.

Santos-Dumont – pioneer extraordinaire

In 1901, Alberto Santos-Dumont gave away most of his 100,000-franc prize for flying seven miles from St-Cloud to the Eiffel Tower and back in under 30 minutes (**1**). An earlier attempt failed when he crashed into the Trocadéro restaurant and was rescued by firemen. Santos-Dumont (**3**) demonstrated his small dirigibles around Europe (**2**).

Santos-Dumont – Pionier der Pioniere

Im Jahre 1901 flog Alberto Santos-Dumont die sieben Meilen von St.-Cloud zum Eiffelturm und zurück in knapp 30 Minuten (**1**); die 100.000 Francs, die er als Preis dafür bekam, verschenkte er fast ganz. Bei einem früheren Versuch stürzte er ins Restaurant Trocadéro und mußte von Feuerwehrleuten gerettet werden. Santos-Dumont (**3**) führte seine kleinen lenkbaren Luftschiffe überall in Europa vor (**2**).

Santos-Dumont – un extraordinaire pionnier

En 1901, après s'être écrasé sur le restaurant du Trocadéro et avoir été sauvé par les pompiers lors d'une précédente tentative, l'aéronaute brésilien Alberto Santos-Dumont (**3**) distribua aux nécessiteux de Paris une grande partie du prix de 100 000 francs qu'il remporta en accomplissant en moins de 30 minutes un circuit aller et retour de 11 km entre Saint-Cloud et la tour Eiffel (**1**). L'aéronaute brésilien présentera par la suite ses petits dirigeables à travers toute l'Europe (**2**).

1

2

Max effort

The Anglo-American inventor Sir Hiram Stevens Maxim (**1**) actually did get this 'plane' off the ground briefly, in Kent in July 1894 (**2**). Basically a test rig biplane powered by two small steam engines, the machine had a wing area of 4,000 square feet and a three-man crew; it weighed 8,000lb. Its main contribution to aviation was as a startling curiosity. Maxim went on to produce a total of 271 inventions including an improved mousetrap and the Maxim machine gun.

Maximal

Der anglo-amerikanische Erfinder Sir Hiram Stevens Maxim (**1**) brachte im Juli 1894 in Kent dieses Monstrum tatsächlich dazu, sich ein kleines Stück vom Boden zu heben (**2**). Der von zwei kleinen Dampfmaschinen betriebene Doppeldecker lief auf einer Versuchsapparatur auf Schienen; er hatte einen Tragflächeninhalt von 370 Quadratmetern, wog 3,6 Tonnen und hatte drei Mann Besatzung. Mehr als ein Kuriosum der Luftfahrtgeschichte war er allerdings nicht. 271 Erfindungen ließ Maxim sich patentieren, darunter eine verbesserte Mausefalle und das Maxim-Maschinengewehr.

L'effort de Maxim

C'est en juillet 1894, dans le Kent, que l'Américain naturalisé anglais Sir Hiram Stevens Maxim (**1**) fit brièvement décoller son «aéroplane». Cette machine (**2**), une cellule biplan propulsée par deux petits moteurs à vapeur, avait une superficie de voilure de 370 m² pour un poids de 3 600 kg et emportait un équipage de trois hommes. Le principal intérêt de cet engin dans l'histoire de l'aviation est d'avoir été une curiosité. On doit à Maxim un total de 271 inventions, parmi lesquelles un piège à souris perfectionné et le fusil automatique qui porte son nom.

Ader's incredible bat-mobile

Claiming to be the first to fly a heavier-than-air machine, the Frenchman Clément Ader (**2**, on left) built the steam-powered machine *Éole* and it actually 'flew' for 160 feet in 1890. But his 1897 twin-boilered Avion III (**1**, as it would have looked in flight, and **3**, with wings folded) never got off the ground. Its best feature was its amazingly powerful steam engine.

Aders unglaubliches Batmobil

Der Franzose Clément Ader (**2**, links) beanspruchte die Ehre für sich, als erster mit einer Maschine geflogen zu sein, die schwerer war als Luft; 1890 hatte er die dampfbetriebene *Éole* gebaut und war damit tatsächlich 50 Meter weit »geflogen«. Sein 1897 entstandenes zwei-keßliges Avion III (**1**, hypothetische Flug-ansicht, und **3**, mit gefalteten Flügeln) bekam er jedoch nie vom Erdboden. Das Beste daran war die Dampfmaschine, die unglaubliche Kraft hatte.

L'incroyable batmobile d'Ader

Le Français Clément Ader (**2**, à gauche) affirme être le premier à avoir fait voler un engin plus lourd que l'air – l'*Éole* – qui, en 1890, propulsé par un moteur à vapeur, «décolla» effective-ment sur 50 mètres. En revanche, son Avion III de 1897 à double hélice (**1** en configuration de vol, et **3** avec les ailes repliées) ne vola jamais. L'élément le plus intéressant de cet aéroplane était son moteur à vapeur d'une puissance étonnante.

Aviation's practical father

If Otto Lilienthal had attached one of the new automobile petrol engines to a larger version of his gliders he would probably have been the first to achieve sustained, controlled, powered flight. Launching himself from a small hill at Lichterfelde, Berlin, in 1894 (**1** and **3**), he used his carefully researched understanding of flight to hang-glide, controlling the flight with his body. He was killed gliding in 1896, but his writings (**2**), and particularly these photographs, helped persuade people that manned flight was possible.

Der Vater der modernen Luftfahrt

Hätte Otto Lilienthal eine größere Ausführung seiner Gleiter gebaut und einen der neuen Verbrennungsmotoren für Automobile hineingesetzt, wäre er wahrscheinlich der erste gewesen, dem ein längerer gesteuerter Motorflug gelungen wäre. 1894 startet er von einem Hügel in Berlin-Lichterfelde zum Gleitflug (**1** und **3**), den er dank ausgiebiger aerodynamischer Studien mit seinem Körper steuern konnte. Lilienthal kam 1896 bei einem Flugexperiment ums Leben, doch seine Schriften (**2**) und Aufnahmen wie diese halfen die Überzeugung durchsetzen, daß Menschen tatsächlich fliegen können.

Le père putatif de l'aviation

Si Otto Lilienthal avait pu construire des planeurs plus grands et les doter d'un des moteurs à essence nouvellement inventés pour l'automobile, il aurait sans doute été le premier à réussir un vol soutenu, propulsé et contrôlé. Après avoir étudié soigneusement et assimilé les rudiments de l'art du vol, Lilienthal perfectionna la technique du vol en planeur, dont il contrôlait l'équilibre par les mouvements de son corps, en s'élançant de nombreuses fois des hauteurs d'une petite colline de Lichterfelde, près de Berlin, comme ici en 1894 (**1** et **3**). Après sa mort, survenue en 1896 lors d'une de ses expériences de «glissade», les plans (**2**) et les documents qu'il a laissés, et notamment les photographies de ses vols, ont contribué à convaincre le public que le vol humain était désormais possible.

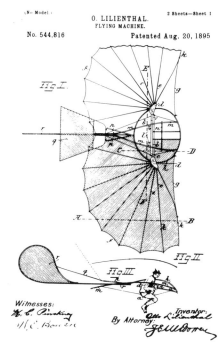

Principles of flight

Most people in the early 1900s thought of flying as an extension of motoring, with the pilot somehow propelling his craft through the air. Disciples of Lilienthal, such as France's Ferdinand Ferber, learned from gliding that aviation involved unique skills – turning, banking and climbing – as shown here in Nice in 1902 (**1**). But after the Wright brothers' success in 1903 he abandoned Lilienthal and in 1904 became the first European to build a glider (**2**) on Wright principles.

Grundprinzipien des Fluges

Die meisten, die sich Anfang des Jahrhunderts mit dem Fliegen beschäftigten, verstanden es als eine Variante des Automobilfahrens – die gleichen Prinzipien, nur daß der Chauffeur seine Maschine durch die Lüfte steuerte. Schüler Lilienthals wie etwa der Franzose Ferdinand Ferber lernten aus dem Gleitflug, daß ein Pilot mehr als das können mußte – er mußte wenden, steigen und sich in die Kurve legen, wie Ferber es hier 1902 in Nizza demonstriert (**1**). Nach dem Erfolg der Gebrüder Wright im folgenden Jahr gab er dann allerdings Lilienthal als Vorbild auf und war 1904 der erste Europäer, der einen Gleiter nach Wrightschem Vorbild baute (**2**).

Principes du vol

Au début des années 1900, la plupart des gens voient dans l'aéronef une sorte d'automobile que l'aviateur conduirait dans les airs. Les disciples de Lilienthal, tel que le Français Ferdinand Ferber – ici à Nice en 1902 (**1**) –, apprirent de leurs expériences en planeur que le vol en aéroplane exigeait des qualités particulières : savoir tourner, virer et grimper. Mais après avoir appris le succès des frères Wright en 1903, Ferber abandonna les traces de Lilienthal et devint en 1904 le premier Européen à construire un planeur (**2**) sur les principes des Wright.

Lilienthal's key disciple

In America, the French-born engineer Octave Chanute carried on where Lilienthal left off. His friend Augustus Moore Herring helped construct a glider and tested it on the dunes near Lake Michigan in 1896 (**1–5**), chased by Chanute's pet dogs. Chanute was by then 64. His novel biplane designs were major influences on the Wright brothers.

Lilienthals bester Schüler

In Amerika setzte der aus Frankreich stammende Ingenieur Octave Chanute die Experimente Lilienthals fort. Sein Freund Augustus Moore Herring half den Gleiter bauen und erprobte ihn 1896 unter reger Beteiligung von Chanutes Hunden in den Dünen am Michigansee (**1–5**). Chanute war damals 64. Seine neuartige Zweidecker-Konstruktion hatte großen Einfluß auf die Gebrüder Wright.

Le principal disciple de Lilienthal

L'ingénieur français Octave Chanute poursuivit aux États-Unis les expériences Lilienthal. Son ami Augustus Moore Herring l'aida à construire un planeur et Chanute, alors âgé de 64 ans, l'essaya sur les dunes proches du lac Michigan en 1896 (**1–5**). La nouvelle conception de ce biplan eut une influence décisive sur les frères Wright.

Kites and gliders

The aeronautic principles of kites, known in China from 1000 BC, were employed for stability in gliders and later aeroplanes. The glider built by the pioneer Ernest Archdeacon being towed aloft in 1905 (**1**). A Puiseux design comprising a kite on a bicycle attracted attention in France in 1909 (**2**), and in California, a monoplane glider built by the scientist John J. Montgomery in flight in 1911 (**3**).

Drachen und Gleiter

Die aeronautischen Prinzipien des Drachen waren in China schon im 1. Jahrtausend vor Christus bekannt; sie verliehen auch den Gleitern der Flugpioniere und später den ersten Flugzeugen ihre Stabilität. Das Gleitflugzeug des Pioniers Ernest Archdeacon wird 1905 an einem Tau in die Luft gezogen (**1**). Puiseux' Fahrraddrachen erregte 1909 in Frankreich Aufsehen (**2**), und in Kalifornien flog 1911 der von dem Wissenschaftler John J. Montgomery konstruierte Eindecker (**3**).

Cerfs-volants et planeurs

Les principes aérodynamiques du cerf-volant, connus en Chine depuis l'an 1000 av. J.C., furent repris et adaptés aux planeurs puis aux aéroplanes afin d'en améliorer la stabilité. Ce sont ces formules que l'on retrouve dans le planeur construit par le pionnier Ernest Archdeacon, ici remorqué en vol en 1905 (**1**), dans le projet de Puiseux de 1909 – un planeur monté sur une bicyclette (**2**) – qui suscita quelque intérêt en France, ou encore dans le planeur monoplan du scientifique John J. Montgomery, volant ici en Californie en 1911 (**3**).

2

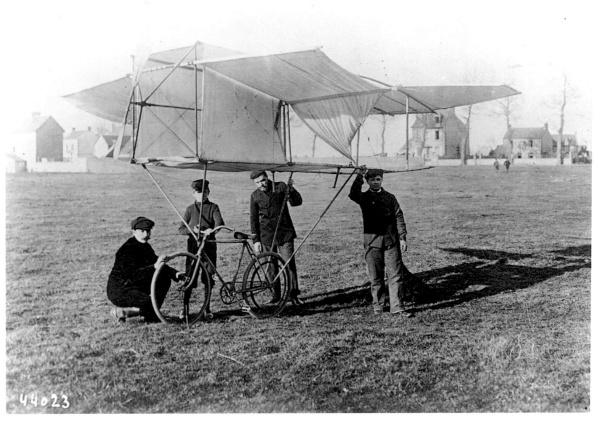

3

2
On a Wing and a Prayer

In 1905 Orville and Wilbur Wright received a letter from the US Army's Board of Ordnance rejecting the brothers' offer to sell it their latest Flyer No. 3 aeroplane. The army wouldn't be interested 'until a machine is produced which by actual operation is shown to be able to produce horizontal flight and to carry an operator'.

It had been nearly two years since the Flyer's historic flight from Kill Devil Hills, and although farmers around Dayton, Ohio, had become used to the Wrights' planes flying around, the US government refused to believe it was being offered a proven flying machine. Officials thought they were being asked to fund a design, much as they had been persuaded to finance Samuel Langley's ill-fated *Aerodrome* machine, which fell into the Potomac in December 1903. The Wrights turned to the British and French governments, but negotiations fell through there, too. On 16 October 1905 the Wrights gave up, and for more than two and a half years, until 6 May 1908, they never once flew in a plane nor allowed any stranger to see their Flyers. They were far ahead of anyone else in aviation, but it was almost as if their historic flight had never been.

Much of the fault was surely their own. The sons of a bishop of the United Brethren Church, the punctilious Wright brothers held to high ethical standards and took little interest in self-promotion. They had no time for the efforts needed to persuade a sceptical world. A photograph and report of their 1903 flight had been sent round the world, but the report was garbled and made little impact. They preferred to spend their time filing patents rather than telling the world exactly how they achieved their success. Perhaps they had a point in trying to protect their Flyers from spies and ruthless commercial competition, particularly after the British government insisted on inspecting and testing the machines without guaranteeing to buy if they met specifications, but their secrecy allowed the aviation world to overtake them.

The Europeans had not grasped just how advanced the Wrights were. In Paris the Aéro-Club de France was sanguine about France's position as leader in aviation, in spite of a detailed lecture from the Wrights' friend Octave Chanute about the brothers' progress. The Irish expatriate lawyer Ernest Archdeacon and Captain Ferdinand Ferber of the French Army did worry about the Wrights, and both men built Wright-type gliders with a front elevator and a tail. But the Europeans didn't learn to fly step-by-step like the Wrights and

they didn't understand the manoeuvrability of wing-warping. Instead, they perceived aviation as an extension of motoring, where the dominant concern was stability in the air.

Ferber, at least, understood what the Wrights were trying to do, and he did get a powered and modified Wright-type Flyer airborne in May 1905. But it was to stability and the box-kites of the Australian Lawrence Hargrave that others turned for their basic flight principles. Gabriel Voisin, in cooperation with Archdeacon and Louis Blériot, built a float-plane that looked a cross between a Wright Flyer and a box-kite. Like the first monoplane, built by the Transylvanian Trajan Vuia, it had great promise for the future but did not really work. It was not until 12 November 1906 that a European aeroplane finally got off the ground, to enormous publicity and euphoria.

It was an airship man, Alberto Santos-Dumont, who did it, and in a craft so strange that it was abandoned after only one further brief hop. Santos-Dumont's 14-bis – so named because he flight-tested it under his airship No. 14 – owed something to Voisin's float-plane, but its longitudinal stability was obtained by moving the elevator and rudder to the front. With a 24hp engine pushing from behind, and standing in a balloon gondola, he flew 722 feet in 21 seconds, won the Aéro-Club de France's 1,500-franc prize for the first flight over 100 metres and was officially credited with making the first powered flight in Europe.

With huge national and international interest awakened, efforts were redoubled. The big goal now was the 50,000-franc Deutsch-Archdeacon prize for the first person to fly a one-kilometre circular course. Voisin struggled with his box-tail designs and, joined by Henry Farman, finally won the big prize in January 1908. But it was hardly a resounding success. The Voisin-Farman 1 was still the only European aircraft that could remain airborne for a whole minute. The Wright brothers' last flight more than two years earlier had taken 39 minutes to do 25 miles.

In Germany Hugo Junkers patented the first of a long line of diesel engines; the first of Zeppelin's military airships, LZ3, took to the skies; and near Lisieux, France, Paul Cornu became the first to fly unaided in the first tentative helicopter. Even in America people began to look beyond the Wrights. Glenn Curtiss, backed by the Aerial Experiment Association of Hammondsport, NY, built on Langley's Aerodrome biplane design, and on 4 July 1908, Independence Day, won a prize for the first American airplane officially to fly more than 1 km.

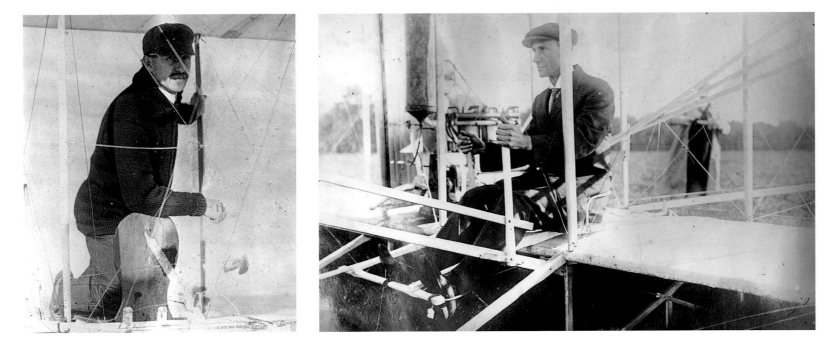

The Wrights finally came off the bench. In February 1908 they signed contracts with the US government and arranged for a French company to build their Flyers under licence. In May, Wilbur travelled to Le Mans to demonstrate his Flyer while Orville went to Washington to convince doubters in the US Army. On 8 August 1908, witnessed by hundreds of the most critical aviation-minded people in France, Wilbur Wright took off, made two graceful circles over one minute 45 seconds and landed smoothly. The audience was stunned. For the first time they saw what flight control was all about. Over the next few months Wilbur flew further and higher, the crowds grew bigger and the cheers louder. In Washington, Orville Wright was having the same impact, even after 17 September when his Flyer crashed and his passenger, Lieutenant Thomas Selfridge, became the first person to be killed in a powered aeroplane. Orville was himself seriously injured.

But it was in Britain that the Wrights first sold their Flyers to be built in series. The entrepreneur Eustace Short heard about Wilbur's flights and went to France to negotiate with him on the spot. Equipped with drawings and a licence, he set up the Short Brothers factory at Shellbeach on the Isle of Sheppey, Kent, and built six Flyers on an assembly line. They were all sold before he finished them.

Britain had been surprisingly slow at aviation, in spite of the fundamental work done by Thomas Cayley over 100 years earlier. It was struggling even with the concept of airships. *Nulli Secundus* (Second to None), built by the British Army, was a non-rigid, underpowered airship that first took to the air in October 1907, got soaked in the rain and never flew again. Fortunately, working on the engine was an American, Samuel Franklin Cody, who persuaded the army to 'loan' him the *Nulli Secundus*' French Antoinette engine for his heavier-than-air machine, later to be nicknamed by soldiers the 'Flying Cathedral'. On 16 October 1908 Cody tested the output of his engine by tying his 'British Army Aeroplane No. 1' to a tree at Farnborough common; he let it go and took to the air. Having achieved the first successful powered flight in Britain, the Aerial Navigation sub-committee of the Committee on Imperial Defence decided that aeroplanes had no military value. Despite a modest outlay of £2,500 a year on aviation, compared to Germany's £400,000, it cancelled Cody's entire programme, allowing him to take his plane away.

By contrast, in France and the rest of Europe Wilbur Wright was still spurring aviators to greater efforts. He moved to Pau in south-western France and set up the first powered flying school. Orville rejoined his brother and together they made flights in Italy and Germany. Louis Blériot developed new models of his monoplane. Santos-Dumont came up with his bamboo-fuselage Demoiselle, with body-operated wing-warping. Hubert Latham had new Antoinettes and Henry Farman produced the Henry Farman biplane, soon to become more popular as a sport plane than even the Wright Flyers.

They were racing each other, with one major new goal – to be the first across the English Channel.

Im Jahre 1905 erhielten Orville und Wilbur Wright ein Schreiben vom Zeugamt der U.S.-Armee, in dem diese das Angebot ausschlug, das neue Flugzeug Flyer Nr. 3 zu erwerben. Die Army werde erst dann interessiert sein, »wenn eine Maschine zur Verfügung steht, welche durch überzeugende Vorführung unter Beweis stellt, daß sie des horizontalen Fluges fähig ist und einen Steuermann tragen kann«.

Beinahe zwei Jahre waren seit dem historischen Flug in den Kill Devil Hills vergangen, und die Farmer von Dayton, Ohio, hatten sich längst daran gewöhnt, Flugzeuge der Brüder Wright vorbeifliegen zu sehen, doch die U.S.-Regierung wollte nicht glauben, daß sie ein flugerprobtes Gerät angeboten bekam. Die Beamten gingen davon aus, daß sie Experimente in der Art Samuel Langleys fördern sollten; dieser hatte sie dazu gebracht, seinen glücklosen *Aerodrome* zu finanzieren, der im Dezember 1903 in den Potomac stürzte. Die Wrights wandten sich danach an die britische und französische Regierung, doch auch dort führten die Verhandlungen zu nichts. Am 16. Oktober 1905 gaben die Brüder auf, und für die nächsten zweieinhalb Jahre bis zum 6. Mai 1908 unternahmen sie keinen Flug mehr und gestatteten auch niemandem, ihre Flyer zu begutachten. Sie waren jedem anderen Flugpionier um Längen voraus, doch war es beinahe, als hätte ihr historischer Flug niemals stattgefunden.

Die Schuld war gewiß zum großen Teil bei den beiden zu suchen. Die peinlich genauen Wrights, Söhne eines Bischofs der Brüdergemeinde, waren sittenstreng erzogen und hielten nichts davon, für sich die Werbetrommel zu rühren. Die Mühen, die es gefordert hätte, eine ungläubige Welt zu überzeugen, war ihnen die Sache nicht wert. Eine Fotografie und ein Bericht über ihren Flug von 1903 waren um die Welt gegangen, doch der Bericht war konfus und blieb fast unbeachtet. Die Brüder verwandten ihre Zeit lieber darauf, Patentschriften einzureichen, als der Welt zu verkünden, wie ihnen das Fliegen gelungen war. Vielleicht war es nur vernünftig, ihre Flyer vor Spionen und rücksichtslosen Konkurrenten zu schützen – gerade nachdem die britische Regierung verlangt hatte, die Maschinen zu inspizieren und zu erproben, ohne im Gegenzug einen Kauf für den Fall zuzusagen, daß sie den Anforderungen entsprachen –, doch dieses Untertauchen hatte zur Folge, daß die Entwicklung der Luftfahrt die beiden überholte.

Die Europäer begriffen gar nicht, wie weit die Wrights ihnen voraus waren. Für den Aéro-Club de France in Paris

war es keine Frage, daß Frankreich in der Entwicklung des Flugwesens führend war, und das obwohl der mit den Wright-Brüdern befreundete Octave Chanute einen Vortrag gehalten hatte, in dem er die Leistungen der beiden in aller Ausführlichkeit beschrieb. Zwei, denen die Wrightschen Fortschritte zu denken gaben, waren Ernest Archdeacon – ein irischer Anwalt, der in Frankreich lebte, und Ferdinand Ferber, Hauptmann der französischen Armee, und beide bauten Gleitflugzeuge nach dem Vorbild der Wright-Flyer, mit einem Höhenruder am vorderen und Leitwerk am hinteren Ende. Doch keiner der Europäer lernte das Fliegen von Grund auf, so wie die Wrights es getan hatten, und keiner verstand die Steuerung durch Verwinden der Tragflächen. Sie sahen das Fliegen nur als eine Variante des Automobilfahrens, bei der alles auf Flugstabilität (dynamisches Gleichgewicht) ankam.

Ferber erkannte immerhin die entscheidende Neuerung der Wrights und brachte einen motorisierten Gleiter nach Wright-Vorbild im Mai 1905 vom Boden. Andere setzten auf Stabilität und die Kastendrachen des Australiers Lawrence Hargrave. Gabriel Voisin baute zusammen mit Archdeacon und Louis Blériot ein Schwimmflugzeug, das wie eine Kreuzung aus Kastendrachen und Wright-Flyer aussah. Wie der vom Transsylvanier Trajan Vuia gebaute erste Eindecker war es ein Schritt in die richtige Richtung, doch wirklich zum Fliegen kamen beide nicht. Erst am 12. November 1906 hob sich unter enormer Publicity und großer Begeisterung endlich ein europäisches Flugzeug in die Lüfte.

Es war ein Luftschiffer, dem es gelang, Alberto Santos-Dumont, und das mit einem so kuriosen Gefährt, daß er nach einem zweiten kurzen Hüpfer keinen weiteren Start mehr damit unternahm. Santos-Dumonts 14-bis – der Name kommt daher, daß er es für Flugversuche unter sein Luftschiff Nr. 14 montierte – hatte eine gewisse Ähnlichkeit mit Voisins Schwimmflugzeug, doch die Längsstabilität erlangte er, indem er Höhen- und Seitenruder nach vorn holte. Mit einem 24-PS-Motor und Druckpropeller flog Santos-Dumont, stehend in einer Ballongondel, 220 Meter in 21 Sekunden und gewann den vom Aéro-Club ausgesetzten Preis von 1.500 Francs für den ersten Flug von mehr als 100 Metern; dieser Flug fand offizielle Anerkennung als erster bemannter Motorflug Europas.

Damit waren das nationale und internationale Interesse nun im großen Stil geweckt, und entsprechend nahmen die Anstrengungen zu. Das nächste große Ziel war der mit 50.000 Francs dotierte Deutsch-Archdeacon-Preis für den ersten,

A passenger-carrying zeppelin operated by the German Delag, the first scheduled airline company, visits France in 1913.

Ein Zeppelin der deutschen Delag, der ersten Passagierfluglinie der Welt, besucht im Jahr 1913 Frankreich.

Un zeppelin de la compagnie allemande Delag, première compagnie aérienne régulière du monde, lors d'une escale en France en 1913.

dem ein Rundflug von einem Kilometer Länge gelang. Voisin mühte sich mit seinen Kastendrachen, und mit vereinten Kräften errangen er und Henry Farman im Januar 1908 gemeinsam den Preis. Ein großer Erfolg war es allerdings nicht. Die Voisin-Farman 1 war nach wie vor die einzige europäische Maschine, die sich eine ganze Minute lang in der Luft halten konnte. Die Brüder Wright waren bei ihrem letzten Flug, der inzwischen über zwei Jahre zurücklag, 40 km in 39 Minuten geflogen.

In Deutschland ließ sich Hugo Junkers den ersten in einer langen Reihe von Dieselmotoren patentieren; das erste Militärluftschiff des Grafen Zeppelin, LZ3, stieg auf und bei Lisieux in Frankreich war Paul Cornu der erste, der ohne weitere Hilfe mit dem Versuchsmodell eines Helikopters flog. Selbst in Amerika waren die Wrights nun nicht mehr das Maß der Dinge. Glenn Curtiss entwickelte mit Unterstützung der Aerial Experiment Association aus Hammondsport, New York, Langleys Aerodrome-Doppeldecker weiter, und am 4. Juli 1908, dem Nationalfeiertag, gewann er den Preis für den ersten öffentlichen Flug in Amerika über mehr als einen Kilometer Distanz.

Bei dieser Konkurrenz konnten die Wrights nicht mehr länger stillhalten. Schon im Februar 1908 hatten sie Verträge mit der U.S.-Regierung unterzeichnet und den Lizenzbau ihrer Flyer durch eine Firma in Frankreich organisiert. Im Mai reiste Wilbur nach Le Mans und führte dort seinen Flyer vor, und Orville zog nach Washington, um die Zweifler in der Army zu überzeugen. Am 8. August 1908 startete Wilbur Wright vor Hunderten von Zuschauern, den kritischsten Fluginteressierten in ganz Frankreich; er zog in einer Minute und 45 Sekunden zwei elegante Kreise und landete dann sanft. Das Publikum war fassungslos. Zum ersten Mal hatten sie gesehen, was es bedeutete, ein Flugzeug wirklich zu steuern. In den folgenden Monaten flog Wilbur immer länger und höher, die Zuschauerzahlen wurden größer, die Beifallsrufe lauter. Orville Wright hatte in Washington ebenso großen Erfolg, den auch ein Absturz am 17. September nicht schmälerte, bei dem sein Passagier, Leutnant Thomas Selfridge, getötet wurde – der erste, der beim Absturz eines Motorflugzeugs ums Leben kam. Orville wurde schwer verletzt.

Doch Großbritannien sollte das erste Land werden, in dem die Wright-Flyer in Serie gingen. Der Unternehmer Eustace Short hörte von Wilburs Flügen und reiste nach Frankreich, um dort an Ort und Stelle mit ihm zu verhandeln. Mit Bauplä-

nen und einer Lizenz ausgerüstet, richtete er die Fabrik der Gebrüder Short in Shellbeach auf der Isle of Sheppey in Kent ein und baute sechs Flyer am Fließband. Alle sechs waren bereits verkauft, bevor sie fertig überhaupt waren.

Die ersten englischen Flugversuche kamen, obwohl Thomas Cayley schon mehr als 100 Jahre zuvor die grundlegenden Vorarbeiten geleistet hatte, überraschend spät. Selbst mit Luftschiffen tat man sich schwer. Das von der britischen Armee gebaute Pralluftschiff *Nulli secundus* (»Nicht seinesgleichen«) war zu schwach motorisiert, wurde beim ersten Aufstieg im Oktober 1907 vom Regen durchtränkt und flog nie wieder. Immerhin war es Glück, daß der Maschinist der Amerikaner Samuel Franklin Cody war, der einen eigenen Flugapparat zur Verfügung hatte, die »fliegende Kathedrale«, wie die Soldaten sie bald nannten; er konnte die Militärs überreden, ihm dafür den französischen Antoinette-Motor der *Nulli secundus* zu »leihen«. Am 16. Oktober 1908 befestigte er sein »British Army Aeroplane No. 1« auf einer Wiese in Farnham an einem Baum, um die Motorleistung zu testen; er gab Gas und hob sich in die Luft. Damit war nun auch in Großbritannien der erste Motorflug geglückt, doch die zuständigen Militärbehörden kamen zu dem Schluß, daß Flugzeuge keinen militärischen Nutzen hätten. Obwohl die Aufwendungen gerade einmal £ 2.500 pro Jahr betragen hatten – in einer Zeit, in der Deutschland jährlich den Gegenwert von £ 400.000 investierte –, wurde Codys Luftfahrtprogramm eingestellt; als Entschädigung durfte er die Maschine behalten.

In Frankreich und anderen Ländern des Kontinents hingegen spornte Wilbur Wright nach wie vor die Flieger zu immer größeren Anstrengungen an. Er zog nach Pau in Südwestfrankreich und gründete dort die erste Motorflugschule. Orville stieß wieder hinzu, und gemeinsam machten die Brüder Vorführungen in Italien und Deutschland. Louis Blériot entwickelte neue Varianten seines Eindeckers. Santos-Dumont stellte seine Demoiselle vor, mit einem Rumpf aus Bambusstäben und einer Steuerung durch Verwinden der Tragflächen, die der Pilot mit seinem Körper vornahm. Hubert Latham konnte mit neuen Antoinettes aufwarten, und Henry Farman stellte seinen Farman-Doppeldecker vor, der als Sportflugzug bald sogar noch die Wright-Flyer überrunden sollte.

Der Wettlauf um das nächste große Ziel hatte begonnen – die Überquerung des Ärmelkanals.

Count Ferdinand von Zeppelin (centre) with Zeppelin captain Hugo Eckener (on left) and Captain Peter Strasser, commander of German Navy airships, 1915.

Ferdinand Graf von Zeppelin (Mitte) mit dem Luftschiffkapitän Hugo Eckener (links) und Kapitän Peter Strasser, dem Kommandeur der deutschen Marineluftschiffe, 1915.

Le comte Ferdinand von Zeppelin (au centre) avec le capitaine de zeppelin Hugo Eckener (à gauche) et le capitaine Peter Strasser, commandant du dirigeable de la Marine allemande, en 1915.

C'est en 1905 qu'Orville et Wilbur Wright reçoivent une lettre du Service du matériel de l'armée des États-Unis rejetant leur offre de vente du Flyer N° III, leur dernier modèle d'aéroplane. L'armée ne saurait s'intéresser à l'aviation, leur explique-t-on, «tant qu'une machine ne sera pas capable d'effectuer un vol horizontal et d'emporter un opérateur».

Il y a près de deux ans qu'a eu lieu le vol historique du Flyer à Kill Devil Hills. Bien que les fermiers de Dayton (Ohio) aient désormais pris l'habitude de voir tourner les avions des Wright au-dessus de leurs champs, le gouvernement américain refuse encore de croire qu'il existe un appareil pouvant réellement voler. L'administration, sans doute échaudée après l'échec de Samuel Langley et du malheureux *Aerodrome*, dont elle s'était laissé persuader de financer la réalisation et qui disparut dans les eaux du Potomac en décembre 1903, pense alors que les Wright lui demandent encore de commanditer un projet. Après de vaines négociations auprès des gouvernements britannique et français qu'ils ont contactés à leur tour, les deux frères abandonnent finalement leurs démarches le 16 octobre 1905 et, pendant plus de deux ans et demi, soit jusqu'au 6 mai 1908, ne montent plus dans un aéroplane et ne permettent à aucun étranger de voir leurs Flyer. Malgré leur extraordinaire avance sur quiconque dans le domaine de l'aviation, c'est comme si leur vol historique n'avait jamais eu lieu.

La faute leur incombe pour une bonne part. Certes, la nouvelle de leur vol de 1903, illustrée par une photographie, a été diffusée dans le monde entier mais le compte rendu a été publié de manière si fantaisiste qu'il n'eut qu'un faible impact. Il est vrai aussi que ces fils d'un prélat de la United Brethren Church s'en tiennent à de hautes valeurs morales et ne se soucient guère de faire leur propre publicité. En outre, ils ne désirent pas perdre leur temps à faire les efforts nécessaires pour persuader les sceptiques et préfèrent déposer des brevets plutôt que d'expliquer comment ils ont pu réussir. Peut-être eurent-ils raison de chercher à protéger leur Flyer d'éventuels espions industriels dans une compétition entre avionneurs qui s'annonce rude; sans doute devinrent-ils particulièrement méfiants après que le gouvernement britannique eut insisté pour examiner et essayer leurs machines sans pour autant garantir de les acheter si elles correspondaient aux spécifications édictées; toujours est-il que leur goût du secret a permis au monde naissant de l'aviation européenne de les devancer.

Les Européens ne saisissent pas tout d'abord quelle est l'avance des Wright, malgré une conférence détaillée que donne à Paris Octave Chanute, l'ami des Wright, sur les réalisations des deux frères. L'Aéro-Club de France se montre même optimiste quant à la position de la France comme chef de file de l'aviation. En revanche, le juriste d'origine irlandaise Ernest Archdeacon et le capitaine d'artillerie français Ferdinand Ferber s'inquiètent des progrès des deux Américains et entreprennent de construire des planeurs de type Wright équipés d'un élévateur à l'avant et d'un gouvernail de direction à l'arrière. Mais les Européens ne procèdent pas par étapes successives à l'instar des Wright et voient mal l'intérêt du système de gauchissement alaire pour la maniabilité. Considérant plutôt l'aviation comme un prolongement de l'automobile, leur principal souci est alors la stabilité du vol.

Ferber, qui comprend ce que les Wright avaient voulu faire, obtient un Flyer Wright, le modifie, l'équipe d'un moteur et décolle à son bord en mai 1905. Pendant ce temps, d'autres préfèrent se consacrer à la stabilité et s'inspirent des principes de vol des cerfs-volants de l'Australien Lawrence Hargrave. Gabriel Voisin, travaillant en coopération avec Archdeacon et Louis Blériot, construit un aéroplane flottant qui évoque un hybride de Flyer Wright et de cerf-volant. Cet appareil, à l'instar du premier monoplan du Roumain Trajan Vuia, est très prometteur mais ne fonctionne pas encore vraiment. Il faudra attendre le 12 novembre 1906 pour voir un aéroplane européen quitter le sol.

Cet exploit, salué par les ovations de la foule et largement exploité à grand renfort de publicité, est réalisé par un «ancien» aérostier, Alberto Santos-Dumont dans un appareil si étrange qu'il en abandonne la formule après un autre vol. Ce 14-bis – qui doit son nom au fait qu'il était suspendu sous le dirigeable N° 14 pour ses premiers tests – s'inspire de l'hydroplane de Voisin mais voit sa stabilité longitudinale assurée en plaçant l'élévateur et la gouverne de direction à l'avant. Disposant d'un moteur de 24 ch placé à l'arrière, il parcourut 220 m en 21 secondes, remporta le prix de 1 500 francs offert par l'Aéro-Club de France pour avoir effectué le premier vol de plus de 100 m et établit officiellement le premier record aérien d'Europe pour un avion propulsé.

Une fois réveillés la curiosité et l'intérêt de tous, tant sur le plan national qu'international, chacun redoubla d'effort. L'objectif était désormais le prix Deutsch-Archdeacon, doté de 50 000 francs, offert au premier à effectuer un vol de d'un kilo-

Towed behind a car, a glider designed by Bélin is prepared for its maiden flight in 1908.

Mit dem Automobil wird im Jahre 1908 ein Gleitflugzeug von Bélin zum Jungfernflug gezogen.

Remorqué par une automobile, un planeur conçu par Bélin se prépare à effectuer son vol inaugural en 1908.

mètre en circuit fermé. Voisin améliora son modèle à caisson de queue et, aidé par Henry Farman qui pilota l'appareil, remporta finalement le prix en janvier 1908. Si le vol eut un certain retentissement, le Voisin-Farman 1 étant encore le seul appareil européen capable de rester une minute en l'air, il fallait bien admettre que le dernier vol des frères Wright, plus de deux ans plus tôt, avait duré 39 minutes et permis de parcourir 40 kilomètres.

En Allemagne, Hugo Junkers fait alors breveter le premier d'une longue série de moteurs diesel, tandis que le premier des dirigeables militaires de Zeppelin, le LZ3, s'élève dans les airs ; en France, près de Lisieux, Paul Cornu est le premier homme à voler sans aide dans le premier hélicoptère expérimental. Aux États-Unis, l'attention se détourne quelque peu des Wright lorsque Glenn Curtiss, soutenu par l'Aerial Experiment Association de Hammondsport (New York), s'inspire du biplan de Langley, l'*Aerodrome*, et le 4 juillet 1908, le jour de la fête de l'Indépendance, remporte le prix attribué au premier avion américain à voler officiellement sur une distance de plus d'un kilomètre.

Les Wright bougent enfin. En février 1908, ils signent plusieurs contrats avec le gouvernement américain et concluent un accord de construction sous licence de leur Flyer avec une société française. En mai, Wilbur arrive au Mans pour effectuer des vols de démonstration de son appareil tandis qu'Orville se rend à Washington pour convaincre les sceptiques de l'armée américaine. Le 8 août 1908, sous les yeux de centaines de spectateurs les plus critiques dans le domaine de l'aviation, Wilbur Wright décolle, effectue deux orbes gracieuses en une minute et 45 secondes et se pose doucement devant l'assistance médusée : pour la première fois, les gens comprennent ce que signifie un vol contrôlé. Au cours des mois suivants, Wilbur vole plus loin et plus haut, devant une foule toujours plus nombreuse et plus enthousiaste. À Washington, Orville Wright conquiert également son public, même après l'accident de son Flyer, le 17 septembre, au cours duquel son passager, le lieutenant Thomas Selfridge, trouve la mort, devenant ainsi le premier passager tué dans un aéroplane motorisé, lui-même étant grièvement blessé.

Mais c'est à la Grande-Bretagne que les Wright parviennent d'abord à vendre le brevet de leur Flyer. L'entrepreneur Eustace Short, ayant entendu parler des vols effectués par Wilbur, se rend en France pour négocier avec lui l'achat des plans et d'une licence de fabrication, puis crée à Shellbeach, dans

l'île de Sheppey (Kent), l'usine Short Brothers où il construit six Flyer sur sa chaîne d'assemblage. Tous les appareils seront vendus avant même d'être terminés.

La Grande-Bretagne est restée jusqu'alors étonnamment prudente à l'égard de l'aviation, malgré l'œuvre fondamentale de Thomas Cayley un siècle plus tôt, et débat encore du concept de dirigeable. Le *Nulli Secundus* (ou «Premier de Tous»), construit par l'armée britannique, est un dirigeable souple et sous-motorisé qui, lors de son vol inaugural en octobre 1907, s'abîme sous la pluie ; il ne volera plus jamais. Par chance, un Américain qui avait travaillé sur le projet, Samuel Franklin Cody, persuade l'armée de lui «prêter» le moteur français Antoinette du *Nulli Secundus* pour l'adapter à son aéroplane, que les soldats surnommeront par la suite la «Cathédrale volante». Le 16 octobre 1908, Cody effectue des essais de puissance de son moteur en attachant son «British Army Aéroplane N° 1» à un arbre du terrain communal de Farnborough puis, montant à bord, décolle et réussit le premier vol motorisé en Grande-Bretagne. Malgré cela, le sous-comité de la Navigation aérienne du Comité de Défense impérial décide que les aéroplanes n'ont aucune valeur militaire et supprime la totalité du programme de recherches de Cody, un modeste budget de 2500 £ par an alloué à l'aviation (à comparer aux 400 000 £ attribuées par l'Allemagne), mais lui permet de garder son avion.

En revanche, en France et dans le reste de l'Europe, Wilbur Wright encourage les aviateurs à poursuivre leurs efforts en s'installant à Pau pour y créer la première école d'aviation motorisée. Lorsqu'Orville rejoint son frère, ils partent tous les deux effectuer des vols de démonstration en Italie et en Allemagne. Pendant ce temps, Louis Blériot développe de nouveaux modèles de son monoplan, Santos-Dumont reparaît avec sa Demoiselle à structure en bambou et un système de gauchissement fixé à la veste du pilote, Hubert Latham fabrique de nouveaux Antoinette et Henry Farman produit le biplan qui deviendra encore plus populaire que le Flyer des Wright.

Tous – ou presque – n'ont plus qu'une seule grande ambition : être le premier à traverser la Manche.

The first eight pilots granted Aéro-Club de France certificates in 1909 included Louis Blériot (top), Ferdinand Ferber, Henry Farman and Léon Delagrange.

Zu den ersten acht Fliegern, die 1909 vom Aéro-Club de France einen Pilotenschein bekamen, zählten (von oben) Louis Blériot, Ferdinand Ferber, Henry Farman und Léon Delagrange.

Louis Blériot (en haut), Ferdinand Ferber, Henry Farman et Léon Delagrange furent, en 1909, parmi les huit premiers aviateurs à obtenir le brevet de pilote délivré par l'Aéro-Club de France.

Wright's gliders

Orville and Wilbur Wright began tests in 1900 by manipulating the wing surfaces of their No. 1 glider to react to the wind (**2**). By 1903 No. 3 glider (**3**) had gained a rudder. (The original glass plate is blemished.) 'Wing warping' – stabilizing – was done by wires to the feet, not always successfully (**1**).

Die Gebrüder Wright

Orville und Wilbur Wright begannen 1900 mit ihren Experimenten, bei denen sie an ihrem Gleiter Nr. 1 verstellbare Tragflächen anbrachten, mit denen der Pilot auf den Wind reagieren konnte (**2**). Gleiter Nr. 3 von 1903 verfügte bereits über ein Höhenruder (**3**; die originale Glasplatte ist beschädigt). Das Verwinden – zur Stabilisierung – wurde mit den Füßen über Drähte gesteuert und gelang nicht immer (**1**).

Les planeurs des frères Wright

En 1900, Orville et Wilbur Wright commencèrent par étudier la réaction au vent de leur planeur N° 1 en jouant sur les surfaces des ailes (**2**). En 1903, le planeur N° 3 (**3**) est pourvu d'une gouverne de direction (la plaque photographique originale est abîmée). Le «gauchissement» de l'aile par torsion s'effectue alors en tirant des câbles avec le pied (**1**).

First flight

Kill Devil Hills, Kitty Hawk, North Carolina, 17 December 1903. After one failure when Wilbur Wright stalled on take-off and crashed, brother Orville opened the throttle of the new, Wright-designed 12hp engine and felt their Flyer lift off its launching rail. With Wilbur running alongside, he covered 120 feet in a flight lasting 12 seconds. It was officially the first sustained, controlled powered flight by a heavier-than-air machine, and it made history.

Der erste Flug

Kill Devil Hills, Kitty Hawk, North Carolina, 17. Dezember 1903. Beim ersten Versuch kommt Wilbur Wright nicht vom Boden und setzt die Maschine unsanft auf. Doch dann zieht sein Bruder Orville den Gashebel des neuen, von den Wright-Brüdern konstruierten 12-PS-Motors und spürt, wie der Flyer sich von der Startschiene hebt. Wilbur läuft neben ihm her, und in einem Flug von 12 Sekunden legt Orville 40 Meter zurück. Dieser Flug ging als erster erfolgreicher Motorflug (der erste längere, gesteuerte Flug in einer Maschine, die schwerer war als Luft) in die Geschichte ein.

Premier vol

Le 17 décembre 1903, dans les collines de Kill Devil près de Kitty Hawk (Caroline du Nord). Après l'échec d'une première tentative, au cours de laquelle Wilbur Wright, en perte de vitesse, s'écrase au décollage sans autres dommages que matériels, son frère Orville s'élance, ouvre la manette des gaz du nouveau moteur Wright de 12 CV, sent le Flyer quitter soudain son rail de lancement et, avec Wilbur courant à côté de l'appareil, parcourt 40 m en restant 12 secondes en vol. Ce «bond» historique est officiellement le premier vol soutenu, contrôlé et propulsé d'un «plus lourd que l'air».

The Wright Flyer

Wilbur Wright demonstrated a 1907 model Flyer at Le Mans in August 1908 (**1**), and showed it to King Edward VII at Pau, France, in 1909 (**3**). Demonstrating a Flyer to the US Army in Virginia in September 1908, however, Orville Wright crashed, killing his passenger, Lt Thomas Selfridge (**4**). In September 1909, a month after these people sheltered under Eugène Lefebvre's new Type A Flyer at Reims (**2**), Lefebvre died – the first pilot to be killed in a plane crash.

Der Wright-Flyer

Im August 1908 führt Wilbur Wright einen Flyer, Modell 1907, in Le Mans vor (**1**) und zeigt ihn 1909 in Pau, Frankreich, dem englischen König Edward VII. (**3**). Orville Wright stürzte im September 1908 in Virginia auf einem Demonstrationsflug für die U.S.-Army ab, und sein Passagier, Lieutenant Thomas Selfridge, kam dabei um (**4**). Im September 1909, einen Monat nachdem dieses Bild in Reims entstand (**2**), fand Eugène Lefebvre mit seinem neuen Type A-Flyer den Tod – der erste Motorflieger, der bei einem Absturz umkam.

Le Flyer des Wright

Après que Wilbur Wright a effectué au Mans, en août 1908, une série de démonstrations en vol de son Flyer modèle 1907 (**1**), en septembre de la même année, Orville s'écrase lors d'une présentation de l'appareil à l'armée américaine en Virginie (États-Unis) et tue son passager, le lieutenant Thomas Selfridge (**4**). En 1909, Wilbur Wright, désormais installé à Pau, présente son appareil au roi Edouard VII d'Angleterre (**3**). Eugène Lefebvre, premier pilote tué dans un accident d'avion, meurt en septembre en testant le nouveau Flyer Type A qu'il a construit, photographié ici à Reims un mois plus tôt (**2**).

First to fly?

The Americans Samuel Langley (**2**, on right) and Charles Manly (**2**, on left) almost had the first flying machine in October 1903, when Langley's *Aerodrome* was catapulted off a houseboat in the Potomac river (**3**). However, Manly, who had built the remarkable radial engine (**1**), flew it straight into the river. In 1914, to counter a copyright lawsuit brought against him by the Wrights, aviation pioneer Glenn Curtiss tried to prove the *Aerodrome* could fly (**4**), but his efforts were discredited by the major modifications he made to the machine.

Waren sie die Ersten?

Die Amerikaner Samuel Langley (**2**, rechts) und Charles Manly (**2**, links) wären den Gebrüdern Wright beinahe zuvorgekommen. Im Oktober 1903 starteten sie Langleys *Aerodrome* mit einem Katapult von Bord eines Hausboots auf dem Potomac (**3**), doch Manly, von dem der bemerkenswerte Sternmotor stammte (**1**), stürzte gleich nach dem Start damit in den Fluß. Um eine Copyrightklage der Wright-Brüder gegen ihn abzuschmettern, versuchte der Flugpionier Glenn Curtiss 1914 zu beweisen, daß die *Aerodrome* tatsächlich fliegen konnte (**4**), doch unterlag er im Rechtsstreit, weil er die Maschine an entscheidenden Stellen modifiziert hatte.

Le premier à voler?

Les Américains Samuel Langley (**2**, à droite) et Charles Manly (à gauche) auraient pu être, dès octobre 1903, les premiers à faire voler un «plus lourd que l'air». Malheureusement, leur *Aerodrome*, conçu par Langley et doté par Manly d'un remarquable moteur en étoile (**1**), bascule du toit de la «maison flottante» sur le Potomac d'où il est catapulté (**3**) et s'abîme directement dans le fleuve. En 1914, Glenn Curtiss, un des pionniers de l'aviation américaine, tente de prouver que ce même *Aerodrome* peut voler (**4**) afin de s'opposer au procès en contrefaçon que lui intentent les frères Wright; mais ses efforts sont discrédités par les modifications importantes qu'il a effectuées sur la machine.

1

2
3

2

Europe's first flight

Europeans remained largely ignorant or indifferent to the Wrights' great advances. In September 1906, three years after Kitty Hawk, Jacob C.H. Ellehammer made tentative hops in a machine tethered to a post in Lindholm, Denmark, powered by his own excellent 18hp radial engine (**1**). But it was in the strange, tail-first box-kite biplane 14-bis, named after a test-flight balloon, that Alberto Santos-Dumont achieved Europe's first flight (**2**) in October 1906. Unlike the Wright Flyer, the 14-bis demonstrated Europe's preoccupation with stability; Santos-Dumont stood upright in a balloon basket.

Der erste europäische Flug

In Europa wurden die Leistungen der Gebrüder Wright kaum bekannt. Im September 1906, drei Jahre nach Kitty Hawk, macht Jacob C.H. Ellehammer im dänischen Lindholm ein paar Luftsprünge mit einer Maschine, die an einem Tau um einen Pfosten kreiste (**1**); angetrieben war sie von Ellehammers ausgezeichnetem 18-PS-Sternmotor. Doch war es der merkwürdige, nach einem Ballon, mit dem er die Testfahrt absolvierte, benannte Kastendrachen 14-bis, mit dem Alberto Santos-Dumont im Oktober 1906 der erste europäische Motorflug gelang (**2**). Anders als der Wrightsche Flyer war die 14-bis, die mit dem Leitwerk voran flog, auf Starrflug konstruiert; Santos-Dumont stand dabei aufrecht in einem Ballonkorb.

Le premier vol en Europe

Les Européens étaient peu au courant des progrès réalisés par les Wright. Trois ans après leurs vols historiques à Kitty Hawk, en septembre 1906, Jacob C.H. Ellehammer effectue, dans l'île de Lindholm (Danemark), quelques bonds sur un appareil relié à un pylône et mû par un excellent moteur en étoile de 18 cv de sa conception (**1**). Un mois après, Alberto Santos-Dumont réussit en revanche le premier vol européen avec son étrange biplan cellulaire de type «canard» (c'est-à-dire avec le gouvernail à l'avant), le 14-bis (2), du nom du dirigeable auquel il l'avait suspendu pour ses essais en vol. Contrairement au Flyer des Wright, le 14-bis manifeste les préoccupations des Européens concernant la stabilité des aéroplanes.

But will they fly?

Europeans in late 1906 still wasted time with odd designs. Most of these tinkerers preferred to put their faith in hope rather than scientific principles; wind tunnels were virtually unheard of. But some pioneers were almost there. In Paris, the Transylvanian Trajan Vuia's bat-winged monoplane (**1**) managed a few hops, but was far too heavy, while Louis Blériot struggled with this ellipsoidal, non-flying biplane (**2**).

Ob sie jemals fliegen?

Noch Ende 1906 vergeudete man in Europa seine Zeit mit kuriosen Konstruktionen. Die vielen Bastler vertrauten fast durchweg auf ihr Glück statt auf wissenschaftliche Prinzipien; Windkanäle waren so gut wie unbekannt. Einige dieser Pioniere hätten es allerdings beinahe geschafft. In Paris gelangen dem Transsylvanier Trajan Vuia einige Hüpfer mit seinem fledermausflügligen Eindecker (**1**), doch die Maschine war viel zu schwer, und auch Louis Blériot bekam seinen Doppeldecker mit elliptischer Tragfläche (**2**) nicht vom Boden.

Voleront-ils?

Fin 1906, les inventeurs européens continuent de perdre leur temps à dessiner d'étranges engins aux géométries bizarres, la plupart d'entre eux se fiant plus à leurs désirs qu'à des principes purement scientifiques, sans compter que les tunnels aérodynamiques leur sont pratiquement inconnus. Tandis que le monoplan à ailes de chauve-souris du Roumain Trajan Vuia (**1**) réussit, malgré son poids, quelques sauts de puce à Paris, Louis Blériot s'efforce – en vain – de faire voler son biplan à voilures elliptiques (**2**).

Optimism

In the absence of solid scientific research, Europeans in the early 1900s did not feel embarrassed at producing odd flying machines. Technology in all fields was advancing at breakneck speed, much of it by trial and error. In 1904 a gentleman named Schmutz unsuccessfully tried this pedal-powered Cycloplane (**1**), and in 1909, M. Vuitton put together a tentative helicopter (**2**), which was along the right lines but far too primitive to be practical.

Optimisten

Da es Anfang des 20. Jahrhunderts kaum eine fundierte wissenschaftliche Forschung gab, wurde mit den verschrobensten Entwürfen experimentiert. Das Tempo des technischen Fortschritts war halsbrecherisch, und meist lernte man durch simples Probieren. Ein gewisser Schmutz versuchte es 1904 vergebens mit diesem Flugfahrrad (**1**), und M. Vuitton baute im Jahr 1909 einen ersten Hubschrauber (**2**), dessen Konstruktion schon in die richtige Richtung wies, der aber in dieser einfachen Form noch nicht flugtauglich war.

Optimisme

Au début des années 1900, les Européens n'hésitent pas, faute d'études et de données scientifiques solides, à concevoir d'insolites machines volantes et contribuent de cette façon à faire rapidement progresser, bien que de manière empirique, la technologie aéronautique dans ses différents domaines d'application. En 1904, un certain Schmutz expérimente ainsi – sans succès – un «Cycloplane» à pédale (**1**) tandis que M. Vuitton construit en 1909 une sorte d'hélicoptère (**2**) qui, bien que sur la bonne voie, demeure bien trop primitif pour être efficace.

45030

Thinking vertically

Vertical flight proved one of the most difficult things to master. The Bertin autogyro tried to get extra lift from a small rotor blade in 1908 (**1**), while in the same year M. Collomb produced a big, wing-flapping ornithopter (**3**) to fly like a bird. Although no ornithopters ever flew, some inventors still had hopes. A contraption introduced at a London exhibition in 1911 (**2**) was known as 'The Bartlett Flapping Machine'.

Das vertikale Prinzip

Kaum eine Aufgabe erwies sich als so schwierig zu meistern wie der vertikale Flug. Bei Bertins Autogyro (Drehflügler) von 1908 sollte ein zusätzlicher Rotor für Auftrieb sorgen (**1**), und im selben Jahr konstruierte M. Collomb seinen imposanten Ornithopter (**3**), der mit den Flügeln schlug wie ein Vogel. Zwar hob sich kein Ornithopter je in die Lüfte, doch manche Konstrukteure setzten weiter ihre ganze Hoffnung auf dieses Prinzip. 1911 wurde auf einer Ausstellung in London die »Bartlett Flapping Machine« gezeigt (**2**).

Voler verticalement

Le vol vertical se révèle rapidement être un problème des plus difficiles à maîtriser. En 1908, Bertin tente d'améliorer la sustentation de son autogyro (giravion) en lui ajoutant une petite hélice de rotor (**1**). Bien qu'aucun ornithoptère ait jamais volé, quelques inventeurs nourrissent quelques espoirs : ainsi M. Collomb, qui construit en 1908 un grand ornithoptère à ailes battantes (**3**), censé voler comme un oiseau, ou Mr. Bartlett qui présenta sa «Bartlett Flapping Machine» à l'exposition de Londres de 1911 (**2**).

Farman's success

Perhaps the second greatest advance, after the Wrights' first flight, was in January 1908, when Henry Farman flew a Voisin biplane over a 1km circular course in France. By Wright standards the achievement was tiny: 1,500 metres over 1 minute 28 seconds. But it was by far the longest flight to date in Europe, and its success forced the shy Wrights back into the public eye.

Farmans Triumph

Vielleicht der zweitgrößte Schritt voran nach dem Flug der Gebrüder Wright wurde im Januar 1908 in Frankreich getan, wo Henry Farman mit einem Voisin-Doppeldecker einen Rundflug von 1.500 Metern in einer Minute und 28 Sekunden absolvierte. Nach Wright-Maßstäben war das keine große Leistung, aber es war der bis dahin mit Abstand längste Flug in Europa, und Farmans Erfolg zwang auch die publikumsscheuen Wrights wieder ins Rampenlicht.

Les succès de Farman

Le plus grand progrès dans l'histoire de l'aviation, après le premier vol des Wright, fut sans doute marqué ce jour de janvier 1908 où Henry Farman effectua le premier kilomètre en circuit fermé sur un biplan Voisin. Si cet exploit – 1 500 mètres en 1 minute 28 secondes – reste modeste comparé à ceux des frères Wright, il s'agit toutefois du plus long vol effectué en Europe, dont le succès contraignit les timides Wright à revenir sur le devant de la scène.

A startling sight

In France in October 1908, people stopped and stared up at an historic sight – aviation pioneer Henry Farman flying his Voisin box-kite aeroplane on Europe's first cross-country flight (**1**). It was nine months after Farman (**2**, on left) and Gabriel Voisin (on right) had flown their record-breaking 1km circular flight. The 16-mile journey from Buoy, near Châlons, to Reims was the first time two towns had been connected by air.

Wie aus einer anderen Welt

Frankreich, Oktober 1908: Passanten halten inne und blicken gen Himmel, um den Flugpionier Henry Farman mit seiner Voisin-Kastendrachen-Maschine auf dem ersten Überlandflug Europas zu sehen (**1**). Neun Monate waren vergangen, seit Farman (**2**, links) und Gabriel Voisin (rechts) ihren 1-km-Rundenrekord aufgestellt hatten. Der 25-Kilometer-Flug von Buoy bei Châlons nach Reims war zugleich der erste Flug von einer Stadt zur anderen.

Une étonnante vision

Quelques Français eurent la chance d'assister à un événement historique : la première liaison aérienne de « ville à ville » – soit 27 km entre Bouy, près de Châlons, et Reims – effectuée par Henry Farman à bord de son aéroplane cellulaire Voisin, en octobre 1908 (**1**). Neuf mois que ce dernier (**2**, à gauche), posant ici avec Gabriel Voisin (à droite), eut établi le premier record de vol en circuit fermé sur 1 km.

2

1

2

Box-kite fever

Voisin-Farman box-kites were all the rage in Europe by 1909. John Moore-Brabazon's made the first flight at Leysdown, Kent (**1**). The Baron de Caters fascinated watchers at Châlons (**2**), and at Reims the British pioneer Claude Grahame-White showed off his 'Baby' model (**3**). The stability of the Voisins made them safer and more popular than the Wright Flyer, but they had no roll control and could only be flown in dead calm weather.

Drachenfieber

Alle Welt wollte 1909 in Europa Kastendrachen von Voisin-Farman. John Moore-Brabazon startet zu seinem ersten Flug in Leysdown, Kent (**1**). In Châlons fasziniert der Baron de Caters die Zuschauer (**2**), und in Reims zeigt der britische Flieger Claude Grahame-White stolz sein »Baby«-Modell (**3**). Die Voisin-Maschinen waren wegen ihrer größeren Flugstabilität beliebter als die Flyer von Wright, doch sie hatten keine Möglichkeit, Rollbewegungen abzufangen, und konnten nur bei völliger Windstille fliegen.

La fièvre du cellulaire

En 1909, les aéroplanes à structure cellulaire Voisin-Farman sont très à la mode en Europe. C'est à bord d'un de ces appareils que John Moore-Brabazon s'apprête à décoller de Leysdown, dans le Kent (**1**), et que le baron de Caters s'envole à Châlons (**2**), tandis qu'à Reims Claude Grahame-White, un des pionniers de l'aviation anglaise, présente son «Baby» (**3**). La stabilité des Voisins les rend plus sûrs et plus populaires que les Flyer des Wright, bien qu'ils ne disposent pas de commande de gauchissement et ne puissent voler que par temps très calme.

America awakes

The American Glenn Curtiss (**5**, on right) produced his *June Bug* – a compromise between Wright manoeuvrability and Voisin stability – and then the successor *Golden Flyer* to put the US back in the frame in August 1909. He won the world speed record at the first international air show at Reims, France (**1**). With success came advertising (**4**), followed by government backing and, in 1911, a warplane for use on the Mexican front (**3**). Orders followed for the first of many float planes (**2**).

Amerika erwacht

Der Amerikaner Glenn Curtiss (**5**, rechts) produzierte die *June Bug* – einen Kompromiß zwischen der guten Steuerbarkeit der Wright-Modelle und der Flugstabilität der Voisin-Konstruktionen –, und mit dem Nachfolger *Golden Flyer* waren die Vereinigten Staaten im August 1909 buchstäblich wieder im Rennen. Auf der ersten internationalen Luftfahrtschau im französischen Reims stellte Curtiss einen Geschwindigkeits-Weltrekord auf (**1**). Mit dem Erfolg kamen auch die Reklame (**4**) und die staatliche Unterstützung, und für den Krieg gegen Mexiko entstand 1911 ein Militärflugzeug (**3**). Es folgte der Auftrag für das erste von vielen Wasserflugzeugen (**2**).

L'Amérique s'éveille

Désireux de ramener les États-Unis sur le devant de la scène, l'Américain Glenn Curtiss (**5**, à droite) construit en août 1909 son *June Bug* – un compromis entre la manœuvrabilité du Wright et la stabilité du Voisin – puis le *Golden Flyer*, avant d'établir dans le même mois le record mondial de vitesse au premier meeting international d'aviation à Reims (**1**). Ces succès, confortés par la publicité (**4**), s'accompagnent bientôt du soutien du gouvernement américain et, en 1911, de la commande d'un avion de guerre destiné au front mexicain (**3**) et d'un des premiers nombreux hydravions (**2**).

T104

Pride of Germany

In parallel with the heavier-than-air developments, Count von Zeppelin's huge, rigid airships were Germany's great national assets. Since the launch of his first airship, LZ1, in 1900, von Zeppelin's mighty machines had held the world spellbound. On Lake Constance in 1906 members of the Reichstag watched preparations for the launch of LZ3 (**3**), while a later model was observed from shore (**1**). The wreck of LZ4 at Echterdingen in 1908 (**2**) immediately bankrupted von Zeppelin, but an outpouring of public and government money saved him. With national backing, in October 1909 the Count formed Delag, the world's first commercial airline company.

Der Stolz des Reiches

Parallel zu den Fortschritten im Flugzeugbau entstanden die gewaltigen starren Luftschiffe des Grafen Zeppelin, auf die man in Deutschland zu Recht stolz war. Seit dem Start des ersten Zeppelins LZ1 im Jahre 1900 hielten die mächtigen Schiffe des Grafen die Welt in Atem. 1906 haben sich Reichtagsmitglieder an Bord eines Bodenseeschiffes versammelt, um den Jungfernflug der LZ3 mitzuerleben (**3**); beim Flug eines späteren Modells stehen die Zuschauer am Ufer (**1**). Der Absturz der LZ4 in Echterdingen im Jahre 1908 (**2**) ruinierte den Grafen, doch öffentliche und private Geldspenden hielten die Firma am Leben. Im Oktober 1909 gründete von Zeppelin mit staatlicher Unterstützung die Delag, die erste kommerzielle Fluggesellschaft der Welt.

Fierté de l'Allemagne

Les immenses dirigeables rigides du comte von Zeppelin représentent le plus grand atout de l'Allemagne face aux progrès réalisés par les «plus lourds que l'air». En effet, les puissants appareils de von Zeppelin fascinent le monde entier depuis l'envol de son premier dirigeable, le LZ1, en 1900. En 1906, le lac de Constance est utilisé pour le lancement du LZ3, auquel quelques membres du Reichstag assistent depuis le pont d'un bateau (**3**), et à celui d'une variante légèrement postérieure de ce même modèle, cette fois observé depuis le rivage (**1**). L'accident du LZ4, en 1908 à Echterdingen (**2**), entraîna immédiatement la faillite de von Zeppelin, qui ne put poursuivre son entreprise que grâce au concours du public et aux subsides du gouvernement allemand. Une souscription nationale, lancée en octobre 1909, permit alors au comte de créer la Delag, première compagnie aérienne commerciale du monde.

Airship appeal

Because of their size, simplicity, majestic flight and ability to carry ordinary passengers, airships continued to attract as much, if not more, attention than the much smaller aeroplanes. The British Army's new *Baby* airship attracted a crowd at Aldershot in May 1909 (**1**). It was an aerodynamic improvement on the army's first airship, *Nulli Secundus*, in 1907 (**2**). Little skill was thought necessary to pilot a balloon, and in January 1910 an unidentified American lady, wearing a long dress and feathered hat, made an ascent in the one-person airship *Dixon* (**3**).

Sympathieträger

Mit ihrer Größe, dem einfachen Bauprinzip, dem majestätischen Flug und der Möglichkeit, Passagiere mitzunehmen, erregten die Luftschiffe nach wie vor ebensoviel Aufmerksamkeit wie die viel kleineren Flugzeuge – vielleicht sogar mehr. Das neue Luftschiff *Baby* der britischen Armee hat im Mai 1909 bei einer Landung in Aldershot die Neugierigen angelockt (**1**). Im Vergleich zum ersten Luftschiff der Army, der *Nulli Secundus* aus dem Jahre 1907, war der Nachfolger aerodynamisch verbessert (**2**). Ballonfliegen galt als einfach, und im Januar 1910 unternimmt eine unbekannte Amerikanerin in langem Kleid und Federhut einen Aufstieg mit dem Einsitzer-Luftschiff *Dixon* (**3**).

L'attrait des aérostats

En mai 1909, une foule nombreuse se presse à Aldershot (**1**) pour assister à la présentation du nouveau dirigeable britannique *Baby*, version aérodynamiquement améliorée du *Nulli Secundus* de 1907, le premier ballon dirigeable militaire anglais (**2**). En effet, les aérostats attirèrent longtemps l'attention du public – autant, sinon plus, que les aéroplanes – en raison de leurs impressionnantes dimensions, de leur majesté, de leur (relative) simplicité et de leur accessibilité à des passagers «ordinaires». Considérant que le pilotage d'un ballon nécessitait peu de qualités particulières, cette Américaine (demeurée anonyme) effectua, en longue robe et chapeau à plumes, une ascension solitaire en janvier 1910 à bord du dirigeable monoplace *Dixon* (**3**).

2

3

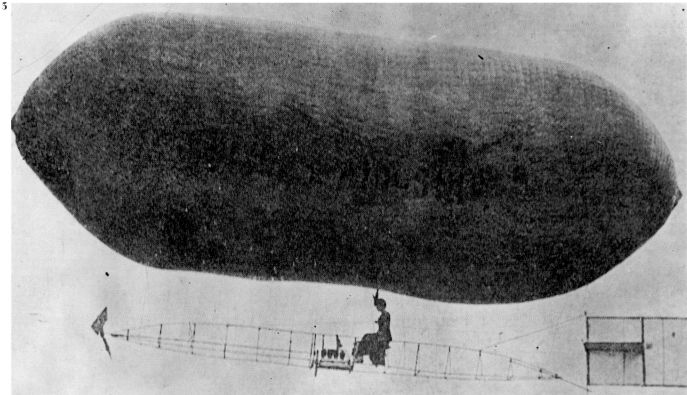

The *Mayfly* disaster

Alarmed by Count von Zeppelin's advances, the British navy ordered its own rigid airship in July 1908. Built by submarine designers in Barrow, it was too heavy and not ready for testing – with its keel reluctantly removed – until September 1911 when it edged slowly out of its waterside shed (**2**). H.M. Airship No. 1 was being towed out to a floating mast (**1**) when a gust of wind tipped it over. With only the new duralumin alloy frame for a structure, it twisted in half (**3**) and was damaged beyond repair. It quickly earned the name *Mayfly*.

Die Eintagsfliege

Von dem Erfolg des Grafen Zeppelin unter Druck gesetzt, gab die britische Marine im Juli 1908 ein eigenes starres Luftschiff in Auftrag. Es entstand in einer U-Bootwerft in Barrow und geriet anfangs zu schwer; unter Bedenken entfernte man den Kiel, und im September 1911 war das Schiff bereit zum ersten Flugversuch. H.M. Airship No. 1 wird vorsichtig aus der Montagehalle gezogen (**1**) und manövriert eben zu einem schwimmenden Mast (**2**), als ein Windstoß es faßt und umwirft. Nur von seinem Skelett aus der neuentwickelten Duralumin-Legierung gehalten, bricht es entzwei und ist nicht mehr zu reparieren (**3**). Schon bald wurde es überall nur noch *Mayfly* genannt, die Eintagsfliege.

Le désastre du *Mayfly*

En juillet 1908, inquiète de l'avance prise par le comte allemand von Zeppelin, la Marine britannique passe commande d'un dirigeable rigide et en confie la construction à l'arsenal des sous-marins de Barrow. L'aéronef se révèle cependant trop lourd et – la quille prévue initialement ayant été enlevée à contrecœur – n'effectue ses premiers essais qu'à partir de septembre 1911, date à laquelle il glisse lentement de son ber (**2**). Le H.M. Airship N° 1, une fois remorqué et amarré à un mât flottant (**1**), est alors pris dans une rafale de vent et bascule brutalement; sa structure en duralumin, un nouvel alliage, ne résiste pas au choc et se plie en deux (**3**). Irréparable, il reçoit très vite le surnom de *Mayfly* («l'éphémère»).

3
Show and Tell:
The Adventurers

In an era of mechanical novelty and excitement, when individuals mattered as much as the machines they made, Samuel Franklin Cody undoubtedly stood out from most of the pioneer aviators. 'Colonel' Cody – he modelled himself on his friend Colonel William F. (Buffalo Bill) Cody – was a big, illiterate Texas cowboy and self-promoter who had been in Wild West shows, international horse-trading and music-hall entertainment before settling down in England. In Western clothes and a stetson hat, with shoulder-length hair, he would ride around Aldershot army base on a grey charger named Bergamo.

For all its conservative rigidity the British Army has always valued a handful of engaging, innovative characters, and when Cody followed the 1894 observation kite experiments of Colonel B.F. Baden-Powell, the army took him on. His 'war kite' was patented in 1901 and officially adopted by the British War Office in 1904. A year later he put an engine and biplane wings on it, and successfully launched it unmanned. Four years later, in his 'Flying Cathedral' aeroplane, he became the first person to fly a manned powered aircraft in Britain. He died on 7 August 1913, testing a new biplane over Farnborough Common.

Cody's contribution to aviation is not so much in technical achievements as in the sheer human enthusiasm and colour he brought to those pioneering days. 'History accords him the prime virtues of courage and perseverance', wrote the Farnborough authorities on his epitaph. The tree his first plane was tethered to was modelled in aluminium and is now in the government's research facilities at Farnborough airfield. Single-handedly, Cody created an 'air-mindedness' in the British government and public that had been conspicuously lacking.

Other flyers did exist in Britain: Alliott Verdon Roe claimed to be the first Briton to fly (Cody was American), though officially he was beaten to that title by J.T.C. Moore-Brabazon in a French-built Voisin in April 1909. While the indefatigable Cody continued to stir public interest in aviation, Moore-Brabazon whimsically took a pig up with him that year to show, he said, 'that pigs can fly'.

It would take something more than gimmicks to rally the British public. Lord Northcliffe, whose *Daily Mail* newspaper had been offering aviation prizes for more than two years, announced a £1,000 prize for the first flight across the Channel. Wilbur Wright was the obvious man to do it, but he declined, characteristically turning down the risk of flying over water as a spectacle for the public when he could make more money selling aeroplanes.

That wasn't the attitude of European aviators. By July 1909, three teams were prepared to go from France: Count Charles de Lambert, who owned two Wright Flyers; Hubert Latham, a Frenchman born and educated in England who had an elegant Antoinette IV monoplane; and Louis Blériot, another Frenchman who had to take out a big loan to pay for his Blériot XI monoplane.

De Lambert crashed in practice and dropped out, but interest in the surviving two reached fever pitch as they waited for the right weather conditions. Along both coasts near Calais and Dover, hotels were booked up, sightseers travelled from London and Paris, and newspapers reported every move. The French government assigned a torpedo boat to accompany the competitors across the Channel. Latham was the first to go, early on 19 July. Crowds filled the streets of Dover, and small boats streamed out of the harbour as Latham's Antoinette climbed into the sky near Sangatte. But as he prepared to take a photograph seven miles out and 1,000 feet up, Latham felt his 50hp engine failing. He glided down and landed gently in the sea, smoked a cigarette and waited for rescue.

It was Blériot's turn. The little man, a bad navigator and worse businessman – he had already lost a fortune on aviation – was the underdog of the race, and never expected to succeed. His aeroplane was underpowered, the smallest and least tested of the three. Hobbling around on crutches, his foot badly burned a few days previously, he didn't look a winner. At 4.35 am on 25 July 1909 Blériot took off, headed out over the Channel at less than 40mph and within ten minutes was lost, unable to see either coast. Then he saw ships heading for Dover and followed them. Blown off course, he found a gap in the cliffs near Dover Castle and dropped down to a meadow, breaking the undercarriage on landing.

He became a hero instantly. Fêted by cheering crowds in London, and a crowd of 100,000 back in Paris, he achieved a fame in aviation perhaps equal only to that of the Wright brothers and later Charles Lindbergh. He won the French Aéro-Club's Gold Medal, Lord Northcliffe's prize, went on to receive more than one hundred orders for Blériot XIs, and galvanized the British. Although many military leaders still distrusted the concept of aeroplanes, the British pioneer Sir Alan Cobham wrote, 'The day that Blériot flew the Channel marked the end of our insular safety, and the beginning of the time when Britain must seek another form of defence besides ships.'

Thrilled by the popping of corks on both sides of the Channel, the great French Champagne houses backed the City of Reims in organizing the Great Aviation Week a month later. On 22 August, at the world's first competitive air show, 22 aeroplanes vied for speed, height, endurance, distance, and passenger-carrying. Hubert Latham won the height prize, Glenn Curtiss won another; Blériot's new Gnome-engined plane was the fastest.

Typically, the Wrights declined to attend. Three of their Flyers were represented, but they themselves preferred to focus on business, forming a professional team of pilots and incorporating the Wright Company in November 1910. By then their direct influence on creative aviation was at an end.

Around the world money poured in to new air shows, and pilots started to earn huge amounts: Curtiss won $10,000 by flying down the Hudson River to New York City. Claude Grahame-White made $50,000 just by appearing at a Boston air show. A year later he used his new fortune to buy land at Hendon, north of London, for an aerodrome, where air shows were staged for many years. There were shows all over Britain. At one, in Doncaster, before thousands of people, Colonel Cody gave up his American citizenship and became British. At Johannisthal airfield in Berlin, the Dutchman Anthony Fokker showed glimpses of his future importance. In Cairo, the lady balloonist Raymonde de Laroche became the world's first woman pilot.

There were deaths: Captain Ferber was killed at Boulogne in a Voisin; Eugène Lefebvre died testing a Type A Wright plane; Charles Rolls, of Rolls Royce, died in a Wright biplane.

With the principles of aviation now firmly established, the floodgates were opened. In 1910 the Imperial Russian Flying Corps was founded. Romania established a Flying Corps. The Frenchman Henri Fabre performed the first take-off from water in a powered seaplane. In November the American Eugene Ely became the first to take off from a ship when he flew his Curtiss pusher from an 83ft platform built over the bows of the cruiser USS *Birmingham*. 1911 saw the first of the long-distance flights: from London to Paris, 250 miles in four hours; Paris to Madrid and Rome; New York to St Louis via Chicago. The opportunities were increasingly obvious – the first airmail run was established in India.

Yet it was the airship to which people still turned for most

Claude Grahame-White takes off from a street outside the White House (right), Washington, in a Farman III biplane, October 1910.

Claude Grahame-White startet im Oktober 1910 mit seinem Farman-III-Doppeldecker von einer Straße vor dem Weißen Haus (rechts), Washington.

En octobre 1910, Claude Grahame-White décolle d'une avenue proche de la Maison Blanche (à droite), à Washington, dans un biplan Farman III.

passenger carrying. Delag, the Deutsche Luftschiffahrts-Aktiengesellschaft, began carrying passengers in 1910, in Zeppelin's new LZ7 between Frankfurt, Baden-Baden and Düsseldorf. The German airship *Suchard* was built for an attempted crossing of the Atlantic in 1912, its passenger compartment designed as a boat which could be detached if the balloon had to come down. Perhaps fortunately, it was never tried out.

As airships started to carry more and more people, and after 1911 the first multi-engined planes appeared, military authorities at last took aviation seriously. If airships and aeroplanes could carry people over great distances, they could carry bombs, and fire machine guns. By 1913 aviation was primed to go to war.

Die Kindertage der Luftfahrt waren eine Zeit, in der jede neue Maschine für Aufsehen sorgte, und die Männer, die sie bauten, waren ebenso populär wie die Apparate, mit denen sie flogen; selbst unter Luftfahrtpionieren war Samuel Franklin Cody ein Mann, der auffiel. »Colonel« Cody – wie er sich nach seinem Freund Colonel William F. Cody (Buffalo Bill) nannte – war ein hünenhafter, ungebildeter Cowboy aus Texas, der als Pferdehändler gearbeitet hatte, in Wildwestshows und Varietés aufgetreten war und sich schließlich in England niedergelassen hatte. In Westernkleidern, mit Stetsonhut und schulterlangem Haar, war er mit seinem grauen Schlachtroß namens Bergamo ständiger Gast auf der Militärbasis Aldershot.

So konservativ und streng geordnet die britische Armee auch ist, hat sie doch immer auch Exzentriker in ihren Reihen geschätzt, und als Cody im Jahr 1894 mit Begeisterung Colonel B. F. Baden-Powells Experimente mit Aufklärungsdrachen verfolgte, nahm die Army ihn offiziell auf. Sein »Kriegsdrachen« wurde 1901 patentiert und 1904 ins Arsenal des Kriegsministeriums aufgenommen. Im folgenden Jahr montierte Cody Motor und Doppeldeckerflügel an seinen Drachen und ließ ihn mit Erfolg unbemannt fliegen. Vier Jahre später wurde er mit seiner »fliegenden Kathedrale« der erste Motorflieger in Großbritannien. Am 7. August 1913 kam er bei einem Versuchsflug mit einem neuen Doppeldecker in Farnborough ums Leben.

Codys Beitrag zur Geschichte der Luftfahrt besteht weniger in technischen Neuerungen; es ist der menschliche Enthusiasmus, die Farbe, die er in diese Tage der Pioniere brachte. »Wir werden ihn für die großen Tugenden des Muts und der Beharrlichkeit im Gedächtnis behalten«, schrieben die Befehlshabenden in Farnborough in seinem Nachruf. Von dem Baum, an den er sein erstes Flugzeug band, wurde ein Abbild in Aluminium geschaffen, das heute das militärische Versuchsgelände des Flugfelds von Farnborough ziert. In zähem Einzelkampf sorgte Cody dafür, daß sich in der britischen Regierung und Öffentlichkeit ein »Fliegersinn« entwickelte.

Es gab allerdings andere: Alliott Verdon Roe beanspruchte die Ehre des ersten britischen Fliegers für sich (Cody war ja Amerikaner), doch offiziell ging dieser Titel an J.T.C. Moore-Brabazon, der im April 1909 in einer französischen Voisin-Maschine geflogen war. Der unerschütterliche Cody versuchte immer wieder, das Publikum für die Fliegerei zu interessieren, doch der launige Moore-Brabazon stieg noch im selben

'Colonel' Samuel Cody carries a map during a break in the *Daily Mail* Round Britain Air Race in 1911.

»Colonel« Samuel Cody mit Landkarte in einer Pause des von der *Daily Mail* veranstalteten Rundum-England-Flugwettbewerbs, 1911.

Le «colonel» américain Samuel Cody consulte une carte lors d'une escale de la Round Britain Air Race organisée par le *Daily Mail* en 1911.

Jahr mit einem Schwein als Kopiloten auf, um zu beweisen, daß, wie er sagte, »selbst Schweine fliegen können«.

Aber es mußte schon mehr als solche Gags sein, bis das britische Publikum wirklich aufhorchte. Lord Northcliffe, dessen Zeitung *Daily Mail* schon seit über zwei Jahren Preise für Flugleistungen aussetzte, stiftete £ 1.000 für den ersten, der den Ärmelkanal überflog. Wilbur Wright wäre der naheliegendste Kandidat gewesen, doch er lehnte ab – es war typisch für ihn, daß er das Risiko nicht einging, für ein Sensationspublikum über Wasser zu fliegen, wo er doch mit dem Verkauf seiner Flugzeuge mehr Geld verdienen konnte.

Europäische Flieger sahen die Dinge anders. Im Juli 1909 waren drei Mannschaften soweit, einen Versuch von Frankreich aus zu wagen: Graf Charles de Lambert, der zwei Wright-Flyer besaß; der Engländer Hubert Latham mit einem eleganten Antoinette-IV-Eindecker; und der Franzose Louis Blériot, der sich schwer verschuldete, um seinen Blériot-XI-Eindecker für das Rennen fertigzustellen.

De Lambert stürzte bei einem Übungsflug ab und zog seine Meldung zurück, doch die beiden anderen Kandidaten warteten nur auf das richtige Wetter, und die Spannung stieg ins Unermeßliche. Die Hotels entlang beider Küsten bei Calais und Dover waren ausgebucht, Schaulustige reisten aus London und Paris an, und die Zeitungen berichteten auch über die kleinsten Aktivitäten. Die französische Regierung stellte ein Torpedoboot bereit, das die beiden Kontrahenten über den Kanal begleiten sollte. Latham startete als erster, am frühen Morgen des 19. Juli. Menschenmengen versammelten sich in den Straßen von Dover, und Boote liefen aus dem Hafen aus, als Lathams Antoinette bei Sangatte in den Himmel stieg. Doch als er, 300 Meter hoch und 11 Kilometer von der Küste, eben dabei war, ein Foto aufzunehmen, spürte Latham, wie sein 50-PS-Motor abstarb. Er segelte abwärts, landete sanft auf dem Wasser und steckte sich eine Zigarette an, bis die Rettungsmannschaft herankam.

Nun war Blériot an der Reihe. Der schmächtige Mann, ein schlechter Flieger und ein noch schlechterer Geschäftsmann war – er hatte mit Flugzeugen schon ein Vermögen verloren –, war der Außenseiter in diesem Rennen, und niemand erwartete, daß er gewinnen würde. Seine Maschine war viel zu schwach, die kleinste und am wenigsten erprobte von den dreien. Er hatte sich ein paar Tage zuvor den Fuß schwer verbrannt, hinkte auf Krücken umher und sah wirklich nicht wie ein Sieger aus. Am 25. Juli 1909 um 4 Uhr 35 morgens machte sich Blériot auf den Weg und flog mit noch nicht einmal 65 Stundenkilometern hinaus auf den Ärmelkanal; binnen zehn Minuten hatte er sich verirrt und konnte in keiner Richtung mehr die Küste sehen. Aber nach einer Weile entdeckte er Schiffe, die nach Dover unterwegs waren, und folgte ihnen. Der Wind brachte ihn vom Kurs ab, doch er fand eine flache Stelle in den Klippen und landete bei Dover Castle, so unsanft, daß er das Untergestell der Maschine demolierte.

Auf Anhieb war er ein Held. Menschenmengen feierten ihn, als er in London eintraf, Hunderttausend begrüßten ihn in Paris, und sein Flug brachte ihm einen Ruhm ein, der wohl nur noch mit dem der Gebrüder Wright und später mit dem Triumph Charles Lindberghs zu vergleichen ist. Er wurde mit der Goldmedaille des Pariser Aéro-Clubs ausgezeichnet und errang Lord Northcliffes *Daily Mail*-Preis, er bekam Aufträge für über 100 Blériot-XI-Maschinen, und die Briten waren in heller Aufregung. Obwohl viele Militärs dem Flugzeug nach wie vor mißtrauten, schrieb der britische Luftfahrtpionier Sir Alan Cobham: »Der Tag, an dem Blériot den Ärmelkanal überflog, war der letzte Tag unserer Sicherheit als Inselvolk und der erste Tag, an dem Großbritannien sich nach anderen Formen der Verteidigung als der Seefahrt umsehen muß.«

Die großen französischen Champagnerkellereien sahen es mit Freuden, als beiderseits des Kanals die Korken knallten, und unterstützten gern die Stadt Reims, als sie im folgenden Monat ihre Große Flugwoche veranstaltete. Am 22. August wetteiferten 22 Flugzeuge auf der ersten Weltausstellung der Luftfahrt um die Ehre des schnellsten, höchsten, längsten und weitesten Fluges, sowie für die Passagierbeförderung. Hubert Latham gewann den Preis für den Höhenflug, ein anderer ging an Glenn Curtiss, und Blériots neue Maschine mit dem Gnome-Motor war die schnellste.

Es war typisch für die Wright-Brüder, daß sie wieder einmal nicht dabei waren. Drei Wright-Flyer waren im Wettbewerb, doch die Konstrukteure widmeten sich lieber dem Geschäft; sie versammelten eine Mannschaft professioneller Piloten um sich und firmierten vom November 1910 an als Wright Company. Ihr direkter Einfluß auf den Fortschritt des Flugwesens ging damit zu Ende.

Weltweit gab es in den neuen Luftfahrtschauen plötzlich viel Geld zu gewinnen, und die Flieger wurden reich: Curtiss erhielt für einen Flug den Hudson River hinunter nach New York $ 10.000. Claude Grahame-White strich $ 50.000 allein dafür ein, daß er auf einer Bostoner Luftfahrtschau auftrat. Da-

von kaufte er ein Stück Land in Hendon nördlich von London, wo ein Aerodrom entstand, das für viele Jahre zum Schauplatz von Luftfahrtveranstaltungen werden sollte. Überall in Großbritannien gab es nun Flugschauen. In Doncaster gab Colonel Cody vor Tausenden seine amerikanische Staatsbürgerschaft auf und erklärte sich zum Briten. Auf dem Flugfeld von Johannisthal in Berlin ließ der Holländer Anthony Fokker erstmals seine zukünftige Größe ahnen. Die Ballonfahrerin Raymonde de Laroche stieg in Kairo als erste Pilotin der Welt auf.

Manche kamen um: Hauptmann Ferber stürzte in Boulogne mit einer Voisin-Maschine ab; Eugène Lefebvre verunglückte beim Probeflug mit einer Wright-Maschine vom Typ A; Charles Rolls, Fabrikant der Rolls-Royce-Automobile, ließ in einem Wright-Doppeldecker sein Leben.

Die Grundbegriffe der Fliegerei standen fest, und der Strom der Flieger wurde immer stärker. 1910 entstand das Kaiserlich-Russische Fliegerkorps, und selbst Rumänien begründete ein Korps. Der Franzose Henri Fabre startete erstmals mit einem Motorflugzeug vom Wasser aus. Im November desselben Jahres flog der Amerikaner Eugene Ely erstmals von einem Schiff aus: Mit seiner Curtiss-Maschine mit Druckpropeller startete er von einer 25 Meter langen Plattform an Bord der USS *Birmingham*. 1911 fand der erste Langstreckenflug statt, von London nach Paris – 402 km in vier Stunden; dann ging es von Paris nach Madrid und Rom und von New York über Chicago nach St. Louis. Vieles ergab sich nun beinahe von selbst, wie etwa die erste Luftpostroute; sie entstand in Indien.

Wenn es jedoch um den Passagierverkehr ging, hielten die meisten sich nach wie vor an das Luftschiff. Die Delag, die Deutsche Luftschiffahrts-Aktiengesellschaft, nahm 1910 mit dem neuen LZ7 des Grafen von Zeppelin die Linie von Frankfurt nach Baden-Baden und nach Düsseldorf erstmals für Passagiere auf. Das deutsche Luftschiff *Suchard* entstand 1912 zur Atlantiküberquerung, und die Gondel war als Boot konstruiert, das allein fahren konnte, wenn das Prallluftschiff notwassern mußte. Es war vielleicht ein Glück für alle Beteiligten, daß es zum Atlantikflug niemals kam.

Luftschiffe beförderten mehr Passagiere denn je, 1911 kamen die ersten Flugzeuge mit mehreren Motoren auf, und nun nahmen auch die Militärbehörden das Fliegen ernst. Wenn Flugzeuge und Luftschiffe Menschen über größere Entfernungen tragen konnten, dann konnten sie auch Bomben transportieren und aus Maschinengewehren feuern. 1913 standen im Luftfahrtwesen alle Zeichen auf Krieg.

Man-flying kites, using Maidot's system developed from Cody's 1899 designs, were still used for observation on the Western Front in 1917.

Bemannte Drachen nach dem System, das Maidot nach Codys Entwürfen des Jahres 1899 entwickelt hatte, waren auch 1917 noch an der Westfront im Aufklärungseinsatz.

Ces cerfs-volants «pilotés», utilisant le système mis au point à partir du dessins de Cody en 1899, étaient encore utilisés en 1917 pour l'observation sur le front Ouest.

En cette nouvelle époque d'engouement pour la mécanique, où les individus comptent au moins autant que les machines qu'ils fabriquent, Samuel Franklin Cody est indubitablement un personnage à part. Le «colonel» Cody, qui a pour modèle son ami le colonel William F. Cody – Buffalo Bill –, est un grand Texan illettré qui s'est mêlé de «Wild West shows», de commerce de chevaux et de spectacles de music-hall avant de venir s'installer en Angleterre. Portant un costume de cow-boy américain et un large Stetson, les cheveux longs tombant sur les épaules, il galope souvent autour de la base militaire d'Aldershot monté sur un cheval gris appelé Bergamo.

En dépit de son conservatisme rigoureux, l'armée britannique a toujours aimé compter dans ses rangs quelques personnages inventifs et attachants. Aussi engage-t-elle Cody en 1894 alors qu'il suit les expérimentations du cerf-volant d'observation du colonel B.F. Baden-Powell. Breveté en 1901, le «cerf-volant de guerre» de Cody est officiellement adopté par le ministère de la Guerre britannique en 1904. L'année suivante, il y adapte un moteur et des ailes de biplan et le lance avec succès dans les airs, bien que sans passager. Quatre ans plus tard, son aéroplane «Cathédrale volante» fait de lui le premier homme à voler en Grande-Bretagne sur un appareil motorisé. Il meurt le 7 août 1913 en testant un nouveau biplan au-dessus de Farnborough Common.

La contribution de Cody à l'aviation s'apprécie moins d'un point de vue technique que pour l'enthousiasme et la coloration particulière qu'il donne à cette époque pionnière en Grande-Bretagne. À lui seul, Cody a fait naître et se développer un «sens de l'aviation» qui manque manifestement au gouvernement et au public anglais. «Que l'histoire lui accorde les vertus premières du courage et de la persévérance», firent inscrire les autorités en épitaphe sur sa tombe. L'arbre auquel fut attaché son premier aéroplane, moulé en aluminium, est aujourd'hui planté à l'intérieur du centre de recherches militaires du gouvernement britannique à l'aérodrome de Farnborough.

Cody n'est cependant pas le seul pionnier de l'aviation en Grande-Bretagne: Alliott Verdon Roe revendique le titre de premier Anglais à avoir volé (Cody étant Américain), bien qu'il ait été officiellement devancé en avril 1909 par J.T.C. Moore-Brabazon sur un avion Voisin. Si Cody entretient l'attention du public pour l'aviation, Moore-Brabazon n'est pas en reste puisqu'il emmène cette année-là un cochon dans son appareil

Adolphe Pégoud (on left) poses with Louis Blériot at Brooklands, England, in September 1913, when Pégoud flew upside down.

Adolphe Pégoud (links) mit Louis Blériot im September 1913 im englischen Brooklands, wo Pégoud auf dem Kopf stehend geflogen war.

Adolphe Pégoud (à gauche) pose en compagnie de Louis Blériot à Brooklands (Angleterre) en septembre 1913, après avoir effectué son célèbre vol sur le dos.

pour prouver, dira-t-il, «that pigs can fly» («que même les cochons volent».

Il faut toutefois plus que quelques blagues pour rallier vraiment le public britannique à la cause de l'aviation. Lord Northcliffe, dont le journal le *Daily Mail* distribue depuis plus de deux ans des prix à l'aviation, annonce qu'il offre 1000 £ au premier aviateur réussissant la traversée de la Manche. Wilbur Wright, qui semble évidemment être l'homme de la situation, décline pourtant l'offre, peu désireux de se donner en spectacle en volant au-dessus de la mer alors qu'il peut gagner plus d'argent en vendant ses aéroplanes.

Les aviateurs européens n'ont pas le même souci. En juillet 1909, trois équipes se tiennent prêtes à décoller de France: le comte Charles de Lambert, qui possède deux Flyer Wright; Hubert Latham, Français né et élevé en Angleterre, qui dispose d'un élégant monoplan Antoinette IV; et Louis Blériot, un autre Français, qui a contracté de lourdes dettes pour acheter son monoplan Blériot XI.

Lambert se retire rapidement de la course après s'être écrasé lors des essais de son appareil. La compétition entre les deux Français restant en lice devient fiévreuse tandis qu'ils attendent de bonnes conditions météorologiques. Les hôtels des côtes française et anglaise, à Calais et à Douvres, affichent complet tant sont nombreux les spectateurs venus de Londres ou de Paris assister à l'événement annoncé en première page par tous les journaux, et la Marine française arme même un contre-torpilleur pour accompagner les concurrents dans leur traversée. Attendu à Douvres par une foule immense, Latham est le premier à partir, tôt le matin du 19 juillet, accompagné par une flottille de petits bateaux lorsque son Antoinette s'élève dans le ciel près de Sangatte. Mais, alors qu'il s'apprête à prendre une photo – à 11 km du départ et à 300 m d'altitude –, Latham sent faiblir et s'arrêter brusquement son moteur de 50 ch. Descendant en vol plané, il parvient néanmoins à amerrir sans casse, il allume alors une cigarette et attend placidement les secours.

C'est désormais au tour de Blériot de tenter l'aventure. Ce petit homme, médiocre pilote et mauvais homme d'affaires – il a déjà perdu une fortune dans l'aviation, est largement donné perdant. Son aéroplane est non seulement sous-motorisé mais aussi le plus petit et le moins préparé des trois. Boitillant sur des béquilles, après s'être brûlé le pied lors d'un vol précédent, il n'a certes pas des allures de vainqueur. Blériot se met en route le 25 juillet 1909 à 4 h 35 du matin, s'engage au-des-

sus de la mer, volant à moins de 65 km/h, et se trouve dix minutes plus tard «perdu dans l'immensité entre le ciel et l'eau»,
toute terre ayant disparu à son regard. Apercevant alors des
navires se dirigeant vers Douvres, il suit leur route puis, dé-
couvrant un creux dans les falaises proches de la forteresse de
Douvres, se pose brutalement sur un champ en brisant le train
de son appareil.

Fêté en véritable héros par la foule qui l'accueille à Londres et acclamé par les 100 000 personnes qui l'attendent à Paris, il obtient une célébrité qui n'a d'égale dans l'aviation que
celle des frères Wright et, plus tard, de Charles Lindbergh. Ce
succès, qui galvanise les Britanniques, lui permet d'empocher
la Médaille d'or de l'Aéro-Club de France, le prix attribué par
lord Northcliffe et, surtout, d'obtenir plus d'une centaine de
commandes pour son Blériot XI. Si de nombreux officiers de
l'armée doutent encore du concept d'aéroplane, sir Alan Cobham écrit: «Le jour où Blériot franchit la Manche marque la
fin de notre sécurité insulaire et le début d'une époque où la
Grande-Bretagne doit rechercher une forme de défense autre
que seulement maritime.»

Profitant de l'occasion qui leur est donnée de se faire de la
réclame des deux côtés de la Manche, les grandes maisons de
champagne s'empressent d'aider la ville de Reims à organiser
la Grande semaine de l'Aviation. Le 22 août, lors de ce premier
meeting aérien international, 22 aéroplanes concourent dans
des compétitions de vitesse, d'altitude, d'endurance, de distance et de transport de passagers. Hubert Latham s'attribue le record d'altitude, Glenn Curtiss remporte la coupe Gordon-Ben-
nett, tandis que Blériot, sur son nouvel avion à moteur Gnome,
se distingue en vitesse.

Si trois de leurs Flyer sont présents, les frères Wright ont
refusé de participer à cette réunion et préférant se consacrer à
la commercialisation de leurs avions, à former une équipe de
pilotes professionnels et à créer, en novembre 1910, la Wright
Company. A partir de ce moment, ils n'auront plus d'influence directe sur le progrès de l'aviation.

Les concours primés et les vols de démonstration se mul-
tiplient dans le monde entier et sont l'occasion de fabuleux
spectacles aériens où les pilotes peuvent gagner de fortes som-
mes: Curtiss remporte ainsi 10 000 $ en descendant l'Hudson
jusqu'à New York et Claude Grahame-White gagne 50 000 $
simplement en se produisant à un meeting d'aviation à Boston. Un an plus tard, il emploie cette fortune pour acquérir des
terrains à Hendon, au nord de Londres, afin d'y créer un aéro-

drome, où se dérouleront pendant plusieurs années de nombreux rassemblements aériens. À Doncaster, en Grande-Bretagne, le colonel Cody renonce devant des milliers de spectateurs à sa nationalité américaine pour devenir citoyen britannique. En Allemagne, le Hollandais Anthony Fokker se produit
avec succès sur l'aérodrome de Johannisthal de Berlin. Au
Caire, l'aérostière française la baronne de Laroche devient la
première femme pilote.

On déplore également plusieurs victimes de l'aviation: le
capitaine Ferber se tue à Boulogne dans un Voisin; Eugène Lefebvre s'écrase au cours d'un vol d'essai sur Flyer A Wright;
Charles Rolls, cofondateur de Rolls-Royce, meurt à bord d'un
biplan Wright.

Malgré cela, l'aviation est désormais dans l'air du temps.
La Russie crée en 1910 le Corps aérien impérial, vite imitée par
la Roumanie. Le Français Henri Fabre effectue le premier décollage depuis un plan d'eau à bord d'un hydroplane motorisé. En novembre, l'Américain Eugene Ely, à bord d'un Curtiss
à hélice propulsive, devient le premier homme à décoller depuis un navire en mouvement, le croiseur USS *Birmingham*, à
la proue duquel a été construite une plate-forme de 25 m de
long. L'année 1911 voit s'effectuer les premiers vols long-courrier: Londres-Paris (402 km en quatre heures), Paris-Madrid
et Paris-Rome, New York-Saint Louis via Chicago. Les oppor-
tunités offertes par l'aviation sont de plus en plus évidentes et
le premier service de poste aérienne est organisé en Inde.

Cependant, c'est encore vers les dirigeables que l'on se
tourne pour le transport des passagers. La Delag – Deutsche
Luftschiffahrts-Aktiengesellschaft – assura depuis 1910 le service régulier des passagers entre Francfort, Baden-Baden et
Düsseldorf dans le nouvel LZ7 de Zeppelin. Le dirigeable allemand *Suchard*, construit en 1912 pour tenter la traversée de
l'Atlantique, dispose d'une cabine de passagers conçue comme
un bateau et pouvant être détachée si le ballon venait à amerrir. Cette solution n'eut heureusement jamais à être essayée.

Maintenant que les dirigeables peuvent transporter de plus
en plus de passagers sur de longues distances, et grâce à
l'apparition des premiers appareils multimoteurs en 1911, les
autorités militaires prennent enfin l'aviation au sérieux en
pensant que, si les dirigeables et les aéroplanes sont capables
de telles prouesses, ils doivent alors pouvoir emporter des
bombes et une mitrailleuse. En 1913, l'aviation est prête à
entrer en guerre.

An aeroplane which crashed onto a
roof in Palmer's Green, London,
demonstrated the frailty of aviation
in December 1912. Two house tiles
were broken.

Diese Aufnahme von einem Flug-
unglück im Dezember 1912 in
Palmer's Green, London, führt vor
Augen, wie zerbrechlich die
Flugzeuge damals waren. Zwei
Dachziegel gingen zu Bruch.

Cet aéroplane, qui s'est écrasé en
décembre 1912 sur le toit d'une
maison de Palmer's Green
(Londres) en cassant deux tuiles,
démontre la fragilité des avions.

Across the Channel
Louis Blériot's XI monoplane looked desperately frail when it crossed the coast near Calais just after dawn on 25 July 1909 (**2**), and Blériot himself looked none too happy when preparing to take off (**1**). He was still nursing a painful foot, burned in a flight a few days before, and half expected to land in the water, like one of his competitors.

Über den Kanal
Klein und zerbrechlich erhebt sich Louis Blériots Eindecker XI kurz nach Sonnenaufgang am 25. Juli 1909 über die Kanalküste bei Calais (**2**), und auch Blériot selbst, kurz vor dem Start aufgenommen (**1**), sieht nicht gerade glücklich aus. Er hatte sich an einem heißen Auspuffrohr den Fuß verbrannt und befürchtete, daß er im Wasser landen würde, wie einer seiner Konkurrenten vor ihm.

À travers la Manche
Le monoplan XI de Louis Blériot semble extraordinairement fragile lorsqu'il franchit les côtes françaises près de Calais, à l'aube naissante du 25 juillet 1909 (**2**). Blériot, photographié au moment du décollage (**1**), n'a pas l'air d'avoir un moral de vainqueur ; il est vrai qu'il s'est récemment brûlé le pied en marchant sur un pot d'échappement et qu'il s'attend à devoir effectuer un amerrissage en catastrophe, à l'instar de l'un de ses concurrents.

Blériot's victory

Louis Blériot landed near Dover Castle on 25 July 1909. An underdog, broke, and with the weakest plane in a three-craft cross-Channel contest, Blériot was such a poor navigator that he almost missed England entirely on his 22-mile flight without instruments or compass. The thoughts of his long-suffering wife (on left), following on a boat, were not recorded. This damaged glass plate negative, recently rediscovered, was taken later that day.

Blériot schafft es

Am 25. Juli 1909 landete Louis Blériot nicht weit von der Burg von Dover. Er war ein Mann aus einfachen Verhältnissen, mittellos, sein Flugzeug war das schwächste der drei Konkurrenten, die zur Kanalüberquerung antraten, und Blériot war ein so schlechter Flieger, daß er England auf dem 35-km-Flug ohne Kompaß und Instrumente beinahe gar nicht gefunden hätte. Die leidgeprüfte Ehefrau (links) folgte per Boot – was sie von dem Abenteuer hielt, ist nicht bekannt. Diese Aufnahme (das Glasnegativ ist beschädigt) entstand später am selben Tag und wurde erst kürzlich wiederentdeckt.

La victoire de Blériot

Après un vol de 35 km sans instruments ni compas, Louis Blériot atterrit à proximité de la forteresse de Douvres (Dover Castle), sur la côte d'Angleterre, le 25 juillet 1909. Souvent malchanceux et donné perdant, désargenté et possédant l'appareil le plus fragile dans cette compétition trans-Manche entre trois aéroplanes, Blériot était si piètre navigateur qu'il faillit manquer l'Angleterre. On ne sait rien des impressions de sa femme (à gauche), qui le suivait en bateau. Retrouvée récemment et abîmée, cette plaque photographique négative fut impressionnée un peu plus tard le même jour.

1

A hero's welcome

Crowds cheered Blériot from Victoria station (**1**) through the streets of London hours after his historic Channel flight. *Daily Mail* publisher Lord Northcliffe, who accompanied him in the open car, paid the £1,000 prize. A year later a memorial marking his landing was photographed near Dover Castle (**2**). Blériot, who was greeted by 100,000 excited people on his return to Paris, made a fortune from sales of his monoplane.

Ein triumphaler Empfang

Die Menschen in den Londoner Straßen jubeln Blériot zu, als er einige Stunden nach seiner historischen Kanalüberquerung am Bahnhof Victoria eintrifft. Neben ihm im Wagen Lord Northcliffe, der Verleger der *Daily Mail*, der den Preis von £ 1.000 ausgesetzt hatte (**1**). Im folgenden Jahr wurde dieses Denkmal aufgenommen, das man an seinem Landeplatz bei Dover Castle errichtet hatte (**2**). Bei seiner Rückkehr nach Paris empfingen 100.000 Menschen Blériot, und der Erfolg seiner Eindecker machten ihn zum reichen Mann.

L'accueil d'un héros

La foule acclame Blériot dans sa traversée des rues de Londres depuis la gare Victoria (**1**), quelques heures après son vol historique au-dessus de la Manche ; près de lui, lord Northcliffe, l'éditeur du *Daily Mail* et organisateur de la compétition qui lui offrit le prix de 1 000 £ réservé au vainqueur. Un an plus tard, un monument marquant l'emplacement de l'atterrissage fut édifié près de Dover Castle (**2**). Blériot, accueilli par 100 000 personnes enthousiastes à son retour à Paris, fit ensuite fortune grâce à la vente de son monoplan.

No prizes for failure

Odds for the Channel crossing race had been on Hubert Latham (**2**, in centre) to beat Blériot. He had more money and flying experience and a more powerful aircraft in his elegant new Antoinette IV (**1**). But Latham's Channel attempt, five days before Blériot's, ended when his engine quit and he crash-landed at sea (**3**). Latham rushed back to Paris for a second Antoinette, but again ditched – two days after Blériot had already succeeded.

Der Verlierer geht leer aus

Die meisten hatten beim Wettrennen um die erste Kanalüberquerung auf Hubert Latham (**2**, Mitte) gesetzt. Er war wohlhabend, hatte mehr Flug-erfahrung als Blériot und eine kräftigere Maschine, die elegante neue Antoinette IV (**1**). Doch Lathams Kanalflug, fünf Tage vor Blériot, endete nach einem Maschinenschaden mit einer Bruchlandung im Wasser (**3**). Latham eilte nach Paris zurück, um eine zweite Antoinette zu holen, aber auch dieser Anlauf, zwei Tage nach Blériot, endete im Kanal.

L'amertume de l'échec

Hubert Latham (**2**, au centre) était le favori de la compétition ouverte pour la traversée de la Manche. Il disposait de moyens financiers plus impor-tants, d'une meilleure expérience de pilote et, avec son nouvel et élégant Antoinette IV (**1**), d'un avion plus puissant que Louis Blériot. Toutefois, sa première tentative de traversée, cinq jours avant celle de Blériot, se solda par un amerrissage forcé (**3**) consécutif à une panne de moteur. Rentré précipitamment à Paris pour prendre un second Antoinette, Latham dut encore une fois se poser en pleine mer – deux jours après le succès de Blériot.

2

3

5/153

Alpine tragedy

Lonely, tiny and slow, the aeroplane of the Peruvian Georges Chavez (**3**) struggled to gain height in the first attempt to cross the Alps between Switzerland and Italy in September 1910 (**1**). Since Blériot's Channel crossing a year earlier, international air connections appeared to be within reach, but no one had tried to fly as high as the Alps. Chavez succeeded in crossing from Brig to Domodossola near the Simplon Pass, but he crashed on landing there (**2**) and died three days later.

Tod in den Bergen

Verloren vor der Bergkulisse, winzig und langsam, gewinnt die Maschine des Peruaners Georges Chavez (**3**) im September 1910 auf ihrem Weg von der Schweiz nach Italien an Höhe: Der erste Versuch, die Alpen zu überfliegen (**1**). Seit Blériots Kanalüberquerung im Vorjahr schienen internationale Flugverbindungen in greifbare Nähe gerückt, doch niemand hatte sich bis dahin mit einem Flugzeug in solche Höhen gewagt. Der Flug von Brig nach Domodossola nicht weit vom Simplonpaß gelang, doch bei der Landung stürzte Chavez ab (**2**) und erlag drei Tage darauf seinen Verletzungen.

Tragédie dans les Alpes

Solitaire, minuscule et volant assez bas au milieu des montagnes lors de la première tentative de franchissement des Alpes entre la Suisse et l'Italie, effectuée en septembre 1910 (**1**), l'aéroplane du Péruvien Georges Chavez (**3**) semble peiner pour gagner en hauteur. S'il semblait envisageable d'établir des liaisons internationales par voie aérienne depuis la traversée de la Manche par Blériot, l'année précédente, personne n'avait encore tenté de voler à des altitudes comme celles des Alpes. Chavez réussit toutefois à relier Brig à Domodossola, près du col du Simplon, mais il s'écrasa à l'atterrissage (**2**) et mourut trois jours plus tard.

This time lucky

The Franco-American John Moisant made a record-breaking flight from Paris to London in August 1910, carrying his mechanic M. Fileux as the first passenger across the English Channel. He crash-landed on an allotment near Rainham, Kent (1), shattering his propeller (2). He crashed again within five days, and another plane crash killed him in New Orleans four months later. But the real image of aviation was undoubtedly that of Count de Lambert flying his Wright aeroplane from Juvisy to Paris and around the Eiffel Tower (3) in October 1909 – mankind advancing ever skywards.

Noch einmal davongekommen

Im August 1910 unternahm der Franko-Amerikaner John Moisant einen Rekordflug von Paris nach London, und sein Mechaniker M. Fileux war der erste Passagier, der über den Kanal geflogen wurde. Moisant mußte in einem Garten bei Rainham in Kent notlanden (1), und der Propeller ging dabei zu Bruch (2). Schon fünf Tage darauf stürzte er ein zweites Mal ab, und ein weiterer Absturz vier Monate später in New Orleans endete tödlich. Doch kaum ein Bild könnte das Abenteuer des Fliegens besser festhalten als die Aufnahme von Graf de Lambert, der im Oktober 1909 in seiner Wright-Maschine von Juvisy nach Paris flog und dabei den Eiffelturm umrundete (3) – das Symbol des Menschen, wie er himmelwärts strebt.

Un coup de chance

L'image la plus symbolique de l'aviation en octobre 1909 est sans aucun doute celle de l'aéroplane Wright du comte de Lambert qui, parti de Juvisy, vole autour du sommet de la tour Eiffel (3) et établit le record d'altitude. Autre record, celui du Franco-Américain John Moisant qui, en août 1910, relie Paris à Londres en effectuant la première traversée de la Manche en aéroplane avec un passager, son mécanicien M. Fileux, avant de faire un atterrissage forcé dans un petit champ près de Rainham, dans le Kent (1), où il casse son hélice (2) ; après avoir subi un autre accident la semaine suivante, il décédera quatre mois plus tard en s'écrasant à la Nouvelle Orléans.

Extending the range

By 1911 steady flights of several hours were regularly being achieved in countries around the world. On 12 April, Pierre Prier (**1**, left) flew his Blériot monoplane from the new airport at Hendon, London, to Issy-les-Moulineaux, Paris, non-stop in 3 hours 56 minutes. On 7 March the French aviator Eugène Renaux won the 100,000 franc Michelin Grand Prix for flying his Farman biplane from Buc (Paris)-Clermont-Ferrand and landing on the summit of the Puy de Dôme (**2**) in the Auvergne, in less than six hours.

Immer länger, immer weiter

1911 gab es in vielen Ländern der Erde bereits mehrstündige Flüge ohne Unterbrechung. Am 12. April flog Pierre Prier (**1**, links) seinen Blériot-Eindecker nonstop in 3 Stunden 56 Minuten vom neuen Londoner Flugplatz Hendon nach Issy-les-Moulineaux bei Paris. Am 7. März flog der Franzose Eugène Renaux in einem Farman-Doppeldecker in knapp 6 Stunden von Buc (Paris)-Clermont Ferrand auf den Gipfel des Puy de Dôme (**2**) in der Auvergne und gewann damit den Großen Michelin-Preis von 100.000 Francs.

Repousser les limites

L'année 1911 voit de nombreux pilotes accomplir régulièrement des vols de plusieurs heures. Ainsi, le 12 avril, Pierre Prier (**1**, à gauche) effectue en 3 heures 56 minutes, sur monoplan Blériot, la première liaison sans escale entre Hendon, le nouvel aérodrome de Londres, et Issy-les-Moulineaux, près de Paris. Le 7 mars, sur le biplan Farman, l'aviateur français Eugène Renaux remporte les 100 000 francs du Grand Prix Michelin pour avoir accompli le trajet Buc (Paris)-Clermont-Ferrand et atterri au sommet du Puy-de-Dôme (**2**) en moins de six heures.

Reims, France: August 1909

Thousands of people flocked to the world's first air show, thrilled at seeing the best aviation had to offer; from now on aviation was exposed to public interest. The Wright brothers were absent but Eugène Lefebvre demonstrated one of six Wright Flyers (**1**), swooping and turning in ways few had ever seen. Robert Esnault-Pelterie had a 60hp engine to drive his steel-framed REP monoplane in the air, but one horse was still needed on the ground (**2**) as André Fournier prepared to take off in his biplane (**3**).

Reims, Frankreich: August 1909

Tausende gespannter Besucher kamen zur ersten Flugzeugschau der Welt, die das Beste versammelte, was die Luftfahrt zu bieten hatte; von nun an nahm auch eine breitere Öffentlichkeit die Fliegerei zur Kenntnis. Die Gebrüder Wright waren nicht dabei, doch gehörten sechs Wright-Flyer zum Aufgebot, und hier führt (**1**) Eugène Lefebvre ihre Wendigkeit mit Kunstflügen vor, wie kaum einer sie je gesehen hatte. Zum Fliegen hatte Robert Esnault-Pelteries REP-Eindecker mit Stahlrahmen einen 60-PS-Motor, doch der Transport am Boden erfolgte nach wie vor mit einer einzigen Pferdestärke (**2**); André Fournier ist mit seinem Doppeldecker bereit zum Start (**3**).

Reims, août 1909

Des milliers de personnes sont venues assister au premier meeting aérien organisé dans le monde – la grande semaine de l'aviation de la Champagne –, où est présenté au public le meilleur de l'aviation internationale. Si les frères Wright sont absents, Eugène Lefebvre fait la démonstration de l'un des six Flyer Wright (**1**), volant en piqué et virant comme peu l'ont déjà vu faire, tandis qu'André Fournier se prépare à décoller à bord de son biplan (**3**). Si Robert Esnault-Pelterie dispose d'un moteur de 60 ch pour propulser en vol son monoplan REP. à structure métallique, le cheval demeure indispensable pour les manœuvres au sol (**2**).

Those magnificent men

Pilots raced each other for fame, thrills and money. Biggest winner in 1911 was the French Lieutenant Jean Conneau, who raced as 'André Beaumont' in his Blériot monoplane. He arrived in Brooklands, near London (1), to win the five-day £10,000 *Daily Mail* Round Britain Air Race and was carried aloft (2) by supporters. Earlier in Paris he won the Circuit of Europe Air Race.

Die tollkühnen Männer

Die Piloten wetteiferten um Ruhm, Geld und Abenteuer. Der größte Gewinner des Jahres 1911 war der französische Leutnant Jean Conneau, der mit seinem Blériot Eindecker unter dem Namen André Beaumont antrat. Hier (1) trifft er als Sieger des fünftägigen, von der *Daily Mail* mit £ 10.000 dotierten Rund-um-England-Wettfluges in Brooklands bei London ein und wird von Verehrern auf die Schultern gehoben (2). Zuvor war er beim Wettflug rund um den Kontinent als erster in Paris eingetroffen.

Ces hommes magnifiques

Les pilotes concouraient pour la gloire, l'argent et le plaisir du risque. L'un des plus grands vainqueurs de 1911 est l'enseigne de vaisseau Jean Conneau, un Français connu sous son pseudonyme de «André Beaumont». Après avoir remporté à Paris le Circuit de l'Europe sur son monoplan Blériot, il gagne à Brooklands, près de Londres (1) la Round Britain Air Race, une course de cinq jours dotée de 10000 £ par le *Daily Mail*, à l'issue de laquelle il est triomphalement accueilli par ses supporters (2).

Not the Wild West
The American 'Colonel' Samuel F. Cody, despite his Wild West image, was one of Britain's foremost aviation pioneers, creating the first British-built aeroplane, and, in 1910, the Cody biplane, on which he posed with passengers at Brooklands (**2**). He won the British Empire Michelin Trophy (**1**) and set new British endurance and distance records.

Nicht der Wilde Westen
Bei allem Wildwest-Image war der Amerikaner »Colonel« Samuel F. Cody doch einer der führenden Flugpioniere in England; er baute das erste britische Flugzeug sowie, im Jahre 1910, den Cody-Doppeldecker, mit dem er sich hier (**2**) mit Passagieren aufnehmen läßt. Er gewann die British Empire Michelin Trophy (**1**) und stellte neue britische Rekorde im Dauer- und Langstreckenflug auf.

Un faux «cow-boy» volant
Le «colonel» Samuel F. Cody, malgré ses allures de cow-boy américain à la Buffalo Bill, fut l'un des plus grands pionniers de l'aviation anglaise. Ayant créé le premier aéroplane de construction britannique et, en 1910, le biplan Cody à bord duquel il se pose ici à Brooklands avec trois passagers (**2**), il remporta le British Empire Michelin Trophy (**1**) et établit les nouveaux records anglais d'endurance et de distance.

Always something different

Air meets often mixed the new, such as George Barnes's Blériot-based Humber flying over Grahame-White's Farman at Brooklands in 1910 (**2**), with the spectacular. In 1913 the stunt pilot Adolphe Pégoud devised a way of taking off and landing without touching the ground at all (**1**). A quick-release device above his Blériot caught a cable stretched between two posts that brought him to a stop in mid-air. He also took off from this hanging position.

Immer etwas Neues

Auf den Luftfahrtschauen – wie hier 1910 in Brooklands, wo George Barnes mit seinem Humber auf Blériot-Basis eben Grahame-Whites Farman über-fliegt (**2**) – kam alles zusammen, was neu und spektakulär war. Der Kunst-flieger Adolphe Pégoud entwickelte 1913 ein Verfahren, mit dem er startete und landete, ohne den Boden zu berühren (**1**). Zwischen zwei Pfosten wurde ein Stahltau gespannt, in das sich eine Kupplung oben an seiner Blériot-Maschine einhakte, so daß er mitten in der Luft zum Stillstand kam. Er startete auch aus dieser Position.

Toujours des nouveautés

Les meetings aériens sont souvent l'occasion de voir des nouveautés, par exemple le Humber sur base Blériot de George Barnes, survolant ici le Farman de Grahame-White à Brook-lands en 1910 (**2**), et d'assister à de spectaculaires démonstrations. Le pilote cascadeur Adolphe Pégoud présente ainsi, en 1913, un moyen de décoller et «d'atterrir» sans toucher le sol (**1**) à l'aide d'un appendice amovible fixé sur son Blériot, lui permettant de crocher dans un câble tendu entre deux pylônes pour être stoppé en l'air.

1

Flying headaches
A pilot's reputation was fragile. Returning from a record-breaking American tour, the pioneer Hubert Latham crashed his Antoinette onto a roof at Brooklands in January 1911 (**1**). Earlier, a little taxiing monoplane crashed into the River Wey at Brooklands (**2**). Neither pilot was seriously hurt. Ground accidents were common; brakes were primitive, grass surfaces were bumpy and there was no standard training.

2

Pilotenglück

Mit dem Ansehen eines Piloten war es schnell vorbei. Nach einer Amerikatournee, auf der er zahlreiche Rekorde brach, flog der Pionier Hubert Latham seine Antoinette im Januar 1911 in ein Dach in Brooklands (**1**). Ebenfalls in Brooklands stürzte dieser kleine Eindecker (**2**) in den Fluß Wey. Beide Piloten kamen ohne größeren Schaden davon. Landeunfälle waren häufig – die Bremsen waren unzureichend, die Rasenpisten uneben, und es gab keinerlei vorgeschriebene Ausbildung.

Accidents de vol

La réputation d'habileté d'un pilote est fragile et les accidents fréquents. Les freins des aéroplanes étaient encore primitifs, les pistes en herbe bosselées et il n'existait pas de formation de base au pilotage. En janvier 1911, après avoir battu plusieurs records, Hubert Latham écrase son Antoinette sur un toit de Brooklands (**1**). Quelque temps plus tôt, ce petit monoplan avait plongé dans les eaux de la Wey lors de manœuvres au sol (**2**). Les deux pilotes ne furent que légèrement blessés.

Looping the loop

With more robust aircraft, pilots became daredevils. Adolphe Pégoud (**3**, on right) won fame as the first to fly upside down on 2 September 1913. He repeated the trick at Brooklands in a strengthened Blériot monoplane (**1**) as people lay on the ground to watch (**2**). Credit for the first loop should actually go to the Russian Lieutenant Nikolaevich Nesterov.

Purzelbäume in der Luft

Je stabiler die Maschinen wurden, desto mehr riskierten die Piloten. Adolphe Pégoud (**3**, rechts) war am 2. September 1913 der erste, der auf dem Kopf stehend flog. Er wiederholte das Kunststück mit seinem Blériot-Eindecker in Brooklands (**1**), und die Zuschauer legten sich zum Beobachten auf den Boden (**2**). Den ersten Looping flog der russische Lieutenant Nikolajewitsch Nesterow.

Les premiers loopings

La robustesse croissante des appareils incite les pilotes à prendre de plus en plus de risques dans leurs évolutions. Adolphe Pégoud (**3**, à droite) devient célèbre le 2 septembre 1913 pour avoir été le premier à voler sur le dos. Il répéta son exploit à Brooklands sur un monoplan Blériot à structure renforcée (**1**), sous les yeux de spectateurs allongés par terre pour mieux apprécier sa voltige (**2**). En réalité, ce fut le lieutenant russe Nikolaïevitch Nesterov qui effectua le premier looping.

Compelling attractions
Contrasting old and new, Claude Grahame-White's flying machine was unloaded at the Hendon Aviation Meeting in May 1911 (**1**). In 1914 Hendon was visited by the First Lord of the Admiralty, Winston Churchill, and his wife Clementine (**2**).

Eine große Attraktion
Alte und neue Transportmittel kommen zusammen: Beim Flugtreffen in Hendon, Mai 1911, wird Claude Grahame-Whites Maschine abgeladen (**1**). 1914 besucht der Erste Lord der Admiralität, Winston Churchill, mit seiner Frau Clementine das Flugfeld von Hendon (**2**).

L'attrait de la nouveauté
La tradition vient au secours de la modernité et la carriole à cheval sert de dépanneuse à l'aéroplane de Claude Grahame-White, accidenté en mai 1911 lors d'un meeting aérien à Hendon (**1**), où se rendirent en 1914 Winston Churchill, alors Premier Lord de l'Amirauté, et sa femme Clementine (**2**).

Bicycles have their uses

People unwilling to pay admission at the 1911 Hendon show stood on bicycles to peer over the perimeter fence (**3**). Their view was probably similar to that at the 1912 Hendon Aerial Derby speed handicap (**4**), involving this Baby Wright racer and Henry Farman biplane.

Wozu man ein Fahrrad braucht

Diese Besucher des Flugtags von Hendon, 1911, wollen das Eintrittsgeld sparen und blicken von ihren Fahrrädern aus über den Zaun (**3**). Sie dürften Ähnliches gesehen haben wie das Aerial Derby im folgenden Jahr (**4**), wo die Maschinen, darunter ein Baby-Wright und ein Doppeldecker von Henry Farman, auf den Start warten.

Du bon usage du vélo

Ces amateurs passionnés ou simplement curieux, juchés sur les selles de leurs vélos pour mieux voir les avions exposés au meeting de Hendon de 1911 (**3**), découvrent probablement un spectacle semblable à celui de la course de vitesse à handicap du Hendon Aerial Derby de 1912 (**4**), à laquelle participaient ce Baby Wright de course et ce biplan Farman.

4

Hendon, 1913
New developments were shown off at Hendon's first international air race on 25 September 1913. Grass airstrips had rapidly developed to become airfields. By 1913 Hendon had solid-looking hangars, production facilities and administrative buildings.

Hendon 1913
Der erste internationale Flugwettbewerb in Hendon fand am 25. September 1913 statt, und die neuesten Maschinen waren zu sehen. Die einfachen Graspisten hatten sich bald zu Flugplätzen entwickelt, und 1913 gab es in Hendon bereits solide wirkende Hangars, Produktionsbetriebe und Verwaltungsgebäude.

Hendon, 1913
La première course aérienne internationale de Hendon, le 25 septembre 1913, est l'occasion de voir les améliorations les plus récentes en matière d'aviation. Les champs d'herbe de Hendon, vite devenus de véritables pistes d'aérodrome, sont désormais bordés de hangars, d'ateliers de production et de bâtiments administratifs en dur.

British pioneers

Claude Grahame-White (**1**), one of a handful of dashing young aviators, was both a great socialite and a shrewd prizewinner. He used his prize to buy land for Hendon airfield in 1911 (**2**). That year he also made the first night flight in Britain, just lost a race to carry airmail from Blackpool to Southport, won the first Gordon Bennett international speed race at Belmont Park, New York, and flew to Washington to land next to the White House.

Britische Pioniere

Claude Grahame-White (**1**) gehörte zu einer Handvoll eleganter junger Flieger aus der feineren Gesellschaft; er war ein Charmeur, wußte aber auch, wie man Preise gewinnt. Mit seinem Preisgeld kaufte er 1911 Land für den Flugplatz Hendon (**2**). Im selben Jahr unternahm er den ersten britischen Nachtflug, unterlag im Luftpost-Wettflug von Blackpool nach Southport nur knapp, gewann den ersten Internationalen Gordon-Bennett-Flugwettbewerb in Belmont Park, New York, und flog nach Washington, wo er gleich neben dem Weißen Haus landete.

Les pionniers britanniques

Claude Grahame-White (**1**), l'un des nombreux et prometteurs jeunes aviateurs anglais, était une des personnalités de la haute société britannique. Habile gestionnaire de ses succès, il employa l'argent des prix qu'il remportait pour acquérir, dès 1911, les terrains nécessaires à l'aérodrome de Hendon (**2**). Cette même année, il effectua également le premier vol de nuit au-dessus de la Grande-Bretagne, perdit la course organisée pour le transport du courrier de Blackpool à Southport, remporta en revanche le prix Gordon Bennett, première course internationale de vitesse, au Belmont Park de New York et, de là, relia Washington où il atterrit près de la Maison Blanche.

Class acts

J.T.C. Moore-Brabazon (later Lord Brabazon of Tara) (**3**), with political advertising on his Wright machine, was the first British resident to become a qualified aeroplane pilot, in December 1908. Thomas Sopwith (**4**, with passenger) began his flying career in October 1910 by crashing on his first-ever flight as a pilot. But in December he won a £4,000 prize for flying 177 miles from England to Belgium in a straight line.

Erste Garde

J.T.C. Moore-Brabazon (später Lord Brabazon of Tara), der hier seine Wright-Maschine mit einem politischen Plakat versehen hat (**3**), war im Dezember 1908 der erste Brite, der sich als Pilot registrieren ließ. Thomas Sopwith (**4**, mit Passagier) begann seine Pilotenkarriere im Oktober 1910 mit einem Absturz gleich auf dem ersten Flug, doch im Dezember errang er den mit £ 4.000 dotierten Preis für einen 285 km langen Luftlinienflug von England nach Belgien.

Des numéros de classe

J.T.C. Moore-Brabazon, devenu lord Brabazon of Tara (**3**), dont le Wright porte une affiche politique, fut le premier résident britannique à obtenir sa licence de pilote, en décembre 1908. Thomas Sopwith (**4**, avec une passagère) commença sa carrière de pilote en s'écrasant lors de son premier vol en solo, en octobre 1910, mais remporta en décembre un prix de 4 000 £ après avoir relié l'Angleterre à la Belgique en parcourant 285 km en ligne droite.

Death of a pioneer

The Hon. Charles S. Rolls (**2**) was already a maker of fine automobiles (Rolls Royce) when he took up ballooning in 1901 and co-founded the Royal Aero Club. In 1909 he bought a Short-built Wright Flyer, and in June 1910 was the first to make a two-way crossing of the English Channel. But at the Bournemouth air meeting on 12 July his French-built Wright biplane, to which he had fitted a defective auxiliary elevator, failed. Shortly after making a turn (**3**) he crashed and was killed (**1**).

Tod eines Fliegers

Charles S. Rolls (**2**) hatte sich als Fabrikant der erlesenen Rolls-Royce-Automobile bereits einen Namen gemacht, als er 1901 seinen ersten Ballonflug unternahm und Mitbegründer des Royal Aero Clubs wurde. 1909 erwarb er einen von Short gebauten Wright-Flyer und war im Juni 1910 der erste, der den Kanal in beiden Richtungen überflog. Doch beim Luftfahrttreffen in Bournemouth am 12. Juli versagte ein zusätzliches Höhenruder, mit dem er ein französisches Exemplar des Wright-Doppeldeckers versehen hatte. Kurz nach einer Wendung (**3**) ging die Maschine zu Boden (**1**), und Rolls kam dabei um.

La mort d'un pionnier

Charles S. Rolls (**2**) était déjà connu comme le constructeur des automobiles de luxe Rolls-Royce lorsqu'il entreprit, en 1901, de faire du ballon et de fonder le Royal Aero Club britannique. En 1909, il acheta un Flyer Wright construit par Short et, en juin 1910, fut le premier à effectuer un aller et retour au-dessus de la Manche. Le 12 juillet, lors du meeting aérien de Bournemouth, il se tua en fin de virage (**3**) à bord d'un biplan Wright de construction française auquel il avait adapté une commande de profondeur auxiliaire défectueuse (**1**).

3

Woman power

On 8 July 1908, a few days after a suffragette dropped leaflets from a balloon on to the House of Commons, Thérèse Peltier flew in Italy as the first woman aeroplane passenger (**4**). Increasingly demanding, she insisted on women being at the forefront of the new aviation industry. When 'Baroness' de Laroche became the first certified woman pilot in March 1910, she was quickly followed by Hélène Dutrieu (**2**) and the American Matilde Moisant (**1**), sister of the doomed show pilot John Moisant. Struggling to be practical in the air, aviatrices developed this new skirt and headpiece (**3**).

Frauen an die Macht

Am 8. Juli 1908 – nur ein paar Tage nachdem eine Suffragette von einem Ballon aus über dem englischen Parlament Flugblätter abgeworfen hatte – erhob sich Thérèse Peltier als erster weiblicher Passagier eines Motorflugzeugs in die Lüfte (**4**). Als Propagandistin forderte sie Frauen an vorderster Front der Luftfahrtbewegung. »Baronesse« de Laroche ließ sich im März 1910 als erste Pilotin registrieren, und bald folgten Hélène Dutrieu (**2**) und die Amerikanerin Matilde Moisant (**1**), die Schwester des Kunstfliegers John Moisant, der bald darauf umkommen sollte. Auf der Suche nach adäquater Flugkleidung entstand dieser Rock mit passender Mütze (**3**).

Les femmes s'envolent

Le 8 juillet 1908, quelques jours après qu'une suffragette a lancé des tracts sur la Chambre des Communes depuis un ballon, Thérèse Peltier devient la première passagère d'un aéroplane au cours d'un vol en Italie (**4**) et revendique avec vigueur une place de premier plan pour les femmes dans l'aviation. L'exemple de la dite «baronne» de Laroche, première femme à obtenir une licence de pilote, en mars 1910, est bientôt suivi par la Belge Hélène Dutrieu (**2**) et l'Américaine Matilde Moisant (**1**), sœur du pilote de voltige John Moisant. Ces aviatrices créèrent ce moderne ensemble combinaison et casque leur permettant de piloter plus à leur aise (**3**).

Noble ladies of flight

Before they had the vote, women aviators found it helped to be aristocratic. Princess Ludwig of Löwenstein-Wertheim learned to fly with the help of a Mr Baumann in 1914 (**1**), while the experienced balloonist and pioneer aviatrice Raymonde de Laroche (**2**) did better as 'Baroness' de Laroche. She was the first woman to fly, in October 1909, and died while testing a new plane in 1919 (**3**).

Fliegende Aristokratinnen

In einer Zeit, als sie noch nicht einmal das Stimmrecht bei Wahlen hatten, war es für Frauen nicht leicht, ans Steuer eines Flugzeugs zu kommen. Für eine Aristokratin waren die Chancen besser. Die Prinzessin von Löwenstein-Wertheim erlernte 1914 bei einem Mann namens Baumann das Fliegen (**1**), und die erfahrene Ballonfliegerin und frühe Pilotin Elise Deroche (**2**) konnte sich besser durchsetzen, als sie sich »Baronesse« de Laroche nannte. Im Oktober 1909 war sie die erste Frau, die selbst flog; zehn Jahre später kam sie beim Testflug mit einer neuen Maschine ums Leben (**3**).

Le vol des aristocrates

En ce début de siècle, il était plus facile aux femmes de devenir pilote que d'obtenir le droit de vote. L'aéronaute confirmée et pionnière de l'aviation Elise Deroche (**2**), plus connue sous le nom de «baronne» de Laroche, fut ainsi la première femme à voler en solo, en octobre 1909, avant de se tuer en 1919 au cours des essais d'un nouvel aéroplane (**3**). Entre-temps, en 1914, la princesse Ludwig von Löwenstein-Wertheim avait à son tour appris à voler en compagnie d'un certain Baumann (**1**).

4

A Technological Revolution

The pioneers of aviation were remarkably unscientific by modern standards. They knew something of the principles of aeronautics, of lift and drag, and power-to-weight ratios, but few were as methodical as the Wright brothers with their wind tunnels, extensive gliding experiments and careful readings of scientific papers.

Most preferred to advance by doing. They were amateurs, tinkerers, businessmen, caught up in the excitement of flying and the money and fame on offer. Brave, yes, foolhardy, even, they were not scientists who understood what they were doing. They copied each other's designs, adjusted them here and there and flew them until they crashed – often fatally. It was perhaps no wonder that so many thousands of people flocked to air shows, their hearts in their mouths as one pioneer after another took to the skies in new designs that might or might not return their pilots to the ground in one piece.

Of all the scores of different aeroplanes that flew until World War I, only a handful demonstrated real advances. Some fundamental misconceptions, such as the Voisin-Farman side-curtained box-kite biplanes, persisted to 1909 because some pioneers thought that the stability of the design was more important than control in Wright's inherently unstable wing-warping Flyer designs. Wing-flapping 'ornithopters' still had a few supporters, and so many weird designs appeared that it was sometimes debatable whether *anybody* should think they might fly.

But fly they did. At least one pioneer was an aviation scientist: as early as 1884 Britain's Horatio Phillips had proved George Cayley's aeronautical theories of 90 years earlier when he built a wind tunnel for the Aeronautical Society and passed steam over a two-surface wing section – an aerofoil. He showed that if a wing is curved more on its upper than its lower surface, air pressure will be higher underneath and the wing will lift. Phillips's writings were of fundamental importance to aviation, but when it came to his own practical work he chose the Multiplane, a machine that looked more like a venetian blind than any aeroplane ever built. In 1907 it did actually fly for 500 feet at Streatham, London, and became Britain's first piloted and powered aeroplane, though it was never officially credited as such.

Another great idea whose time had not yet come was the helicopter. The concept of a vertically directed airscrew appears to date from the 12th century, refined by Leonardo da Vinci in about 1490. A prototype competed against or-

nithopters in the 1870s and the concept finally got off the ground in France as Breguet-Richet Gyroplane No. 1 in 1907. Credit for the first free-lifting helicopter, however, goes to the French engineer Paul Cornu, who at the same time built a tandem-rotor machine driven by a water-cooled 24hp Antoinette engine. Both Cornu and Louis Breguet failed to solve problems of stability and power, and it was not until 1936 that the first practical helicopter flew.

And the first jet plane? A Romanian called Henry Coanda knew about that in 1910. This was not the turbo-jet design of the 1930s and 40s, but a centrifugal air compressor, driving air backwards inside a nose cowling and itself driven by a 50hp Clerget engine. The aircraft's sleek shape and cantilevered, varnished plywood wings were advanced, too. Whether it actually flew is debatable, but Coanda claimed to have a barely controlled hop in it near Paris.

Engines were the weakest part of early aeroplanes. Big and heavy, they were made of cast iron and steel, weighing about 8lb per horsepower developed. With the added weight of a water-tank for cooling, water-pipes, a heavy wooden propeller, strain caused by torque in the drive shaft and intermittent bangs of the cylinders, an engine sometimes broke off its mountings or caused the aircraft itself to break up. Until 1908 aviators could counter engine weight only by making their aircraft lighter and producing greater lift from more wing area. Thus the biplane became the triplane. Alliott Verdon Roe was the first Briton to fly in a British aeroplane: 100 feet over Lea Marshes, Essex, in a paper-covered machine that had triplane forward wings and rear elevators. The Brazilian-French pioneer Santos-Dumont built the tiny Demoiselle, a monoplane that was the first successful light aircraft with a bamboo fuselage, and the Englishman John Dunne built a tailless, V-winged biplane that appeared to be all lift.

In 1908 a wholly new engine appeared that greatly improved aviation. The Gnome rotary engine was built by Laurent and Louis Séguin to do away with the continuously flowing water-cooling radiator. Instead, it used cooling fins around each cylinder to dissipate heat into the air. Instead of the crankshaft shaking the aeroplane as it spun, the engine itself moved round with the propeller. The result was a smooth-running flywheel that ran like a sewing machine and was less than half the weight of the water-cooled engine. Instead of 30 or 50hp it gave 70 or 80, and quickly became one of the best-selling engines in the world.

The Gnome became Le Rhône, with versions later built by Bentley, Clerget and BMW. It was the mainstay of many aircraft throughout World War I, including the British Sopwith Camel. It was with a 140hp Gnome engine that a streamlined Deperdussin Monocoque monoplane, whose shell fuselage carried most of the aircraft's loads, achieved a world record speed of 108 mph at Chicago in 1912.

Increasingly, it was wealthy shipping businesses which saw advantages in aviation, and Henri Fabre, the scientist son of a French shipowner, seized on the new 50hp Gnome engine to power his remarkable Hydravion float-plane off Marseilles in 1910. Fired by Fabre's success, the American Glenn Curtiss the following January fitted a float to his plane and flew the first successful seaplane off San Diego.

Already acutely interested in the possibilities of aviation, the US Navy in November 1910 arranged for one of Curtiss's pilots, Eugene Ely, to make the first flight from the deck of the cruiser USS *Birmingham*, anchored at Hampton Roads, Virginia. In January 1911, he landed back on the USS *Birmingham* using a hook to catch on to an outstretched rope. Later that year a new Curtiss seaplane took off from the deck of the cruiser USS *Pennsylvania* supported by a thickly-greased cable – the first catapult launch.

Curtiss would ultimately make most of his fortune from the military. But where was the other big source of income – fare-paying passengers? Anxiously looking at Count von Zeppelin's ever-bigger airships and regular passenger services, aircraft designers knew the answer had to be bigger, multi-engined planes. For safety's sake, in any case, two or more engines had to be better than one. In 1911 the Short Brothers in England built the Triple Twin biplane, powered by two 50hp Gnome engines, one pushing behind the cockpit, the other in front driving twin wing-mounted propellers by chains. The two occupants each had flying controls. In Russia at the same time, Igor Sikorsky built the even bigger *Bolshoi* (known as *Le Grand*, a four-engined, 92ft wingspan passenger-carrying biplane with the first enclosed cabin. The *Ilya Mourometz* which followed in 1914 was bigger still, with a passenger promenade deck, a toilet, and meals served at table.

Before 1914 came the first air-to-ground radio transmission, the first airspeed indicator, sprung undercarriages and other safety improvements. There was, too, a demonstration of the first parachute. In August 1913, Adolphe Pégoud, a daredevil pilot for the Blériot company who had been one of the

An early, unsuccessful model of Léon Levavasseur's Antoinette monoplane appeared in August 1907. His later Antoinettes set the monoplane standard.

Eine erste, noch erfolglose Ausführung von Léon Levavasseurs Antoinette Eindecker erschien im August 1907. Spätere Antoinettes sollten zum Vorbild aller weiteren Eindecker werden.

Datant d'août 1907, ce prototype de Léon Levavasseur ne fut pas une réussite mais préfigura déjà l'Antoinette, qui déterminera par la suite le modèle du monoplan.

first to fly upside down, safely jumped out of a plane that was already assigned to the scrapheap.

Ironically, the parachute was to be the one significant advance that British, French – and some German – officials ignored as war clouds gathered. Single-seat planes were soon to be snapped up as fighters, twin-seaters for reconnaissance, and multi-engined aircraft for bombers. But parachute development stayed in limbo, partly because governments feared pilots would too easily abandon their valuable machines if they knew they could jump.

The cruel lack of parachutes would cost the lives of thousands of aviators – including many a pioneer – in the coming war. Adolphe Pégoud was one of them.

First 'club' plane

Alberto Santos-Dumont's tiny 1909 Demoiselle monoplane (**2**, **3**) was the first of its kind, with a wingspan of under 17 feet and a 20hp two-cylinder Antoinette engine (**1**). It appealed to those who wanted an aeroplane for the fun of 'dropping in' on their friends. The pilot flew it rather like a motorized hang-glider and it well matched the personality of the adventurous but diminutive (five feet tall) Santos-Dumont (**3**).

Das erste »Amateurflugzeug«

Alberto Santos-Dumonts winziger Demoiselle-Eindecker von 1909 (**2**, **3**) war das erste Flugzeug seiner Art, mit einer Spannweite von nur knapp über 5 Metern und einem 20-PS-Antoinette-Zweizylindermotor (**1**). Es wandte sich an jene, die ein Flugzeug wollten, mit dem sie im Garten ihrer Freunde landen konnten. Der Pilot flog es wie einen motorisierten Hanggleiter, und die Demoiselle paßte gut zur Persönlichkeit ihres Erbauers, der zwar wagemutig, aber nur 1 Meter 52 groß war (**3**).

Le premier avion de loisirs

Le petit monoplan Demoiselle modèle 1909 (**2**, **3**)
correspondait parfaitement à la personnalité aventurière
et à la taille (1,52 m) de Santos-Dumont (**3**). Avec une
envergure de à peine plus de 5 m et un moteur
Antoinette bi-cylindre de 20 ch (**1**), cet appareil fut le
premier de son genre. Se pilotant comme un planeur
motorisé, il intéressait tous ceux qui désiraient un
aéroplane de «loisirs» leur permettant de passer voir
des amis à la campagne.

Early Blériot

Louis Blériot's debt-inducing aviation efforts before his famous Channel crossing reveal not only his extraordinary energy but his technological progression. After unsuccessful biplanes No. III and No. IV in 1906, he built his first monoplane, the tail-first No.V *L'Oiseau* (**2**), in March 1907. That was quickly abandoned in July for the No. VI *Libellule* (**3**), which at least experimented with wing-tip ailerons. Then in November came the vital No. VII (**4**), which he soon abandoned, although it established the future shape of all tractor-monoplanes. The two-seater XII, seen in June 1909 (**1**), immediately followed his Channel-crossing XI.

Blériots Anfänge

Aus Louis Blériots ruinösen Experimenten der Zeit vor der berühmten Kanalüberquerung lassen sich nicht nur seine enorme Tatkraft, sondern auch seine technischen Fortschritte ablesen. Nach den glücklosen Doppeldeckern Nr. III und Nr. IV des Jahres 1906 war im März 1907 sein erster Eindecker fertig, Nr. V *L'Oiseau* mit Frontleitwerk (**2**). Doch schon im Juli hatte er ihn zugunsten von Nr. VI aufgegeben, der *Libellule* (**3**), die immerhin versuchsweise Querruder an den Tragflächenenden hatte. Im November kam der Durchbruch mit Nr. VII (**4**), das er zwar ebenfalls binnen kurzem aufgab, mit dem er jedoch die Grundform für alle zukünftigen Eindecker mit Frontmotor fand. Die zweisitzige Nr. XII, hier im Juni 1909 aufgenommen (**1**), nahm er gleich nach der Kanalüberquerung (mit einer Nr. XI) in Angriff.

Les premiers Blériot

Les efforts de Louis Blériot en faveur de l'aviation avant sa célèbre traversée de la Manche témoignent non seulement de son extraordinaire énergie mais également de son évolution technologique. Après les échecs de ses biplans N° III et N° IV en 1906, il construit en mars 1907 son premier monoplan de type canard, le N° V dit *L'Oiseau* (**2**), rapidement remplacé en juillet par la *Libellule* (**3**), un N° VI pourvu d'ailerons en extrémité d'aile. C'est en novembre qu'il réalise le N° VII (**4**), aéroplane fondamental qui, bien qu'également abandonné, définira la forme future de tous les monoplans à hélice tractive. Le N° XII, un avion biplace photographié ici en juin 1909 (**1**), suivit immédiatement le N° XI avec lequel il avait traversé la Manche.

2

3

4

Father of the Antoinette

Léon Levavasseur (**1**) built his first, unsuccessful biplane in 1903, and might
have left aviation for motorboat racing had it not been for the increasing
popularity of his excellent Antoinette engines – named after the daughter of
his industrialist sponsor, Jules Gastambide. Levavasseur's first monoplane
was the Gastambide-Mengin I, seen here in December 1907, with Jules
Gastambide and Gabriel Mengin standing on the wings (**3**). It was the
forerunner of the famous Antoinette monoplane, photographed over Châlons
in 1910 (**2**).

Der Vater der Antoinette

Léon Levavasseur (**1**) baute seinen ersten, erfolglosen Doppeldecker 1903 und hätte sich von da an vielleicht ganz auf Rennboote konzentriert, wäre nicht sein ausgezeichneter Antoinette-Motor gewesen, der sich immer größerer Beliebtheit erfreute; benannt war er nach der Tochter seines Geldgebers, des Industriellen Jules Gastambide. Levavasseurs erster Eindecker war der Gastambide-Mengin I, hier im Dezember 1907 mit Jules Gastambide und Gabriel Mengin auf den Tragflächen aufgenommen (**3**). Es war der Vorgänger der berühmten Antoinette, hier 1910 im Flug über Châlons festgehalten (**2**).

Le père de l'Antoinette

Léon Levavasseur (**1**) construisit son premier biplan en 1903. Il aurait pu abandonner l'aviation pour les courses de bateau à moteur si ses excellents moteurs Antoinette – du nom de la fille de Jules Gastambide, l'industriel qui le commanditait – n'avaient été si appréciés. Le premier monoplan de Levavasseur fut le Gastambide-Mengin I, que l'on voit ici en décembre 1907 avec Jules Gastambide et Gabriel Mengin sur ses ailes (**3**) et qui servit de «prototype» au célèbre monoplan Antoinette, photographié en vol au-dessus de Châlons en 1910 (**2**).

Flawed pioneer

Robert Esnault-Pelterie (2) was a first-class French scientist-engineer who nevertheless probably retarded aviation development in Europe. He attended Octave Chanute's vital 1903 Paris lecture describing the Wrights' simultaneous use of wing-warping and rudder, built a flawed copy of their glider and, in a widely recorded lecture in 1905, denounced the Wright design as structurally dangerous. He was, however, the first to put ailerons on a Wright-type Flyer and he is remembered for his 1907 monoplane REP No. 1 (1), and as the inventor of the joystick and seatbelts. He was later famed for developmental work on space flight.

Pionier mit kleinen Fehlern

Robert Esnault-Pelterie war ein erstklassiger französischer Wissenschaftler und Ingenieur, doch trotzdem warf er wahrscheinlich die Entwicklung des europäischen Flugwesens zurück (2). Im Jahre 1903 hielt Octave Chanute einen entscheidenden Vortrag über die Gebrüder Wright und deren Steuerung von Flugzeugen durch Verwinden der Tragflächen zusätzlich zum Ruder. Esnault-Pelterie baute daraufhin eine Kopie des Wrightschen Gleitflugzeugs, die jedoch fehlerhaft war, und prangerte in einem weithin bekannt gewordenen Vortrag im Jahre 1905 die Wrightsche Konstruktion als gefährlich an. Andererseits war er der erste, der an den Tragflächenenden eines Flyer Querruder montierte; außerdem ging er mit seinem 1907 entstandenen Eindecker REP Nr. 1 (1) sowie als Erfinder von Steuerknüppel und Sicherheitsgurten in die Flugzeuggeschichte ein. In späteren Jahren stellte er wichtige Forschungen zur Raumfahrt an.

Un pionnier imparfait

Robert Esnault-Pelterie (2), ingénieur et inventeur français de premier ordre, est sans doute à l'origine du retard pris en Europe dans le développement de l'aviation. En effet, après avoir assisté à l'importante conférence donnée par Octave Chanute à Paris en 1903, où ce dernier décrivait le système jumelant gouverne et gauchissement alaire mis au point par les frères Wright, il réalisa une copie de leur planeur avant de dénoncer comme dangereuse, en 1905, lors d'une conférence très remarquée, la conception structurelle de l'avion des Wright. Outre son monoplan REP N° 1 (1), de 1907, il cependant resté célèbre pour avoir été le premier à adapter des ailerons à un Flyer Wright et à inventer le manche à balai et la ceinture de sécurité. Il se fit ensuite connaître par ses études sur le vol spatial.

Wright impact

Europeans and the US government were stunned when the Wrights resumed demonstrating their Flyers in 1908–9, four years after their first flight. At Fort Myer, Virginia, Orville Wright (**1**, on right) checked over his craft during government demonstrations. By 1908, assisted take-offs like this one in France (**2**), involving heavy counterweights pulled to the top of a derrick, were well out of date.

Die Wrights melden sich zurück

Als die Brüder Wright 1908/09, vier Jahre nach ihrem Erstflug, wieder mit den Flyers zu Demonstrationsflügen erschienen, waren europäische und amerikanische Regierungen verblüfft von den Leistungen dieser Flugzeuge. Orville Wright (**1**, rechts) vergewissert sich bei einer Vorführung für die U.S.-Regierung in Fort Myer, Virginia, daß seine Maschine in Ordnung ist. Flugzeuge, die zum Starten einen Flaschenzug und schwere Gegengewichte brauchten, waren 1908, als diese Aufnahme (**2**) in Frankreich entstand, hoffnungslos veraltet.

L'influence des Wright

Les Européens et les autorités américaines furent stupéfiés par le Flyer lorsque les Wright reprirent leurs démonstrations dans les années 1908–1909, soit quatre ans après leur premier vol. À Fort Myer, en Virginie, Orville Wright (**1**, à droite) inspecte son appareil avant une demonstration devant le gouvernement. En 1908, les décollages effectués à l'aide d'un lourd contrepoids tombant du haut d'un pylône, comme ici en France (**2**), étaient déjà bien démodés.

Flight training
Horses had to be tightly controlled (3) when Wilbur Wright and Wright team member Paul Tissandier practised at their new flying school at Pau, France, in 1909.

Flugausbildung
Die Pferde waren an den Betrieb in der neugegründeten Wright-Flugschule im französischen Pau noch nicht gewöhnt (3) – hier 1909 Wilbur Wright und sein Mitarbeiter Paul Tissandier.

Entraînement en vol
En 1909, les chevaux sont encore à peine habitués à l'avion lorsque Wilbur Wright et Paul Tissandier, un des élèves de sa nouvelle école de pilotage, s'entraînent à Pau (3).

1

2

3

4

The new rage: monoplanes

A fashion for monoplanes developed after Blériot's 1909 Channel crossing. Deperdussin's monoplane (**1**) of October 1910 was a Blériot imitation. 'Le Plus Petit' of Raoul Vendôme (**3**), also of 1910, owed more to Santos-Dumont's successful little Demoiselle. In England in 1909, newcomer Frederick Handley Page built his first aircraft, the monoplane *Bluebird* (**2**). Germany, fascinated by von Zeppelin's airships, finally started to produce good aeroplanes, including Etrich-Wels' monoplane in 1908 (**4**) and Etrich's birdlike Rumpler Taube (dove) (**5**), seen in 1914.

Die neue Mode: Eindecker

Nach Blériots Kanalüberquerung von 1909 wollte alle Welt Eindecker. Deperdussins Maschine (**1**) vom Oktober 1910 war ein Blériot-Imitat. Raoul Vendômes 'Le Plus Petit' desselben Jahrs (**3**) hängte sich eher an den Erfolg von Santos-Dumonts kleiner Demoiselle an. In England trat 1909 der Neuling Frederick Handley Page mit seiner ersten Maschine an, dem Eindecker *Bluebird* (**2**). Auch in Deutschland, das bis dahin ganz im Bann von Zeppelins Luftschiffen gestanden hatte, kamen nun gute Flugzeuge auf, darunter Etrich-Wels' Eindecker (**4**) 1908 und seine vogelartige Rumpler-Taube (**5**) 1914 fotografiert.

5

La nouvelle vogue du monoplan

L'engouement pour les monoplans est apparu après la traversée réussie de la Manche par Blériot en 1909. Ainsi le monoplan de Deperdussin (**1**), datant d'octobre 1910, est-il une imitation du Blériot ; en revanche, Le Plus Petit de Raoul Vendôme (**3**), également de 1910, tient plutôt du petit Demoiselle de Santos-Dumont. En Angleterre, Frederick Handley Page construit en 1909 son premier avion monoplan, le *Bluebird* (**2**). L'Allemagne, fascinée par les dirigeables de von Zeppelin, se décide à son tour à produire de bons aéroplanes, notamment le monoplan de Etrich et Wels de 1908 (**4**) et le bien nommé Rumpler Taube (colombe) de Etrich (**5**), ici photographié en 1914.

Take-offs

It is hard to exaggerate the risks – and fear – faced by the early aviators in testing new aeroplanes. Ferdinard Ferber tried out this craft (**1**) in July 1908, and was killed a year later when his Voisin hit a ditch taxiing at speed at Boulogne. Charles and Gabriel Voisin built a classic type of push-engine biplane, the second example of which in February 1907 took a few hops before its fuselage broke up. Its first successful flight was on 30 March 1907 (**2**).

Der erste Start

Die Risiken, die von den Flugpionieren bei Versuchen mit neuen Maschinen eingegangen wurden, und die Ängste, die sie dabei ausstanden, waren ungeheuer. Ein Jahr nach diesem Versuchsflug im Juli 1908 (**1**) kam Ferdinand Ferber ums Leben, als seine Voisin beim Anrollen in Boulogne in einen Graben geriet. Charles und Gabriel Voisin bauten eine Variante des klassischen Doppeldeckers mit Druckpropeller, deren zweites Modell im Februar 1907 nach einigen Sprüngen mit zerbrochenem Leitwerk zu Boden ging. Der erste erfolgreiche Flug fand am 30. März 1907 statt (**2**).

Décollages

On imagine mal les risques – et la peur – que devaient affronter les premiers aviateurs en essayant de leurs nouveaux aéroplanes. Ferdinand Ferber testa son appareil (**1**) en juillet 1908 et il se tua un an plus tard lorsque son Voisin capota dans un fossé en roulant à toute vitesse sur une piste de Boulogne. Le biplan à propulsion de type classique, construit par Charles et Gabriel Voisin et dont le second exemplaire fit quelques bonds en février 1907 avant de briser son fuselage, effectua son premier vol réussi le 30 mars 1907 (**2**).

Experimenters

In November 1910, an experimental biplane with lattice structure that could be dismantled (**1**) was tested by Louis Paulhan, winner of the *Daily Mail* prize for the first London to Manchester flight. René Caudron's little biplane (**2**) became one of the significant aircraft of World War I. Gomez da Silva had less success with his pusher biplane (**3**) in October 1910, and a triple-deck Tandem Boutaric in September 1909 (**4**).

Experimente

Im November 1910 testete Louis Paulhan, der Gewinner des *Daily-Mail*-Preises für den ersten Flug von London nach Manchester, einen zerlegbaren Zweidecker aus Gitterwerk (**1**). René Caudrons kleiner Doppeldecker (**2**) sollte eines der wichtigsten Flugzeuge des Ersten Weltkriegs werden. Weniger Glück hatte Gomez da Silva – weder sein Zweidecker mit Druckpropeller vom Oktober 1910 (**3**) noch sein Dreidecker Tandem Boutaric vom September 1909 (**4**) setzten sich durch.

Expérimentateurs

Un an après le triplan Tandem Boutaric de septembre 1909 (**4**), c'est en novembre 1910 que ce biplan expérimental à structure démontable en treillis (**1**) fut testé par Louis Paulhan, vainqueur du prix du *Daily Mail* pour le premier vol Londres-Manchester. Si le petit biplan de Caudron (**2**) devint l'un des « grands » avions de la Première Guerre mondiale, Gomez da Silva eut, en octobre 1910, moins de succès avec son biplan à propulsion (**3**).

Birth of a classic

The classic World War I biplane fighter owes much to the French Goupy II, first flown in March 1909 (**1**). Built by Louis Blériot to follow an earlier Voisin aeroplane made for Ambroise Goupy, it was the first to have staggered wings. The Briton Alliott Verdon Roe followed the Goupy and abandoned his unsuccessful 1908 Roe I biplane (**2**) to build two triplanes. Early engines were still unreliable, and men such as Bellamy at Weybridge in 1907 (**3**) had to make do with limited power.

Geburt eines Klassikers

Die französische Goupy II, die zu ihrem Erstflug im März 1909 startete (**1**), ist der Urahn aller Doppeldecker-Kampfflugzeuge des Ersten Weltkriegs. Die von Louis Blériot für Ambroise Goupy auf der Basis eines früheren Voisin-Modells gebaute Maschine war die erste mit versetzten Tragflächen. Der Brite Alliott Verdon Roe nahm sich für den Nachfolger seines erfolglosen Roe-I-Doppeldeckers (**2**) die Goupy zum Vorbild und entwarf zwei Dreidecker. Die frühen Motoren waren noch unzuverlässig, und Männer wie Bellamy, hier in Weybridge im Jahr 1907 (**3**), mußten sich mit geringer Leistung zufriedengeben.

Naissance d'un classique

Le classique chasseur biplan de la Première Guerre mondiale doit beaucoup au Goupy II français, dont le premier vol eut lieu en mars 1909 (**1**). Construit par Louis Blériot en s'inspirant d'un ancien aéroplane Voisin réalisé pour Ambroise Goupy, ce fut le premier avion à disposer d'ailes décalées. Le Britannique Alliott Verdon Roe adopta le Goupy en abandonnant son malheureux biplan Roe I de 1908 (**2**) pour construire deux triplans. Les premiers moteurs étaient encore peu fiables et des hommes tels que Bellamy, ici à Weybridge en 1907 (**3**), devaient s'accommoder d'une puissance limitée.

2

The future arrives early

Tail-less flying wings, such as America's new B-2 Stealth bomber, have their origin in the Englishman John William Dunne's remarkable swept-wing biplanes. The first, D1, based on the winged Zanonia seed from Java, was built for the British government in secret in 1907. It failed, but his Gnome-engined D5, with Dunne in the cockpit, flew well at Eastchurch, England, in 1910 (**2**) and his D8 flew from Eastchurch to Paris in 1913 (**1**).

Schon damals die Zukunft

Nurflügelflugzeuge wie der neue amerikanische Bomber B-2 Stealth haben ihren Ursprung in den merkwürdigen Doppeldeckern des Engländers John William Dunne mit ihrer abwärtsgewandten Pfeilform. Dunne ließ sich bei der D1, die er 1907 als Geheimprojekt für die britische Regierung konstruierte, von den geflügelten Samen der Zanonia (Bandelierfrucht) inspirieren, eines Gewächses aus Java. Die ersten Versuche scheiterten, doch die von einem Gnome-Motor angetriebene D5 bestand 1910 ihre Probe im englischen Eastchurch mit Dunne am Steuer (**2**), und die D8 flog 1913 von Eastchurch nach Paris (**1**).

Un avenir précoce

Les ailes volantes sans empennage, comme le moderne bombardier américain B-2 Stealth, trouvent une lointaine origine dans les remarquables biplans à ailes en flèche de l'Anglais John William Dunne. Le premier appareil de ce type, le D1, inspiré des graines de zanonia de Java, fut construit en secret pour le gouvernement britannique en 1907. Si cet avion fut un échec, un D5 à moteur Gnome, piloté par Dunne, vola à Eastchurch (Angleterre) en 1910 (**2**) tandis que son D8 relia Eastchurch à Paris en 1913 (**1**).

Biplanes to triplanes

Gabriel Voisin's Goupy box-kite No. 1 was the first triplane, in May 1908 (**1**), but it barely flew and was abandoned. In the same year Henry Farman's Voisin added a top 'wing' horizontal stabilizer (**2**), but it, too, was soon abandoned.

Vom Doppel- zum Dreidecker

Gabriel Voisins Goupy Nr. 1 vom Mai 1908 war der erste Dreidecker (**1**), doch der Kastendrachen kam kaum vom Boden. Auch Henry Farman gab die Voisin-Maschine mit zusätzlichem Stabilisator (**2**) bald wieder auf.

Des biplans aux triplans

Si le Goupy N° 1 à structure cellulaire de Gabriel Voisin fut, en mai 1908, le premier triplan construit (**1**), il vola à peine et fut abandonné, tout comme ce Voisin de Henry Farman, auquel avait été ajouté un stabilisateur horizontal (**2**).

Better success

A.V. Roe's *Avroplane* (**4**), modelled on the Goupy triplane, was the first all-British aeroplane to fly, on 23 July 1909. With only a tiny 9hp JAP engine, it was extraordinarily light, weighing 399lb, including Roe himself, and its fuselage fabric was made of thick paper. By the time of the big Tarrant in 1919 (**3**) the triplane had had its day.

Erste Erfolge

A.V. Roes *Avroplane* (**4**), nach dem Vorbild des Goupy-Dreideckers gebaut, war das erste rein britische Flugzeug, das flog – am 23. Juli 1909. Die von einem winzigen 9-PS-JAP-Motor angetriebene Maschine war extrem leicht – mit Roe an Bord wog sie nur 181 Kilogramm, und die Bespannung des Rumpfes bestand aus kräftigem Papier. Als 1919 die gewaltige Tarrant vorgestellt wurde (**3**), war die große Zeit der Dreidecker schon vorbei.

Les débuts du succès

L'*Avroplane* (**4**) de A. V. Roe, inspiré par le triplan Goupy, fut le premier aéroplane de construction entièrement britannique à voler (23 juillet 1909). Disposant d'un petit moteur JAP de 9 ch, cet appareil extraordinairement léger, au fuselage recouvert de papier résistant, ne pesait que 181 kg, pilote compris. En 1919, le triplan est déjà passé de mode lorsque sort l'énorme Tarrant (**3**).

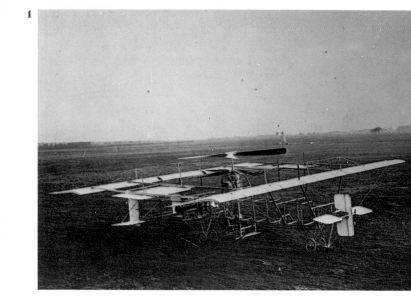

First helicopters

Two machines vied for the title of first practical helicopter in late 1907, but neither really qualified because the problems of stability were not be solved for another 30 years. Nevertheless, the Breguet brothers' four-rotor gyroplane No. 1 (**1**) did rise two feet off the ground with a man on board on 19 September, although it was supported by four men at each corner. On 13 November Paul Cornu rose vertically for a few seconds on his twin-rotor machine (**2**), and is reckoned the victor because his craft hovered unassisted.

Die erste Hubschrauber

Zwei Maschinen wetteiferten Ende 1907 darum, als erste das Hubschrauber-prinzip umzusetzen, doch keine schaffte es wirklich, und es sollte noch dreißig Jahre dauern, bis die Stabilitätsprobleme gelöst waren. Der mit vier Rotoren versehene Gyroplane Nr. 1 der Brüder Breguet (**1**) erhob sich am 19. September mit einem Mann an Bord rund einen halben Meter über den Boden, wurde allerdings an den vier Enden von Helfern gehalten. Am 13. November hob sich Paul Cornu mit seiner Zwei-Rotoren-Maschine (**2**) für einige Sekunden vom Boden und gilt als Sieger dieses Wettstreits, weil er ohne Unterstützung schwebte.

Premiers hélicoptères

Fin 1907, deux machines se disputent le titre du premier hélicoptère vraiment utilisable : le 19 septembre, soutenu par quatre hommes à ses extrémités, le Gyroplane N° 1 à quatre ailes planantes des frères Breguet (**1**) s'élève à 60 cm du sol avec son pilote ; le 13 novembre, Paul Cornu s'envole quelques secondes sur un appareil à double voilure tournante (**2**). Si ce dernier est reconnu vainqueur de la compétition parce que son appareil s'est élevé sans aide, il faudra pourtant attendre près d'une trentaine d'années avant que ne soient vraiment résolus les problèmes de stabilité des appareils à vol vertical.

3

The extraordinary multiplane
Some inventors determined to test the aerofoil-lifting ideas of the Englishman Horatio Phillips, patented in 1884. His 'Venetian blind' multiplane, powered by steam engine, hopped off the ground in 1893. He built a four-frame 'flying runner bean frame', which actually did fly for 500 feet in 1907. A single-frame recreation was made in 1911 (**1**). Alexander Graham Bell's 5,000-cell multiplane glider was tested unsuccessfully in Nova Scotia in 1907 (**2**), as was the Roshon multiplane (**3**).

Der unglaubliche Vieldecker
1884 ließ sich der Engländer Horatio Phillips das Tragflächenprinzip mit verschiedener Krümmung an Ober- und Unterseite patentieren, und einige Erfinder stellten ihre Experimente damit an. Phillips' von einer Dampfmaschine angetriebener Vieldecker hob sich mit seinem Jalousienflügel 1893 tatsächlich vom Boden. Das »fliegende Bohnengerüst« von 1907 flog mit vier solchen Flächen immerhin 150 Meter weit. 1911 versuchte er es noch einmal mit einer einzelnen Fläche (**1**). Alexander Graham Bell testete seinen Multiplan mit 5.000 Zellen nach dem Kastendrachen-Prinzip 1907 in Neuschottland (**2**), doch ohne Erfolg, und auch der Roshon-Vieldecker (**3**) scheiterte.

D'extraordinaires multiplans
Certains inventeurs se décident à essayer les idées de sustentation par voilure multiple de l'Anglais Horatio Phillips, brevetées en 1884. Après que son appareil multiplan «à persiennes», propulsé par un moteur à vapeur, s'est soulevé du sol en 1893, il construit un nouveau Multiplane à quadruple châssis de cellules à profils superposés qui vole sur 150 m en 1907. Il reprendra cette idée, mais avec un cadre unique, en 1911 (**1**). Le planeur multiplan en nid d'abeilles composé de 5000 tétraèdres d'Alexander Graham Bell, essayé en Nouvelle-Écosse en 1907 (**2**), sera un échec, tout comme d'ailleurs le multiplan de Roshon (**3**).

Odd shapes that just might fly

The Marquis d'Ecquevilly thought he might have some luck with a fan-type multiplane in 1908 (**1**). Wing shapes were still experimental, and the designer of the Vendôme (**2**) in 1908 still had great hopes for bird-like tailplanes. The Diapason Schreick monoplane of 1910 (**3**) clearly took the Taube wing-tip aileron idea to an extreme. None were successful.

Vielleicht fliegt es ja doch?

Der Marquis d'Ecquevilly rechnete sich 1908 Chancen mit einem fächerförmigen Multiplan aus (**1**). Überall experimentierte man noch mit Tragflächenformen, und im selben Jahr setzten die Konstrukteure der Vendôme (**2**) große Hoffnungen auf die Vogelform. Der Schreick-Eindecker, Diapason, von 1910 (**3**) trieb das Prinzip der Rumpler Taube mit Leitwerken auf den Flügelspitzen ins Extrem. Keine dieser Maschinen bewährte sich.

D'étranges appareils qui devraient voler

Toutes les formes de voilures furent sans doute expérimentées : depuis le multiplan «ventilateur» du marquis d'Ecquevilly (**1**) et le Vendôme à empennage d'oiseau (**2**), tous deux de 1908, jusqu'à ce monoplan Schreick de 1910, le Diapason (**3**), où était reprise, poussée à l'extrême, l'idée de la queue du Taube de Etrich. Tous ces appareils furent un échec.

Winging it
Some with little understanding of aerodynamics tried anything that looked as if it might fly. In January 1909, the Robart's monoplane Papillon was to be seen – on the ground – at Amiens (**1**), while a Mr Stoeckel thought this monoplane might work in April 1909 (**2**).

Gedankenflüge
Manche versuchten es ohne aerodynamische Kenntnisse mit allem, was aussah, als ob es fliegen könnte. Im Januar 1909 war in Amiens Robarts Eindecker Papillon zu bewundern (**1**) – doch nur am Boden –, und ein gewisser Stoeckel wollte sich im April 1909 mit diesem kuriosen Eindecker (**2**) in die Lüfte heben.

Faire pousser des ailes
Certains inventeurs essayèrent en vain, et sans grande connaissance de l'aérodynamique, de faire voler toute machine pourvue d'ailes : par exemple ce monoplan de Robart, le Papillon, visible – au sol – à Amiens en janvier 1909 (**1**) ou, en avril 1909, ce bizarre monoplan de Stoeckel (**2**).

Almost successful

M. Bertrand was ambitious, but unsuccessful, with this barrel monoplane the UNIC No. I R.B. in March 1910 (**3**), while Jacques de Lesseps tried the opposite tack to Robart's aeroplane with his Blériot-based, drooped-wing *Le Frégate* in February 1910 (**4**).

Nahe dran

M. Bertrand zeigte diesen ehrgeizigen, doch glücklosen Eindecker, der UNIC Nr. I R.B. mit Faßrumpf im März 1910 (**3**), und Jacques de Lesseps versuchte es bei seiner auf Blériot-Basis gebauten *Frégate* vom Februar desselben Jahres mit den Robart-Flügeln, nur diesmal mit den Spitzen nach unten (**4**).

Un quasi succès

Après Jacques de Lesseps qui, en février 1910, prend le contre-pied de l'avion de Robart avec sa *Frégate* à aile basse sur base Blériot (**4**), Bertrand présente, en mars, un monoplan tubulaire ambitieux, l'UNIC N° I R.B., qui restera un échec (**3**).

Military testing

The armed forces of all nations had a direct and increasingly urgent interest in military aviation as aeroplanes became more reliable and powerful. By September 1912, a few months after the first air display at Hendon, naval and military craft were lined up for examination and tests (**1**). In army aeroplane tests on Salisbury Plain a month earlier 31 aircraft were entered for comparison, including a Martinsyde monoplane (**2**). Brakes were not always effective and soldiers had to hang on after the propeller started (**3**).

Militärversuche

Als die Flugzeuge stärker und zuverlässiger wurden, begannen sich auch die Militärs aller Nationen zusehends für die Maschinen zu interessieren. Im September 1912, nur wenige Monate nach der ersten Luftfahrtschau in Hendon, sind dort Marine- und Militärflugzeuge zu Begutachtung und Probeflügen zusammengekommen (**1**). Einen Monat zuvor waren auf der Ebene von Salisbury 31 Maschinen zu Tests versammelt, darunter der Martinsyde-Eindecker (**2**). Die Bremsen halfen nicht immer, und die Soldaten mußten die Maschinen festhalten, wenn die Propeller angeworfen wurden (**3**).

Essais militaires

Les états-majors de toutes les nations se mirent à porter un intérêt croissant à l'aviation à mesure qu'augmentaient la fiabilité et la puissance des aéroplanes. Ainsi, les qualités de 31 appareils, dont un monoplan Martinsyde (**2**), furent comparées lors d'importants concours militaires et séances d'essai organisés par l'armée anglaise à Salisbury Plain, en août et septembre 1912 (**1**), quelques mois après le premier salon aéronautique de Hendon. Les freins n'étant pas toujours très efficaces, les soldats devaient maintenir l'avion en ligne au point fixe une fois son moteur lancé (**3**).

First float plane

The American Glenn Curtiss owed a debt to the first man to fly a powered aircraft from water, the Frenchman Henri Fabre. It was Fabre, a friend of Gabriel Voisin, who built and flew the remarkable hydroplane *Canard* near Marseilles on 28 March 1910, here seen piloted by Jean Bécu the following year (**1**, **2**). The machine had three 'lifting' floats. Voisin – who had been the first to take off from water in a boat-towed box-kite glider in 1905 – later used them on the earliest successful amphibious aircraft.

Das erste Wasserflugzeug

Der Amerikaner Glenn Curtiss verdankte seine Kunst dem Franzosen Henri Fabre – dem ersten, der ein Motorflugzeug vom Wasser aus startete. Fabre, ein Freund Gabriel Voisins, baute das erstaunliche Wasserflugzeug *Canard* und flog es erstmals am 28. März 1910 nicht weit von Marseille, hier geflogen von Jean Bécug im darauffolgenden Jahr (**1**, **2**). Die Maschine verfügte über drei Schwimmer, die für den Auftrieb sorgten. Später verwendete Voisin – der 1905 als erster mit einem vom Boot gezogenen Kastendrachen vom Wasser aufgestiegen war – dasselbe Prinzip für das früheste gebrauchstüchtige Wasserflugzeug.

Le premier avion flottant

L'Américain Glenn Curtiss doit beaucoup au Français Henri Fabre. Ami de Gabriel Voisin, Fabre fut le premier homme à avoir volé sur un avion motorisé en décollant le 28 mars 1910 à partir d'un plan d'eau, en l'occurrence l'étang de Berre près de Marseille. Ce remarquable hydroaéroplane *Canard* qu'il avait construit est ici piloté par Jean Bécu l'année suivante (**1**, **2**). Le système à trois flotteurs adopté par Fabre sera repris par Voisin – premier, en 1905, à décoller depuis l'eau dans un planeur à structure cellulaire et carène de bateau – pour ses appareils amphibies.

Over and under
Eugene B. Ely was the first to fly a powered aircraft from a ship, on 14 November 1910. He launched his Curtiss pusher from a platform built over the bows of the USS *Birmingham* and landed on shore. He was photographed taking off from the deck of the USS *Pennsylvania* in January 1911 (**2**). In August 1912, Frank McClean heralded the new sport of stunt flying when he manoeuvred a Short pusher hydroplane through Tower Bridge, London (**1**).

Drunter und drüber
Eugene B. Ely war der erste, der ein Motorflugzeug vom Schiff aus startete. Am 14. November 1910 erhob er sich mit seiner Curtiss mit Druckpropeller von einer über dem Bug der USS *Birmingham* errichteten Plattform und landete am Ufer. Die Aufnahme zeigt ihn bei einem Start von Deck der USS *Pennsylvania* im Januar 1911 (**2**). Im August 1912 steuert Frank McClean, einer der ersten Kunstflieger, sein ebenfalls mit einem Druckpropeller versehenes Short-Wasserflugzeug unter der Londoner Tower Bridge hindurch (**1**).

Sens dessus dessous
Eugene B. Ely fut, le 14 novembre 1910, le premier à voler sur un avion motorisé – un Curtiss à propulsion – ayant décollé depuis le pont d'un navire: une plate-forme construite à la proue de l'USS *Birmingham*. On le voit ici photographié en janvier 1911 lors de son envol depuis le pont de l'USS *Pennsylvania*, où il se posera peu après (**2**). En août 1912, passant au milieu de Tower Bridge, à Londres, aux commandes d'un hydravion Short à propulsion, Frank McClean inaugure un nouveau «sport»: la cascade en vol (**1**).

The Schneider Trophy

When the French industrialist Jacques Schneider offered a significant trophy for the most seaworthy and speedy seaplanes in 1912 he started a long battle to establish the world's fastest aircraft. Winner of the first Schneider Trophy at Monaco in 1913 was Maurice Prévost in the Blériot-type Deperdussin Monocoque (**1**). It was streamlined and used its fuselage body to provide strength. Its 160hp Gnome engine ultimately gave a record 126mph. A year later Howard Pixton in a British Sopwith Tabloid won the trophy at 92mph (**2**).

Der Schneider-Pokal

Im Jahr 1912 setzte der französische Industrielle Jacques Schneider einen großen Preis für das schnellste und seetüchtigste Wasserflugzeug aus und brachte damit einen langen Wettkampf um den Geschwindigkeits-Weltrekord in Gang. Den ersten Wettbewerb um den Schneider-Pokal, 1913 in Monaco, gewann Maurice Prévost mit einem Deperdussin-Monocoque nach Blériot-Vorbild (**1**). Der aerodynamisch gestaltete Rumpf hatte bei dieser Maschine auch tragende Funktion. Mit dem 160-PS-Gnome-Motor erreichte sie eine Rekordgeschwindigkeit von 203 Stundenkilometern. Im folgenden Jahr gewann Howard Pixton in einer britischen Sopwith Tabloid die Trophäe mit 148 Stundenkilometern (**2**).

Le trophée Schneider

Lorsque l'industriel français Jacques Schneider propose, en 1912, une forte récompense à l'hydravion le plus rapide et le plus navigable du monde, une intense compétition s'engage entre les nations. Le vainqueur du premier trophée Schneider, en 1913 à Monaco, fut Maurice Prévost sur un monocoque Deperdussin de type Blériot, dont le fuselage aérodynamique lui assure une bonne rigidité (**1**). Le même appareil, disposant d'un moteur Gnome de 160 ch, lui permettra d'établir le record de vitesse à Reims (203 km/h). Howard Pixton remportera le trophée Schneider 1914 sur un Sopwith Tabloid britannique à la vitesse de 148 km/h (**2**).

2

Schneider farce

The next Schneider Trophy contest at Bournemouth, England, in September 1919 was dogged by bad weather and controversy. Competitors including Harry Hawker in his Sopwith (**2**) had to start from the beach amidst thronging crowds. The French withdrew, the British floundered in the dense fog, leaving only the Italian Guido Janello to finish in his Savoia S13 (**1**). But uncertainty over whether he completed the correct course forced him to do an extra lap, and the judges awarded the following year's contest to Italy.

Schneider-Farce

Der nächste Schneider-Wettbewerb im September 1919 im englischen Bournemouth war von Streit und schlechtem Wetter beherrscht. Die Teilnehmer, darunter Harry Hawker mit seiner Sopwith (**2**), mußten vom Strand mitten zwischen den Zuschauern starten. Die Franzosen zogen ihre Meldung zurück, die Briten mußten in dichtem Nebel aufgeben, nur der Italiener Guido Janello in seiner Savoia S13 kam ans Ziel (**1**). Doch da nicht sicher war, ob er den vorgeschriebenen Kurs wirklich geflogen war, mußte er eine Extrarunde drehen, bevor er den Preis bekam und Italien den nächsten Wettbewerb ausrichten durfte.

Un trophée contesté

Le trophée Schneider suivant, qui a lieu en septembre 1919 au départ de Bournemouth (Angleterre), sera marqué par le mauvais temps et les contestations. Les concurrents, dont l'Anglais Harry Hawker sur Sopwith (**2**), durent partir de la plage au milieu d'une foule gigantesque. Le Français ayant abandonné et le Britannique s'étant perdu dans un épais brouillard, seul l'Italien Guido Janello finit la course avec son Savoia S13 (**1**). Toutefois, peu sûrs qu'il ait effectué le parcours complet, les juges l'obligèrent à effectuer un tour supplémentaire avant d'annuler l'épreuve et de remettre le prix en jeu l'année suivante en Italie.

A major industry
By 1919 aviation was a huge new industry employing many women. Workers at Short Brothers'
seaplane works take a break (**1**); building wings at the Short works in Rochester (**2**); applying
dope to wing fabric at the Short works (**3**); fitting a propeller to the Rolls Royce engine of a
Shorts' seaplane (**4**); launching the completed seaplane (**5**).

Eine Großindustrie
1919 war der Flugzeugbau bereits ein einträglicher Industriezweig, in dem viele Frauen arbeiteten. Arbeiterinnen in den Wasserflugzeugwerken der Gebrüder Short machen eine Pause (**1**);
Montage von Tragflächen in den Short-Werken in Rochester (**2**); der Stoff für die Tragflächen
wird, ebenfalls bei Short, mit Spannlack überzogen (**3**); der Propeller wird an den Rolls-Royce-
Motor montiert (**4**); das fertige Short-Wasserflugzeug läuft vom Stapel (**5**).

Une industrie essentielle

En 1919, l'aviation était devenue une nouvelle et importante industrie qui employait de nombreuses femmes, comme ces ouvrières de l'usine d'hydravions Short Brothers lors d'une pause (**1**). Ces photos illustrent les différentes étapes de construction d'un avion Short à Rochester : assemblage des panneaux d'ailes (**2**) après enduction du tissu de voilure (**3**) ; fixation de l'hélice au moteur Rolls-Royce (**4**) et, enfin, mise à l'eau de l'hydravion achevé (**5**).

First passenger carriers

By 1914, aviation aimed to compete with ships and trains by building ever larger. In France a Breguet biplane was lengthened to carry five passengers (**2**). At Hendon in 1913 Claude Grahame-White prepared to carry five passengers (**3**). In Russia in 1914 Igor Sikorsky built the world's biggest, and first four-engined, plane, the *Ilya Mourometz*, with a cabin, washroom and space for 16 passengers, who could even stand on a promenade deck (**1**)!

Die ersten Passagierflugzeuge

1914 hatte die Flugzeugindustrie bereits Ambitionen, es beim Passagiertransport mit Schiff und Eisenbahn aufzunehmen. Bei Bréguet in Frankreich entstand ein Doppeldecker mit längerem Rumpf, der fünf Fluggäste befördern konnte (**2**). Claude Grahame-White ist in Hendon 1913 zum Start mit fünf Passagieren bereit (**3**). In Rußland baute Igor Sikorsky 1914 das größte Flugzeug der Welt (und das erste viermotorige), die *Ilya Mourometz* (**1**), die über eine Kabine für 16 Fluggäste, eine Waschraum und sogar ein Promenadendeck verfügte!

Les premiers avions de passagers

L'avion commence dès 1914 à concurrencer le bateau et le train grâce à la construction d'appareils toujours plus grands. En France, le poste de pilotage d'un biplan Bréguet se voit ainsi allongé pour pouvoir emporter cinq passagers (**2**), de même qu'à Hendon, en 1913, sur l'appareil de Claude Grahame-White (**3**), tandis que le Russe Igor Sikorsky construit en 1914 le premier quadrimoteur au monde, l'*Ilya Mourometz*; cet appareil, qui peut transporter 16 passagers, dispose d'une cabine, d'un cabinet de toilettes et même d'un «pont promenade» (**1**)!

5
World War I

On 1 November 1911, 2nd Lieutenant Giulio Gavotti of the Italian Air Flotilla flew over the Taguira Oasis in Libya and dropped several grenades on enemy Turkish troops below. It was the first time bombs had been dropped from an aeroplane in war, and it marked a massive change from a year earlier, when an experimental observation flight over army manoeuvres on Salisbury Plain, England, was criticized for 'unnecessarily frightening the cavalry's horses'.

In just that one year the naive view of aviation was dispelled as governments realized its new power. The Americans alone showed how aircraft could be flown from battleships, how planes could receive radio messages and drop written messages to troops on the ground, and even how a machine gun could be fired from a Wright Model B biplane.

By the end of 1912 Turkey had formed its own Army Aviation Section, Bulgaria had an Aviation Corps, Japan had a Naval Air Service. Britain, slow to catch up, formed the Royal Flying Corps with 50 aircraft on 13 May 1912, well behind the world leader, France, which already had 200 planes, several hundred personnel and well-established operational procedures. Germany, preoccupied with airships, also caught up and on 1 October 1912 formed its Military Aviation Service with about 100 planes and several airships.

All had their own budgets, and plane-making was booming. But exactly what they would be used for was still unclear, except for reconnaissance. Even the few pioneers who appreciated the military value of aircraft failed to realize just what war in Europe would mean for aviation. The Frenchman Roland Garros, who had earlier splattered a Mexican artillery battery with oranges in a bombing demonstration near Mexico City, spent much of the summer of 1914 in Germany giving aerobatic displays in his Morane Bullet monoplane and naively expounding his theories on military flying to fascinated German newspapers. On the day war was declared he escaped, shocked, back to France by a perilous night flight via Switzerland.

The allies went to war not with combat planes, but with machines such as A.V. Roe's Avro 504 biplane, built with staggered wings to enable the pilot and observer to see the ground as they flew along; with French Henry Farman biplanes, Maurice Farman Longhorns, Voisin pusher bombers and even old Blériot monoplanes. Germany had the Aviatik, the Albatros and the Rumpler Taube monoplane, with swept-back, birdlike wings; at least 30 long-range Zeppelin airships, and new Fokker Eindecker E1 monoplanes.

Almost all began by photographing enemy trenches and troop movements, observing and correcting shellfire and occasionally dropping small bombs or darts on to enemy troops. Air combat was by shooting pistols and rifles at each other from open cockpits. Front-mounted machine guns on pusher planes such as the Vickers FB5 Gunbus helped, but only if they could be flown fast enough to engage enemy planes. Fast, single-seat Eindecker, Morane-Saulnier and Sopwith Tabloid scout planes could do the job, but that meant shooting forwards through the propeller, an apparent impossibility.

It was Garros who first solved the problem. With the manufacturer Raymond Saulnier he fitted metal deflector plates to the propeller of his Morane-Saulnier, and on 1 April 1915 fired a Hotchkiss machine gun directly through the propeller, shooting down a German Albatros. Within 16 days he had downed five German aircraft and became the first air ace. On 19 April, however, he was forced down behind enemy lines and failed to destroy his plane before he was captured.

The allies' 'secret weapon' was secret no more. Within days the Dutchman Anthony Fokker, builder of the German Eindeckers, had studied Garros's plane and designed an engine interrupter lever that allowed a machine gun bullet to fire through the propeller without striking it. In August 1915, Max Immelmann and Oswald Boelcke used the device to shoot down several allied aircraft. In September Germany had control of the air over the western front as allied planes turned away from the 'Fokker scourge'.

By January 1916, Boelcke and Immelmann had each shot down eight aircraft – the latter famous for his 'Immelmann turn', which enabled a pilot to outmanoeuvre a pursuer and get on his tail – and the German public hailed them as heroes. It was the start of a tit-for-tat personalization of the air war that would create legends: the 'Red Baron' – Baron Manfred von Richthofen; France's Captain René Fonck and Captain Georges Guynemer; Britain's Major Edward 'Mick' Mannock and Captain Albert Ball; Canada's Major William Bishop; and America's Captain Eddie Rickenbacker.

By the summer of 1916 the allies had regained control of the skies over the Western Front. France had new, fast, Nieuport 11 single-seater scouts with machine guns that fired over the propeller. Britain had FE2bs and DH2s, both with guns facing forward, and the Sopwith 1½ Strutter, with

synchronized guns firing through the propeller. More and more fighters were built: the British had the Sopwith Pup, Sopwith Camel and SE5A; the Germans built the Albatros DIII and the Pfalz DIII; the French countered with the SPAD.

Less glamorous, but perhaps of more fundamental political and strategic importance, were the bombers. From the start the allies feared the long-range reconnaissance and bombing potential of Germany's Zeppelins, and even though it was a German Taube monoplane which was the first to drop bombs – on Paris on 30 August 1914 – Germany's Zeppelin sheds quickly became the allies' first major targets. The Royal Naval Air Service launched the first-ever air attack from a ship when it sent seven Short seaplanes against Zeppelin sheds at Cuxhaven on Christmas Day 1914. Within months the navy had its first seaplane carrier, the *Vindex*, launched seaplane torpedo attacks in the Dardanelles, and in August 1917 launched a fighter off the flat deck of the first aircraft carrier, HMS *Furious*.

But this did not stop the high-flying, quiet, powerful Zeppelins from raiding Britain. The first attacks began against east coast towns in January 1915. But once Lieutenant W. Leefe-Robinson shot down a Zeppelin near London in September 1915, encouraging 15 others to retreat, large-scale airship raids ceased. As British defences improved, the Germans switched to new Gotha bombers, killing scores in Paris. Fourteen Gothas attacked London on 13 June 1917, killing 162 and injuring 432. Many were children. To counter public outrage, the South African General J.C. Smuts brought two squadrons of Sopwith Camels across from France. They dealt with the Gothas, in both day and night attacks, but Smuts

went further. He not only recommended retaliatory air strikes against German industrial and civilian centres but, to keep the flyers free from interference by generals and admirals, suggested air power should have its own independent force.

It was military aviation's biggest political opportunity. The British Prime Minister, David Lloyd George, seeing the collapse of Russia, indiscipline in the French Army, America's involvement not yet decisive, and needing a quick route to victory, agreed to create the Royal Air Force on 1 April 1918. By June, new Handley Page 0/400 bombers powered by two 360hp Rolls Royce engines and able to drop up to 4,000lb of bombs had made 57 raids into Germany. They did little to interrupt industrial production, and many were shot down, but, as with the Gotha raids on Britain, they brought badly needed fighters back from the front and caused German civilian morale to plunge.

By the last few months of the war allied air forces became fully part of land and sea operations around the world, bombing and strafing in support of ground troops, though taking heavy losses against such excellent German aircraft as the Junkers J4 and Fokker DVII. In September 1918, led by the American Brigadier-General 'Billy' Mitchell, 1,483 aeroplanes of all types were brought to bear in a single operation against the Saint Mihiel Salient.

Yet within a year of war's end in November 1918, Mitchell was struggling to make his case in Washington, and the RAF – the largest and most independent air force in the world, with 3,300 aircraft in service and almost 300,000 men – was decimated by demobilization. Traditional ideas of land and sea power would take more time to overcome.

Am 1. November 1911 überflog Lieutenant Giulio Gavotti von der Italienischen Luftflottille die libysche Oase Taguira und warf Granaten auf die feindlichen türkischen Bodentruppen ab. Zum ersten Mal wurden in einem Krieg Bomben vom Flugzeug aus geworfen – noch im Vorjahr hatten britische Militärs einen Beobachtungsflug über einem Manöver auf der Ebene von Salisbury als »unnötiges Erschrecken der Kavalleriepferde« kritisiert.

Binnen nur eines Jahres waren solche naiven Vorstellungen verschwunden, und die Regierungen der Länder hatten begriffen, welche Möglichkeiten die Fliegerei bot. Die Amerikaner führten vor Augen, wie man Flugzeuge von Schlachtschiffen aus starten konnte, wie Flugzeuge Funknachrichten empfangen und schriftliche Nachrichten zu Bodentruppen abwerfen konnten, und sogar, wie sich mit einem Maschinengewehr von Bord eines Wright-Doppeldeckers, Modell B, feuern ließ.

Als das Jahr 1912 zu Ende ging, hatte die türkische Armee bereits ihre eigene Flugabteilung, Bulgarien hatte ein Fliegerkorps gebildet, ebenso die japanische Marine. Großbritannien, das lange hinterherhinkte, gründete das Royal Flying Corps mit 50 Maschinen am 13. Mai 1912, lange nach der weltweit führenden Nation, den Franzosen, die bereits über 200 Maschinen, mehrere Hundert Mann und eine gut funktionierende Organisation verfügten. Deutschland, bis dahin ganz mit Luftschiffen beschäftigt, holte ebenfalls auf und bildete am 1. Oktober 1912 eine Fliegertruppe innerhalb des Heeres mit etwa 100 Flugzeugen und mehreren Luftschiffen.

Jede dieser neuen Einheiten war mit finanziellen Mitteln ausgestattet, und die Luftfahrtindustrie blühte. Wozu sich Kriegsflugzeuge außer zu Aufklärungszwecken wirklich einsetzen ließen, war allerdings nach wie vor unklar. Selbst die wenigen unter den Pionieren, die einen militärischen Einsatz begrüßten, konnten sich nicht vorstellen, was ein Krieg in Europa für die Fliegerei wirklich bedeuten würde. Der Franzose Roland Garros, der zuvor eine mexikanische Artilleriestellung in Mexiko-Stadt mit Apfelsinen beworfen hatte, um die Möglichkeiten eines Bombardements vor Augen zu führen, reiste im Sommer 1914 durch Deutschland, führte mit seinem Morane-Bullet-Eindecker Flugkunststücke vor und legte den begeisterten deutschen Zeitungen seine Vorstellungen von einem Luftkrieg dar. Trotzdem traf ihn der Kriegsausbruch völlig unerwartet, und er floh in einem riskanten Nachtflug über die Schweiz zurück nach Frankreich.

Die Alliierten gingen nicht mit speziellen Kampfflugzeugen in den Krieg, sondern mit Maschinen wie A. V. Roes Avro-504-Doppeldecker (der versetzte Tragflächen hatte, damit Pilot und Beobachter beim Flug die Erde unter sich sehen konnten); mit französischen Doppeldeckern von Henry Farman, den Longhorns von Maurice Farman, mit Voisin-Bombern mit Druckpropellern und selbst mit alten Blériot-Eindeckern. In Deutschland gab es Aviatik, Albatros und den Rumpler-Taube-Eindecker mit seinen nach hinten geschwungenen Vogelflügeln; außerdem hatten die Deutschen mindestens 30 langstreckentaugliche Zeppelin-Luftschiffe und die neuen Fokker-E1-Eindecker.

Fast alle begannen damit, daß sie Stellungen und Truppenbewegungen des Feindes fotografierten, den eigenen Granatenbeschuß überwachten und dirigierten und gelegentlich auf feindliche Truppen kleine Bomben oder Speere abwarfen. Beim Luftkampf wurde aus den offenen Cockpits mit Pistolen oder Gewehren aufeinander geschossen. Maschinengewehre am Vorderende von Flugzeugen mit Druckpropeller, etwa bei der Vickers FB5 Gunbus, waren nur nützlich, wenn sie schnell genug flogen, um die feindlichen Maschinen zu stellen. Dazu brauchte man schnelle, einsitzige Eindecker, Morane-Saulnier und Sopwith Tabloid, aber sie mußten vorwärts durch den Propeller schießen, und das schien unmöglich.

Garros war der erste, der diese Aufgabe löste. Zusammen mit dem Konstrukteur Raymond Saulnier ersann er für den Propeller seiner Morane-Saulnier Metallplatten, von denen die Kugeln abprallten, und am 1. April 1915 feuerte er zum ersten Mal mit einem Hotchkiss-Maschinengewehr durch den Propeller und schoß einen deutschen Albatros ab. Binnen 16 Tagen hatte er fünf deutsche Flugzeuge zur Strecke gebracht und war das erste Flieger-As der Geschichte. Am 19. April wurde er jedoch zur Landung hinter den feindlichen Linien gezwungen und konnte seine Maschine nicht rechtzeitig zerstören.

Die »Geheimwaffe« der Alliierten war nun kein Geheimnis mehr. Der Holländer Anthony Fokker, Konstrukteur der deutschen Eindecker, studierte Garros' Maschine und entwarf eine Synchronisation, die es ermöglichte, mit dem Maschinengewehr durch den Propellerkreis zu schießen, ohne daß die Blätter getroffen wurden. Im August 1915 schossen Max Immelmann und Oswald Boelcke mit dieser neuen Vorrichtung mehrere alliierte Maschinen ab. Im September beherrschte Deutschland den Luftraum über der Westfront, denn die alliierten Maschinen suchten vor »Fokkers Geißel« das Weite.

Bis Januar 1916 hatten Boelcke und Immelmann – letzterer berühmt für seinen »Immelmann-Überschlag«, mit dem ein

A German searchlight tracks an allied plane on the Western Front in January 1917. Night flying was new and highly dangerous then.

Ein deutscher Suchscheinwerfer hat ein alliiertes Flugzeug geortet, Januar 1917 an der Westfront. Nachtflüge, damals noch ein Novum, waren ausgesprochen gefährlich.

Un projecteur allemand traque un avion allié sur le front Ouest en janvier 1917. Les vols de nuit sont encore nouveaux et risqués.

Pilot sich einem Verfolger entzog und sich dann selbst hinter ihn setzte – jeder acht Abschüsse zu vermelden und waren deutsche Nationalhelden geworden. Es war der Anfang eines Kults des Luftkriegs als Kampf Mann gegen Mann, der aus den erfolgreichen Fliegern des Ersten Weltkriegs Legenden machte: der »Rote Baron«, Baron Manfred von Richthofen; die Kapitäne René Fonck und Georges Guynemer in Frankreich; die Briten Major Edward »Mick« Mannock und Captain Albert Ball; der Kanadier Major William Bishop sowie Captain Eddie Rickenbacker aus Amerika.

Im Sommer 1916 war der Luftraum über der Westfront wieder von den Alliierten beherrscht. Die Franzosen hatten die neuen, schnellen einsitzigen Nieuport-11-Aufklärer mit Maschinengewehren, die über den Propeller hinwegfeuerten. In England gab es die FE2b und die DH 2, beide mit vorwärtsgerichteten Gewehren, und die Sopwith 1½ Strutter, deren synchronisiertes Maschinengewehr durch den Propellerkreis feuerte. Immer mehr Jagdflugzeuge kamen hinzu: Die Briten verfügten über Sopwith Pup, Sopwith Camel und SE5A; die Deutschen bauten die Albatros DIII und die Pfalz DIII; die Franzosen konterten mit der SPAD.

Weniger schneidig, doch vielleicht von größerer politischer und strategischer Bedeutung waren die Bomber. Das erste deutsche Flugzeug, das Bomben abwarf, war ein Taube-Eindecker – am 30. August 1914 über Paris –, doch was die Alliierten vor allem fürchteten, waren die Zeppeline, die sich als Aufklärer und Bomber über weite Distanzen einsetzen ließen, und bald zählten die Luftschiffhallen zu den Hauptzielen der alliierten Angriffe. Der britische Royal Naval Air Service ging mit dem ersten Luftangriff von einem Schiff aus in die Geschichte ein: Am Weihnachtstag 1914 wurden fünf Short-Wasserflugzeuge vor Cuxhaven ausgesetzt, die dann einen Angriff gegen die dortigen Luftschiffhallen flogen. Nur Monate darauf hatte die Navy bereits ihren eigenen Träger für Wasserflugzeuge, die *Vindex*, und flog mit Wasserflugzeugen Torpedoangriffe auf die Dardanellen; im August 1917 stiegen Jagdflugzeuge vom Startdeck des ersten Flugzeugträgers auf, der HMS *Furious*.

Das konnte allerdings die Zeppeline – leise, kraftvoll, für große Flughöhen gebaut – nicht von ihren Angriffen auf England abhalten. Die ersten Attacken wurden im Januar 1915 gegen die Städte der Ostküste geflogen. Doch nachdem Lieutenant W. Leefe-Robinson im September 1915 einen Zeppelin bei London abschoß und damit 15 andere zum Rückzug brachte, wurden die größeren Luftschiffangriffe eingestellt. Angesichts

einer immer besseren britischen Verteidigung verließen sich die Deutschen nun auf ihre neuen Gotha-Bomber, deren Einsätze in Paris zahlreiche Menschenleben gefordert hatten. Am 13. Juni 1917 flogen 14 Gothas einen Angriff auf London, bei dem 162 Menschen umkamen, 432 wurden verletzt. Viele der Opfer waren Kinder. Auf den allgemeinen Ruf nach Vergeltung brachte der südafrikanische General J. C. Smuts zwei Staffeln mit Sopwith Camels nach Frankreich. Von da an waren sie Tag und Nacht gegen die Gothas im Einsatz. Smuts und empfahl Vergeltungsschläge gegen deutsche Industrieanlagen und zivile Einrichtungen, und schlug vor, daß die Lufteinheiten eine eigene, von Generälen und Admiralen unabhängige Streitmacht bilden sollten.

Eine solche politische Chance hatte die Militärfliegerei noch nie gehabt. Der britische Premierminister David Lloyd George, der den Zusammenbruch Rußlands sah, die undisziplinierte Armee Frankreichs, das Zaudern der Amerikaner, und der auf einen raschen Sieg angewiesen war, willigte in die Schaffung der Royal Air Force zum 1. April 1918 ein. Bis zum Juni hatten die neuen Handley-Page-0/400-Bomber, angetrieben von zwei 360-PS-Rolls-Royce-Motoren und mit einer Traglast von 1.800 Kilogramm Bomben, bereits 57 Angriffe auf deutsche Ziele geflogen. Sie beeinträchtigten die Industrieproduktion kaum, und viele wurden abgeschossen, doch genau wie bei den Gotha-Angriffen auf England zogen sie Jagdflugzeuge von der Front ab, wo sie dringend gebraucht wurden, und untergruben die Moral der Zivilbevölkerung.

In den letzten Kriegsmonaten waren die alliierten Lufteinheiten zum festen Bestandteil der Land- und Seeoperationen überall auf der Welt geworden. Sie bombardierten zur Unterstützung der Bodentruppen und deckten sie im Tiefflug, wobei die ausgezeichneten deutschen Maschinen wie die Junkers J4 und die Fokker DVII ihnen schwere Verluste beibrachten. Im September 1918 waren unter dem Kommando des amerikanischen Brigadegenerals »Billy« Mitchell 1.483 Maschinen verschiedenster Bauart in einer einzigen Operation vereint, dem Schlag gegen den deutschen Frontvorsprung Saint-Mihiel.

Und doch hatte Mitchell schon ein Jahr nach Kriegsende im November 1918 Mühe, die Stellung der U.S.-Luftwaffe in Washington zu verteidigen, und die Royal Air Force – mit 3.300 Maschinen und fast 300.000 Mann die größte und eigenständigste Luftwaffe der Welt – wurde zum großen Teil demobilisiert. Bis althergebrachte Vorstellungen von Land- und Seemacht wirklich überwunden waren, sollte es noch lange dauern.

The new Iron Cross insignia of the German Air Service displayed on a biplane's wings at St Quentin, France, in September 1914.

Das Eiserne Kreuz, das neue Abzeichen der deutschen Luftwaffe, wird im September 1914 auf Doppeldeckerflügeln in St.-Quentin, Frankreich, vorgeführt.

Ces ailes de biplan, ici à Saint-Quentin (France) en septembre 1914, sont frappées de la Croix de Fer, nouvel insigne de l'Armée de l'Air allemande.

Le 1er novembre 1911, le sous-lieutenant Giulio Gavotti de la Flottille de l'Air italienne vole au-dessus de l'oasis de Taguira, en Lybie, et lance plusieurs grenades sur les troupes turques: c'est la première fois que des bombes sont larguées depuis un aéroplane en guerre. Cet événement marque un tournant dans l'aviation et témoigne du changement des mentalités depuis ce jour de l'année précédente, où des officiers anglais avaient protesté contre le passage d'un avion lors d'un exercice de reconnaissance aérienne au-dessus des troupes à Salisbury Plain (Angleterre) pour avoir «inutilement effrayé les chevaux de la cavalerie».

Ayant fini par réaliser le potentiel de l'aviation, les gouvernements ont en effet abandonné, en l'espace d'un an, la vision quelque peu naïve et simpliste qu'ils pouvaient avoir de celle-ci. Seuls les Américains s'étaient montrés jusque-là plus pragmatiques en démontrant que les avions pouvaient décoller d'un porte-avions, qu'il était possible de communiquer avec le pilote par radio et de faire parvenir des messages aux troupes au sol, et même que l'on pouvait tirer à la mitrailleuse depuis un biplan Wright B.

À la fin de 1912, la Turquie a formé une Section aérienne, la Bulgarie possède un Corps d'aviation et le Japon une Unité aéro-navale. La Grande-Bretagne, plus lente à se mettre à niveau, ne forme le Royal Flying Corps, doté de 50 appareils, que le 13 mai 1912, bien après la France qui aligne déjà 200 avions, plusieurs centaines d'hommes et a instauré de solides procédures opérationnelles. L'Allemagne, plus favorable au dirigeable, rattrape également son retard et crée une Force aérienne le 1er octobre 1912, à laquelle sont affectées une centaine d'appareils environ et plusieurs dirigeables.

Ces corps d'armée, qui disposent tous d'un budget propre, encouragent la construction aéronautique. Mais l'utilité de l'aéroplane reste, à l'exception des missions de reconnaissance, encore assez mal définie. Même les quelques aviateurs qui discernent l'avantage militaire à tirer de l'avion ne réalisent pas vraiment les conséquences d'une guerre en Europe pour l'aviation. Le Français Roland Garros, qui avait organisé près de Mexico un simulacre de bombardement, à coups d'oranges, sur une batterie d'artillerie mexicaine, passe une grande partie de l'été 1914 en Allemagne à faire des demonstrations d'acrobatie dans son monoplan Morane Bullet et à exposer ses théories sur le vol militaire à des journalistes allemands fascinés. Le jour de la déclaration de guerre, il parvient à s'enfuir d'Allemagne et à rentrer en France après un périlleux vol de nuit via la Suisse.

Lorsque les Alliés entrent en guerre, ils n'ont pas encore de véritables avions de combat mais des machines comme le biplan Avro 504 de l'Anglais A. V. Roe, dont les ailes décalées permettent au pilote et à l'observateur de voir le sol, les biplans français de Henry Farman, les Longhorns de Maurice Farman, les bombardiers Voisin à propulsion et même les vieux monoplans Blériot. L'aviation allemande se compose alors d'Aviatik, d'Albatros et de monoplans Rumpler Taube, aux ailes «à rémiges» comme celles d'un oiseau, en plus de nouveaux monoplans Fokker Eindecker E1 et d'une trentaine de zeppelins long-courriers.

Presque tous assignent aux aviateurs des missions de photographie des tranchées ennemies et des mouvements de troupe, d'observation et de correction des tirs d'artillerie, parfois de harcèlement des adversaires en lançant de petites bombes ou des flèches explosives. Les duels aériens se déroulent encore entre pilotes au pistolet ou à la carabine. Les mitrailleuses montées tout à l'avant des avions à hélice propulsive, par exemple le Vickers F.B.5 Gunbus, ne se révèlent efficaces que s'il est possible d'être assez rapide pour s'approcher de l'appareil ennemi. Les avions de reconnaissance rapides – le Eindecker, le Morane-Saulnier et le Sopwith Tabloid entre autres – pourraient être employés mais il leur faut alors pouvoir tirer à travers l'hélice avant. Le problème était ardu.

C'est Garros qui, assisté par le constructeur Raymond Saulnier, trouva la solution en adaptant sur les pales de l'hélice de son Morane-Saulnier des déflecteurs en acier déviant les balles qui ne parvenaient pas à passer. Le 1er avril 1915, il réussit à abattre avec sa mitrailleuse Hotchkiss ainsi un Albatros allemand puis, pendant les 16 jours suivants, à descendre cinq autres appareils ennemis, victoires qui firent de lui le premier as de l'aviation. Le 19 avril, contraint de se poser derrière les lignes allemandes, il fut capturé sans avoir eu le temps de détruire son appareil.

L' «arme secrète» des Alliés n'en était plus une. En l'espace de quelques jours, le Hollandais Anthony Fokker, auteur du Eindecker allemand, a étudié l'avion de Garros et conçu un système d'interrupteur qui assurait la synchronisation du tir à travers l'hélice. Utilisant ce dispositif en août 1915, Max Immelmann et Oswald Boelcke purent abattre facilement plusieurs appareils alliés. En septembre, les avions alliés cherchant désormais à échapper au «fléau Fokker», abandonnèrent la maîtrise du ciel à l'Allemagne sur le front Ouest.

En janvier 1916, Boelcke et Immelmann – devenu célèbre

Top-scoring American air ace Eddie Rickenbacker in the cockpit of his French-built SPAD 13 fighter in 1918.

Der amerikanische Meisterflieger Eddie Rickenbacker im Cockpit seines französischen SPAD 13-Jägers, 1918.

L'as américain Eddie Rickenbacker dans le cockpit de son chasseur, un SPAD 13 français, en 1918.

pour la figure de voltige qui porte son nom et permet à un pilote de se retrouver derrière son poursuivant – ont chacun abattu huit avions et sont acclamés par le public allemand. La guerre aérienne allait désormais avoir ses héros et ses légendes: le «Baron rouge» allemand Manfred von Richthofen, les capitaines français René Fonck et George Guynemer, le major Edward «Mick» Mannock et le capitaine Albert Ball britanniques, le major canadien William Bishop et le capitaine américain Eddie Rickenbacker.

L'aviation alliée s'impose de nouveau sur le front Ouest à l'été 1916 grâce à des appareils plus performants. La France dispose du nouveau et rapide Nieuport 11, un monoplace de reconnaissance avec armement avant synchronisé; la Grande-Bretagne possède des FE2b et des DH 2 à hélice propulsive avec canons à l'avant, ainsi que du Sopwith 1½ Strutter, équipé de deux mitrailleuses tirant à travers l'hélice. On construit également un grand nombre de chasseurs: le Sopwith Pup, le Sopwith Camel et le SE5A en Grande-Bretagne, l'Albatros DIII et le Pfalz DIII en Allemagne, et les SPAD en France.

Les bombardiers, bien que moins prestigieux, se révèlent avoir une plus grande importance stratégique et politique. Les Alliés craignent depuis le début de la guerre le potentiel des zeppelins allemands dans des missions de reconnaissance et de bombardement à long rayon d'action. Dans cette optique, et même si ce fut un monoplan Taube allemand qui fut le premier à larguer des bombes – sur Paris le 30 août 1914 –, les zeppelins devinrent rapidement la cible principale des Alliés. Le Royal Naval Air Service organise la première attaque aérienne depuis un navire le jour de Noël 1914 en envoyant sept hydravions Short bombarder les hangars des dirigeables à Cuxhaven. Quelques mois plus tard, la Marine anglaise dispose du premier «porte-hydravions», le Vindex, et lance des torpilles à partir d'hydravions dans les Dardanelles. En août 1917, elle fait décoller un chasseur depuis le pont du HMS *Furious*, premier porte-avions de l'histoire.

Cela n'empêche pas les puissants zeppelins, capables de voler silencieusement en altitude, d'effectuer des raids sur la Grande-Bretagne. Leurs premières attaques visent les villes de la côte est de l'Angleterre en janvier 1915, mais cessent rapidement après septembre 1915, lorsque le lieutenant W. Leefe-Robinson abat un zeppelin près de Londres et met en fuite 15 autres dirigeables. Les défenses britanniques s'améliorant, les Allemands envoient leurs nouveaux bombardiers Gotha bombarder Paris, provoquant des centaines de victimes, puis atta-

quer Londres où, le 13 juin 1917, un raid de quatorze Gotha tue 162 personnes et fait 432 blessés, parmi lesquels nombre d'enfants. Pour venger l'outrage, le général sud-africain J.C. Smuts expédie deux escadrilles de Sopwith Camel en France pour combattre les Gotha lors d'attaques de jour comme de nuit. Smuts va plus loin: non seulement il recommande d'effectuer des frappes aériennes de représailles contre les centres civils et industriels allemands mais, afin de dégager les pilotes de l'autorité de l'armée de Terre et de la Marine, suggère que les forces aériennes soient regroupées sous un commandement unique.

Le Premier ministre britannique, David Lloyd George, devant l'effondrement de la Russie à l'est, l'indiscipline d'une partie de l'armée française, la participation encore peu décisive des États-Unis et ayant besoin d'une victoire rapide, accepte le 1er avril 1918 de créer la Royal Air Force. En juin, les nouveaux bombardiers Handley Page 0/400, équipés de deux moteurs Rolls-Royce de 360 ch et capables d'emporter jusqu'à 2 tonnes de bombes, ont accompli 57 missions sur l'Allemagne. Ces raids, malgré les pertes subies et leur faible influence sur la production industrielle allemande, obligent toutefois l'Allemagne à dégarnir le front d'un certain nombre de ses chasseurs et contribuent, à l'instar des bombardements de Gotha sur la Grande-Bretagne, à saper le moral des civils allemands.

Les forces aériennes alliées, malgré les lourdes pertes subies face aux excellents avions allemands que sont les Junkers J4 et Fokker DVII, participent à part entière aux opérations terrestres et navales des derniers mois de la guerre en bombardant et en mitraillant les troupes au sol. Ainsi, en septembre 1918, conduits par le général de brigade américain «Billy» Mitchell, 1483 avions alliés de tous modèles apportèrent leur soutien lors de l'offensive contre le saillant de Saint-Mihiel.

Malgré cela, pendant l'année qui suivit la fin de la guerre, en novembre 1918, Mitchell dut se battre à Washington pour faire valoir ses arguments en faveur de l'aviation tandis que la RAF – la plus importante force aérienne indépendante au monde, avec 3300 appareils en service et près de 300000 hommes – se trouvait décimée par la démobilisation. Il faudra attendre encore longtemps avant que les militaires acceptent l'idée d'une «troisième arme», autre que terrestre et maritime.

A US Army film cameraman catches a Nieuport 28 taking off from an airfield in France in 1918.

Ein Filmkameramann der U.S.-Armee hält 1918 eine Nieuport 28 beim Start von einem Flugfeld in Frankreich fest.

Ce cameraman de l'armée américaine filme un Nieuport 28 au décollage, quelque part en France en 1918.

Zeppelins under attack

Fearing long-range Zeppelin attacks against Britain, on 21 November 1914 three Royal Navy Avro 504s took off from Belfort, France (2), flew 125 miles up the Rhine Valley and attacked the huge Zeppelin sheds at Friedrichshafen (1). It was the world's first strategic bombing mission and each plane dropped four 20lb bombs, damaging the sheds, an airship and the adjacent hydrogen plant. Zeppelin sheds were attacked throughout the war, one of the last being at Tondern in July 1918, when two airships were destroyed (3).

Zeppeline unter Beschuß

Um Angriffe durch die langstreckentauglichen Zeppelin-Luftschiffe zu vereiteln, schickten die Engländer am 21. November 1914 drei Avro-504-Bomber der Royal Navy vom französischen Belfort aus (2), von wo sie 200 Kilometer das Rheintal hinaufflogen und die gewaltigen Zeppelinhallen in Friedrichshafen (1) bombardierten. Es war das erste strategische Bomberkommando der Geschichte; jede Maschine warf vier Neun-Kilo-Bomben ab, und die Hallen, ein Luftschiff und die zugehörige Wasserstoffanlage wurden beschädigt. Während des ganzen Krieges wurden Angriffe auf Zeppelinhallen geflogen, einer der letzten im Juli 1918 in Tondern, wo zwei Luftschiffe zerstört wurden (3).

Les zeppelins attaqués

Craignant les raids des zeppelins contre la Grande-Bretagne, trois Avro 504 de la Royal Navy décollèrent le 21 novembre 1914 de Belfort (France) (2), remontèrent la vallée du Rhin sur 200 km et attaquèrent les gigantesques hangars de l'usine de dirigeables de Friedrichshafen (1). Au cours de cette première mission de bombardement stratégique au monde, chaque avion largua quatre bombes de 9 kg, endommageant les hangars, un dirigeable et l'usine d'hydrogène voisine. Pendant toute la durée de la guerre, les bâtiments abritant les zeppelins firent périodiquement l'objet de bombardements, dont l'un des derniers, effectué sur Tondern en juillet 1918, détruisit deux dirigeables (3).

3

1

Balloons at war

Tethered balloons had long been used for observing enemy troop dispositions. This French-made whale-like balloon (**2**) was put to use in Serbia in 1914. Never before, however, had balloons been used to try to stop attack from the air. 'Balloon aprons' were erected over London to catch aeroplanes and Zeppelins in their steel nets (**1**), or force attackers to fly too high for accurate bombing. But their weight kept them from reaching an effective height.

Ballons im Krieg

Fesselballons wurden schon seit langem zur Beobachtung von Truppenbewegungen des Feindes verwendet. Der walförmige französische Ballon (**2**) kam 1914 in Serbien zum Einsatz. Neu waren allerdings Ballons als Schutz vor einem Luftangriff – über London errichtete »Ballonschürzen« (**1**) sollten mit ihren Stahlnetzen die feindlichen Flugzeuge oder Zeppeline aufhalten oder sie in Höhen zwingen, aus denen sie nicht mehr gezielt bombardieren konnten. Sie erwiesen sich jedoch als zu schwer und erreichten nie die erforderlichen Höhen.

Les ballons de défense passive

Les ballons captifs ont servi pendant longtemps à l'observation des troupes ennemies, comme ce ballon «baleine» français (**2**) employé en Serbie en 1914. Toutefois, ils n'avaient encore jamais été utilisés pour tenter de stopper une attaque aérienne. Des «ballons tablier», censés prendre les aéroplanes et les zeppelins ennemis dans leurs filets d'acier, ou forcer les attaquants à voler trop haut pour effectuer un bombardement précis, furent ainsi arrimés au-dessus de Londres (**1**). Leur poids les empêchait toutefois d'atteindre une altitude vraiment efficace.

2

Aerial reconnaissance

From the first day of the war reconnaissance by aircraft was vital to both sides; fighters were originally developed to shoot them down. Aerial photography provided evidence of widespread bomb and shell damage to Ypres in September 1915 (**1**). Much intelligence was gathered from the deep trenches, mine craters and shell strikes on an important sector of the Hindenburg Line (**2** and **3**), and from the growing network of defences at Le Plantin (Windy Corner) in September 1915 (**4**).

Luftaufklärung

Für beide Seiten war die Luftaufklärung vom ersten Kriegstag an von großer Bedeutung; Jagdflugzeuge wurden ursprünglich entwickelt, um Aufklärer abzuschießen. Ein Luftbild zeigt das Ausmaß der Schäden, die Bombardement und Artilleriebeschuß im September 1915 in Ypern angerichtet haben (**1**). Aus den Aufnahmen von tiefen Gräben, Minentrichtern und Granateneinschlägen eines wichtigen Sektors der Hindenburglinie (**2** und **3**) ließen sich zahlreiche militärische Informationen ablesen, ebenso von Bildern der immer weiter ausgebauten Verteidigungsanlagen in Le Plantin im September 1915 (**4**).

Reconnaissance aérienne

Les opérations de reconnaissance aérienne se révélant essentielles dès le début de la guerre, les deux partis en présence conçurent des chasseurs spécifiquement destinés à ce rôle. La photographie aérienne permettait non seulement de constater les importants dommages causés par les bombes et les obus, subis ici par la ville d'Ypres en septembre 1915 (**1**), mais également d'obtenir des renseignements utiles sur le système et la profondeur des tranchées, les mines et les impacts d'obus – par exemple dans un secteur important de la Ligne Hindenburg (**2** et **3**) – ou sur l'extension du réseau défensif au Plantin en septembre 1915 (**4**).

Awaiting the call

Aircrews at war, it was hoped, would be civilized gentlemen, like these British pilots of B flight, 3 Squadron RFC, at Larkhill, England, in 1913 (**1**). The reality by 1918 was more like these suited-up American pilots (**2**), awaiting a call to action in a cold tent in France.

Warten auf den Einsatz

Piloten stellte man sich gern als kultivierte Gentlemen vor, wie hier der 2. Schwarm der 3. Staffel des Royal Flying Corps im englischen Larkhill, 1913 (**1**). Die Realität von 1918 sah eher aus wie bei den amerikanischen Fliegern, die in voller Montur im ungeheizten Zelt in Frankreich auf den Einsatzbefehl warten (**2**).

En état d'alerte

Les aviateurs devaient être des gentlemen civilisés, à l'exemple de ces pilotes britanniques du 3e escadron de bombardement du Royal Flying Corps basé à Larkhill (Angleterre) en 1913 (**1**). En 1918, la réalité est tout autre et correspond plutôt à cette image décontractée de pilotes américains en tenue de vol, attendant leur ordre de mission sous une tente, quelque part en France (**2**).

Technical training
Germany entered the war with a sense of reverence for technology. Young recruits in 1914 received instruction on the engine of an aeroplane dressed, not in overalls, but in full military uniform (**3**).

Technische Ausbildung
Technik spielte für das deutsche Militär schon bei Kriegsbeginn eine zentrale Rolle. Die jungen Rekruten des Jahres 1914 erscheinen zum Unterricht über Flugmotoren nicht im Overall, sondern in voller Uniform (**3**).

Entraînement
Le grand respect pour la technologie manifesté par l'Allemagne ne se dément pas pendant la guerre. Ainsi, ces jeunes recrues de 1914 étudient-elles un moteur d'avion vêtues non pas d'un bleu de mécanicien mais en grand uniforme (**3**).

Dogfight

Aerial combat in World War I was at first a question of observers in opposing planes taking potshots with pistols and rifles (**1**). It ended with heavily armed fighters shooting directly at each other in swirling masses (**2**) as equipment and tactics changed out of all recognition. Much of the leadership in aerial combat came from Germany, which introduced propeller-synchronized machine guns, 'Flying Circus' hunting packs, and the tight, evasive 'Immelmann turn'.

Luftkampf

Zu Anfang des Ersten Weltkriegs beschränkte sich der Luftkampf darauf, daß die Kopiloten mit Pistolen und Gewehren aufs Geratewohl auf die feindlichen Maschinen schossen (**1**). Er endete mit schwer bewaffneten Jagdflugzeugen, die sich in wirbelnden Schwärmen unter gezielten Beschuß nahmen (**2**), und Taktik wie Gerät waren am Ende des Krieges nicht mehr wiederzuerkennen. Vorreiter war fast immer Deutschland, von wo die mit dem Propeller synchronisierten Maschinengewehre, das Prinzip der rotierenden Staffeln und der halsbrecherische »Immelmann-Überschlag« stammten, mit dem ein Flieger sich dem feindlichen Beschuß entzog.

Combat aérien

Les combats aériens du début de la Première Guerre mondiale se résumaient souvent à des duels que se livraient, en tirant à vue au pistolet ou à la carabine, et sans grande précision, les pilotes lors des vols de reconnaissance (**1**). Les premiers avions d'observation étant devenus, grâce aux progrès du matériel et à l'évolution de la tactique, de véritables chasseurs lourdement armés, les affrontements devinrent des ballets confus, tournoyants et meurtriers (**2**). La mise au point de la mitrailleuse à tir synchronisé à travers l'hélice, la formation des escadrilles de chasse la figure de voltige d'Immelmann contribuent, dans un premier temps, à assurer la suprématie aérienne de l'Allemagne.

2

Bomb gone

In 1914 and 1915 aeroplanes were seen to be of greater value as reconnaissance for the army than as combat aircraft. Small bombs were dropped inaccurately by hand, or released singly by the pilot or observer, as in this photo of a German bombing mission (**1**).

Bombe über Bord

1914/15 sahen die Militärs das Einsatzgebiet für Flugzeuge noch eher im Aufklärungs- statt im Kampfbereich. Kleine Bomben wurden ohne zu zielen von Hand geworfen, oder sie wurden vom Piloten oder Kopiloten einzeln ausgeklinkt, wie bei dieser Aufnahme eines deutschen Bombereinsatzes (**1**).

Bombe larguée

En 1914 et 1915, les aéroplanes sont encore considérés comme plus intéressants pour la reconnaissance et l'observation qu'en tant qu'unité de combat. Cependant, ils pouvaient parfois être utilisés à des missions de bombardement (**1**) au cours desquelles des petites bombes étaient soit lancées à la main par le pilote ou l'observateur, soit simplement larguées de leurs fixations le long du fuselage.

Balloonist gone

Parachuting from an observation balloon, as this German did in 1918, was considered acceptable if it was shot down (**2**). But senior officers thought pilots might not try to save their aeroplanes if they were allowed to jump out, and many hundreds of good airmen died as a result.

Ballonflieger über Bord

Der Fallschirmabsprung aus einem Aufklärungsballon, wie hier bei einem Deutschen im Jahr 1918, galt nicht als ehrenrührig, wenn der Ballon abgeschossen wurde. Den Flugzeugpiloten erlaubten die Befehlshaber den Absprung jedoch nicht, weil sie befürchteten, die Flieger würden dann nicht versuchen, ihre Maschinen zu retten. Hunderte guter Piloten kamen dadurch um. (**2**)

Touché? Sautez!

Le saut en parachute d'un aérostier depuis son ballon d'observation, comme pour cet Allemand en 1918 (**2**), était accepté si le ballon était touché. Dans l'aviation, en revanche, les officiers de l'État-major l'interdisaient, craignant que les pilotes n'essaient plus de sauver leur appareil si on les autorisait à sauter. Des centaines de bons aviateurs moururent à cause de ce principe.

Chief architect of air combat
Hauptmann Oswald Boelcke (**1**) introduced 'hunting packs' of fighters in 1915, and his basic rules of fighting – in force, sun at pilot's back, attack from above and behind, make every shot count – greatly countered allied air superiority. Credited with 40 'kills' before himself being killed in a collision during air combat in October 1916, he and Max Immelmann were the first German air aces.

Der Stratege des Luftkampfs
Hauptmann Oswald Boelcke (**1**) organisierte 1915 als erster Kampfflugzeuge zu »Jagdstaffeln«, und seine Grundregeln des Luftkampfes – Formationsflug, die Sonne im Rücken, Angriff von oben und von hinten, nur gezielte Schüsse – machten den Alliierten trotz größerer Maschinenzahl schwer zu schaffen. 40 Abschüsse gingen auf sein Konto, bevor er im Oktober 1916 bei einem Zusammenstoß im Luftkampf umkam. Boelcke und Max Immelmann waren die ersten deutschen Fliegeridole.

Le tacticien du combat aérien
Le capitaine Oswald Boelcke (**1**) préconisa la création de «patrouilles» de chasseurs dès 1915 et, en définissant les règles de base de la chasse – attaquer en nombre, en venant derrière et au-dessus de l'ennemi avec le soleil dans le dos et faire que chaque coup porte –, fit beaucoup pour contrer la supériorité aérienne des Alliés. Titulaire de 40 victoires avant d'être lui-même tué au cours d'un combat aérien en octobre 1916, il fut avec Max Immelmann le premier as de l'aviation allemande.

3

Richthofen's 'Flying Circus'

Baron Manfred von Richthofen (2), the 'Red Baron', was a protégé of Boelcke's who had already shot down 16 allied planes when he took over the elite Jasta 11 in January 1916. Operating from French airfields such as this (3), von Richthofen in his red fighter led brightly coloured Albatros, Fokker and Halberstadt machines in skilful, aggressive air attacks. In 'Bloody April', 1917, the Royal Flying Corps outnumbered German aircraft by three to one, but lost 151 aircraft to the Germans' 70. Richthofen downed a world record 80 planes before being shot down and killed in April 1918.

Richthofens Geschwader

Baron Manfred von Richthofen (2), der »Rote Baron«, war ein Schützling Boelckes und hatte bereits 16 Abschüsse alliierter Maschinen aufzuweisen, als er im Januar 1916 die Elite-Jagdstaffel 11 übernahm. Von französischen Flugfeldern wie diesem (3) führte Richthofen in seinem roten Jagdflugzeug die bunten Albatros-, Fokker- und Halberstadt-Maschinen zu wagemutigen und geschickten Luftangriffen. Im »blutigen April« des Jahres 1917 überwogen die alliierten Maschinen drei zu eins, doch die Alliierten verloren 151 Flugzeuge, die Deutschen nur 70. Richthofen konnte 80 Abschüsse verbuchen – eine absolute Rekordzahl –, bevor er im April 1918 selbst abgeschossen wurde.

Le «Cirque volant» de von Richthofen

Le baron Manfred von Richthofen (2), protégé de Boelcke et surnommé le «Baron Rouge», avait déjà abattu 16 appareils alliés lorsqu'il prit le commandement de l'escadrille d'élite Jasta 11 en janvier 1916. Opérant à partir d'aérodromes français comme ce jour (3), von Richthofen dans son triplan écarlate entraînait des Albatros, des Fokker et des Halberstadt peints de couleurs vives dans des attaques adroites et agressives, comme ce jour d'avril 1917 où le Royal Flying Corps, malgré son surnombre de trois contre un, perdit 151 appareils et les Allemands seulement 70. Von Richthofen, titulaire d'un record de 80 victoires, fut abattu à son tour et tué en avril 1918.

British heroes

Lieutenant Albert Ball, VC (**1**), scored 44 enemy aircraft and was the archetype of the lone fighter. He was only 20 when a German infantryman shot him down in May 1917. Major James McCudden, VC (**2**), had 57 victories, twice shooting down four planes in a day, before dying in a flying accident in 1918.

Britische Helden

Lieutenant Albert Ball (**1**), Träger des Victoria-Kreuzes, konnte 44 Abschüsse verbuchen und war der Inbegriff des einsamen Kämpfers. Er war gerade erst 20, als ein deutscher Infanterist ihn im Mai 1917 abschoß. Major James McCudden (**2**), ebenfalls mit dem Victoria-Kreuz ausgezeichnet, blieb bei 57 Luftkämpfen erfolgreich, und zweimal holte er vier Maschinen bei einem einzigen Einsatz vom Himmel. 1918 starb er bei einem Flugunglück.

Héros britanniques

Le lieutenant Albert Ball (**1**), porteur de Victoria Cross (VC), qui compte 44 victoires en combat aérien, fut l'archétype du chasseur solitaire; il n'avait que 20 ans lorsqu'un soldat de l'infanterie allemande l'abattit en mai 1917. Le major James McCudden, VC (**2**), est titulaire de 57 victoires – il descendit quatre avions deux fois le même jour – lorsqu'il meurt en 1918 dans un accident d'avion.

American hero

Major Raoul Lufbery (**3**) flew with the French in 1915 and was one of a core group of Americans that formed the Lafayette Escadrille before transferring to a US squadron when America entered the war in 1917. He had 17 'kills'.

Amerikas As

Major Raoul Lufbery (**3**) flog seit 1915 für die Franzosen – eine Gruppe von Amerikanern gab den Kern des Lafayette-Geschwaders ab. Als die Vereinigten Staaten 1917 in den Krieg eintraten, schloß er sich einem U.S.-Geschwader an. Er konnte 17 Abschüsse verbuchen.

Héros américain

Le major Raoul Lufbery (**3**) vola avec les Français en 1915 et fut l'un des Américains qui formèrent l'escadrille Lafayette avant son transfert dans un escadron US à l'entrée en guerre des États-Unis, en 1917. Il est titulaire de 17 victoires.

French air aces

Aviation pioneer Roland Garros (**4**) was France's first ace, in 1915. Captured with his secret plane, which shot bullets through a propeller, he eventually escaped but was killed in 1918. Captain Georges Guynemer (**5**) was perhaps France's most popular ace. Sickly, but with 54 'kills', he disappeared on a combat flight in 1917.

Französische Meisterflieger

Der erste Fliegerheld der Franzosen war 1915 Roland Garros (**4**). Mit seinem geheimen Modell, dessen Geschütz durch den Propeller schoß, geriet er in die Hände der Deutschen, konnte jedoch wieder entkommen. 1918 kam er um. Capitaine Georges Guynemer (**5**) war vielleicht der populärste französische Flieger. Als kranker Mann brachte er noch 54 Gegner zur Strecke, bevor er 1917 von einem Einsatz nicht zurückkehrte.

As français

Roland Garros (**4**), l'un des pionniers de l'aviation, fut, en 1915, le premier as français; fait prisonnier par les Allemands avec son avion, pourvu d'un dispositif secret de tir à travers l'hélice, il parvient à s'échapper et trouve la mort en 1918. Le capitaine Georges Guynemer (**5**) fut peut-être l'as le plus populaire de France; malgré une constitution maladive, il compte 54 victoires; il disparut lors d'un combat aérien en 1917.

French survivors

Lieutenant Charles Nungesser (**6**), impetuous and adventurous, was frequently wounded and shot down. He survived the war with 45 'kills'. Captain René Fonck (**7**) was the allies' highest-scoring pilot with 75 'kills' – six in one day and three in a single ten-second burst; he also survived the war.

Ein paar kamen durch

Lieutenant Charles Nungesser (**6**), stürmisch und abenteuerlustig, wurde vielfach abgeschossen und verwundet, stieg jedoch immer wieder auf. Er holte 45 feindliche Maschinen vom Himmel und überlebte den Krieg. Capitaine René Fonck (**7**) war mit 75 Abschüssen der erfolgreichste Pilot der Alliierten – mit sechs abgeschossenen Gegnern in einem Tag und dreien in einer einzigen Zehn-Sekunden-Salve; auch er überstand den Krieg.

Survivants français

Le lieutenant Charles Nungesser (**6**), fougueux et épris d'aventure, fut souvent blessé et abattu, mais survécut à la guerre en totalisant 45 victoires. Le capitaine René Fonck (**7**) détient le record des victoires alliées, avec 75 appareils abattus – six en un jour et trois autres en une seule rafale de dix secondes.

Fog of war

Artificial fog swirled around a captured British tank used by German troops moving up to British positions, supported by a German biplane (**1**). Low-level reconnaissance and bombing missions harassed German trenches near Cambrai in 1917 (**3**), but the cost was high. In 13 weeks during 1918 a French bomber escadrille lost 45 planes and 116 men – the highest casualty rate of any squadron in the war. A German photographer caught this unidentified plane about to crash near Hamel, Belgium, in July 1918 (**2**).

Nebel des Krieges

Deutsche Truppen haben einen britischen Panzer erbeutet und nähern sich damit, von einem deutschen Doppeldecker unterstützt und in künstlichen Nebel gehüllt, den britischen Linien (**1**). Aufklärungs-tiefflüge und Bomberangriffe setzten 1917 den Deutschen in ihren Gräben bei Cambrai zu (**3**), doch die eigenen Verluste waren hoch. 1918 verlor ein französisches Bombergeschwader in nur 13 Wochen 45 Maschinen und 116 Mann – die höchste Verlustrate eines einzelnen Geschwaders im ganzen Krieg. Ein deutscher Fotograf hielt im Juli 1918 den Absturz einer nicht identifizierten Maschine bei Hamel in Belgien fest (**2**).

Brumes de guerre

Capturé, ce char anglais est utilisé par les troupes allemandes avançant vers les positions britanniques à couvert d'un brouillard artificiel et avec le soutien d'un biplan allemand (**1**). Les opérations de harcèlement des tranchées allemandes par des missions de bombardement à basse altitude, comme ici à Cambrai en 1917, ou de reconnaissance (**3**), coûtaient cher. Ainsi, en 13 semaines de l'année 1918, une escadrille de bombardiers français perdit 45 appareils et 116 hommes – la plus grosse perte d'une escadrille pendant la guerre. Nombre de pilotes se tuèrent en s'écrasant comme cet avion (non identifié), photographié par un Allemand près de Hamel (Belgique), en juillet 1918 (**2**).

Grim endings

Soldiers on the ground were slaughtered in thousands, but aircrew deaths in World War I, owing to the individual nature of aeroplanes and the heroic status of the early pioneers, were generally accorded greater respect. German soldiers look at the body of a British pilot (**1**). A German pilot died when his plane crashed on a rooftop (**3**). A British pilot escaped when his seaplane ditched and sank (**2**).

Selten ging es gut aus

Soldaten, die am Boden kämpften, wurden zu Tausenden hingeschlachtet, doch da Flugzeuge im Ersten Weltkrieg immer noch etwas Besonderes waren und die ersten Flieger als Helden verehrt wurden, wurde ihr Tod meist noch mit Achtung aufgenommen. Deutsche Soldaten betrachten den Leichnam eines britischen Piloten (**1**). Beim Sturz dieser Maschine auf ein Hausdach (**3**) ließ ein deutscher Pilot sein Leben. Der Brite am Steuer des versinkenden Wasserflugzeugs (**2**) kam davon.

Des fins atroces

Dans l'immense hécatombe des soldats de la Première Guerre mondiale, les morts de l'aviation furent particulièrement honorés – même par les ennemis, à l'exemple de ces soldats allemands contemplant avec respect le corps d'un pilote britannique (**1**) – autant en raison de la nature «mythique» des aéroplanes que du statut de héros et de pionnier des pilotes. Si ce pilote anglais a pu s'échapper lors de l'amerrissage forcé de son hydravion (**2**), cet aviateur allemand a eu moins de chance en s'écrasant sur un toit (**3**).

Evolution of bombing

From the puny, hand-held efforts of the crew of a British De Havilland BE2c observation plane in 1914 (**1**), allied forces went on to load a score of incendiary or high-explosive bombs into the hold of a Handley Page bomber in April 1918 (**2**). The largest British bomb dropped during the war was a 1,650-pounder (**3**) dropped by a Handley Page 0/400 on Le Cateau railway station on the night of 13 September 1918.

Die Entwicklung des Bombers

Von bescheidenen Anfängen im Jahre 1914, als die Besatzung eines britischen De Havilland BE2c-Aufklärungsflugzeuges die Bomben von Hand abwarf (**1**), waren die alliierten Streitkräfte im April 1918 zum Handley Page-Bomber gekommen, der zwanzig Brand- oder hochexplosive Bomben an Bord hatte (**2**). Die größte britische Bombe, die im Krieg abgeworfen wurde, war dieser Dreivierteltonner (**3**), den eine Handley Page 0/400 in der Nacht des 13. September 1918 auf den Bahnhof Le Cateau warf.

Évolution du bombardement

Après les bombardements effectués à la main, à l'exemple de cet équipage britannique d'un avion d'observation De Havilland BE2c en 1914 (**1**), les progrès techniques réalisés en avril 1918 permirent aux forces alliées de charger des bombes incendiaires ou explosives dans les soutes d'un bombardier Handley Page (**2**). La plus grosse bombe anglaise larguée pendant la guerre pesait 825 kg (**3**); elle fut lâchée par un Handley Page 0/400 sur la gare du Cateau dans la nuit du 13 septembre 1918.

3

2

THIS HOUSE
contains a
fairly good sized
CELLAR,
in the event of an
AIR RAID
passers by are
welcome to what
shelter it affords.

Civilian war

For the first time in almost a thousand years, British civilians found themselves under direct attack from a foreign power. In July 1917, women and children looked at a notice offering the use of a cellar as an air-raid shelter (**1**).

Krieg der Zivilisten

Zum ersten Mal seit fast tausend Jahren war die britische Bevölkerung unmittelbar durch eine fremde Macht bedroht. Eine Frau mit Kindern liest einen Anschlag im Juli 1817, mit dem der Keller eines Hauses für den Fall eines Luftangriffs den Passanten zum Schutz angeboten wird (**1**).

La guerre des civils

Pour la première fois en près de mille ans, les civils britanniques furent directement la cible des attaques d'une puissance étrangère. En juillet 1917, cette femme et ses enfants lisent une affiche indiquant la présence dans cette maison d'un abri antiaérien (**1**).

2

3

Downed Zeppelins

Germany gave up Zeppelin raids on London after 2 October 1916, when navy airship L31 was shot down at Potters Bar, just to the north (**2**). The craft had plummeted in flames from 12,000 feet. A month later Zeppelin L21 was destroyed off Yarmouth, Norfolk (**3**).

Zeppeline am Ende

Deutschland gab die Zeppelin-Luftangriffe auf London auf, nachdem am 2. Oktober 1916 das Marineluftschiff L31 in Potters Bar gerade nördlich der Stadtgrenze abgeschossen wurde (**2**). Das Luftschiff war brennend aus 3.600 Metern Höhe heruntergestürzt. Einen Monat darauf wurde die L21 vor der Küste von Norfolk bei Yarmouth zerstört (**3**).

Zeppelins abattus

L'Allemagne abandonna ses raids de zeppelins sur Londres à partir d'octobre 1916, lorsque le dirigeable L31 fut abattu près de Potters Bar, juste au nord de la capitale (**2**). L'aéronef en flammes piqua vers le sol depuis une altitude de 3 600 m. Un mois plus tard, le Zeppelin L21 était à son tour détruit à Yarmouth, dans le Norfolk (**3**).

Zeppelin damage

London was the main target of Zeppelin raids in 1915 and 1916, in which 5,907 bombs killed 528 people, mostly civilians. Buildings and a roadway were destroyed in central London in September 1915 (1), while a grocer looked over damage to his store in 1916 (4). Les Halles in Ypres, Belgium, was hit by German shells and bombs (3), while a soldier in France in October 1917 operated a roof-top air-raid siren (2). German Gotha bomber raids caused further casualties in Britain and France, but RAF bombers inflicted heavy damage on German towns.

Zeppelin-Schäden

London war das Hauptziel der Zeppelinangriffe von 1915/16, deren 5.907 Bomben 528 Menschen zum Opfer fielen, größtenteils Zivilisten. Bei einem Angriff im September 1915 haben Gebäude und Straßendecke in der Innenstadt schweren Schaden genommen (1), und 1916 mustert ein Kaufmann die Schäden an seinem Laden (4). Die historische Tuchhalle im belgischen Ypern ist von deutschen Bomben und Minen getroffen (3), und in Frankreich warnt im Oktober 1917 ein Soldat mit einer Sirene vor dem Luftangriff (2). Auch andernorts in England und Frankreich richteten die Angriffe der deutschen Gotha-Bomber Verwüstungen an, doch im Gegenzug fügten die Bomber der Royal Air Force auch deutschen Städten schweren Schaden zu.

Les destructions des zeppelins

Londres fut la principale cible des raids de zeppelins en 1915 et 1916, années au cours desquelles 5 907 bombes tuèrent 528 personnes, pour la plupart des civils, détruisant comme ici en septembre 1915 des immeubles et une rue du centre de Londres (1) ou endommageant en 1916 la vitrine d'une épicerie (4). Tandis qu'un soldat français actionne, en octobre 1917, une sirène d'alerte aérienne installée sur un toit (2), les Halles d'Ypres (Belgique) sont touchées par des bombes et des obus allemands (3). Si les raids des bombardiers allemands Gotha provoquèrent de nombreuses victimes en Grande-Bretagne et en France, les bombardiers de la RAF infligèrent également de lourdes pertes aux villes allemandes.

1 British BE2c

Built summer 1914 for reconnaissance. Safe but slow and unwieldy. Nicknamed 'Fokker Fodder' in 1915.

Im Sommer 1914 als Aufklärer gebaut. Sicher, doch langsam und unhandlich. Erhielt 1915 den Spitznamen »Fokker-Futter«.

Construit à l'été 1914 pour la reconnaissance. Fiable mais lent et peu maniable. Surnommé «Fokker Fodder» en 1915.

2 British Airco DH2

Delivered January 1916. Single-seat fighter with Lewis gun. Some success against Fokkers. Withdrawn 1917.

In Dienst gestellt Januar 1916. Einsitziger Jäger mit Lewis-Maschinengewehr. Erfolge gegen die Fokker. Seit 1917 außer Dienst.

Mis en service en janvier 1916. Chasseur monoplace à canon Lewis. Quelques succès contre les Fokker. Abandonné en 1917.

3 British Sopwith Strutter 1½

Delivered April 1916. Multi-purpose. First British plane with propeller-synchronized machine gun.

In Dienst gestellt April 1916. Allzweckflugzeug. Erste britische Maschine mit propellersynchronisiertem Maschinengewehr.

Mis en service en avril 1916. Polyvaleur. Premier avion britannique doté d'une mitrailleuse à tir synchronisé avec l'hélice.

4 French Nieuport 11

Delivered summer 1915, also used by British. Lewis gun on top wing. Overcame 'Fokker Scourge'.

In Dienst gestellt Sommer 1915, auch von den Briten geflogen. Lewis-Gewehr auf der Tragfläche. Bot Fokkern erstmals Paroli.

Mis en service à l'été 1915. Employé aussi par les Britanniques. Canon Lewis sur l'aile supérieure. Surpassa le Fokker.

5 French SPAD VII

Delivered October 1916. Synchronized machine gun, fast turns, helped restore allied balance against Fokkers.

In Dienst gestellt Oktober 1916. Synchronisiertes Maschinengewehr, wendig, stellte Gegengewicht zu Fokkern her.

Mis en service en octobre 1916. Mitrailleuses synchronisées. Il aida à rétablir l'équilibre des forces par rapport aux Fokker.

6 French Farman F40

Delivered early 1916. Reconnaissance and bombing but vulnerable in daylight and switched to night attacks.

In Dienst gestellt Anfang 1916. Aufklärer und Bomber, doch bei Tag leicht verletzbar. Später nur noch im Nachteinsatz.

Mis en service au début 1916. Avion de reconnaissance et de bombardement. Affecté aux attaques nocturnes.

7 German Junkers J1

'Tin Donkey'. Delivered early 1915. First all-metal monoplane. Used as patrol plane.

Der »Blechesel«. In Dienst gestellt Anfang 1915. Erster Ganzmetall-Eindecker. Als Aufklärer genutzt.

Surnommé «Tin Donkey». Mis en service au début 1915. Premier monoplan entièrement métallique. Utilisé en patrouille.

8 German Fokker EIII, Eindecker

Most common variant of Fokker E1, delivered summer 1915 with first synchronized machine gun.

Die am weitesten verbreitete Variante der Fokker E 1, mit erstem synchronisiertem Maschinengewehr.

La variante la plus répandue du Fokker E.I, mis en service à l'été 1915 avec la première mitrailleuse synchronisée.

9 German Albatros D1

Delivered September 1916. Fast, powerful scout/fighter used to great advantage by von Richthofen's 'Flying Circus'.

In Dienst gestellt September 1916. Schneller, kräftiger Aufklärer /Jäger, verhalf von Richthofens Staffel zum Erfolg.

Mis en service en septembre 1916. Chasseur/éclaireur puissant, avec succès par le «Cirque Volant» de von Richthofen.

10 British Handley Page 0/100
Delivered November 1916. Four-seat bomber carrying up to 2,000lb bombs. With SE5 fighter.

In Dienst gestellt November 1916. Bomber mit 4 Mann Besatzung und bis zu 900 kg Bombenlast. Begleitet von SE5-Jägern.

Mis en service en novembre 1916. Bombardier quadriplace pouvant emporter 1 000 kg de bombes. Assisté du chasseur SE5.

11 British Sopwith Camel
Delivered July 1917. Single-seat fighter. Named for hump which covers Vickers machinegun.

In Dienst gestellt Juli 1917. Einsitziger Jäger. Hat seinen Namen vom Höcker, der das Vickers-Maschinengewehr schützt.

Mis en service en juillet 1917. Chasseur monoplace. Doit son nom aux carénages couvrant ses mitrailleuses Vickers.

12 RAF SE5a
Delivered March 1917. Outstanding single-seat fighter. Fast, tough, well-armed, scourge of German Jastas.

In Dienst gestellt März 1917. Einsitziger Jäger. Schnell, stabil, gut bewaffnet, der Schrecken der deutschen Jagdstaffeln.

Mis en service en mars 1917. Ce chasseur monoplace, rapide, solide et bien armée, fut la terreur des Jastas allemands.

13 French Morane-Saulnier L
Delivered 1913, later with machine gun. Used by British and Russians throughout 1915.

In Dienst gestellt 1913, später mit Maschinengewehr. 1915 auch in britischen und russischen Diensten.

Mis en service en 1913 et ensuite équipé d'une mitrailleuse. Utilisé par les Britanniques et les Russes en 1915.

14 French Voisin pusher
Delivered early 1914, also for British. Reconnaissance only, but later main bomber to 1916.

In Dienst gestellt Anfang 1914, auch für Briten. Zunächst nur Aufklärer, später wichtigster Bomber bis 1916.

Mis en service début 1914, aussi chez les Anglais. Avion de reconnaissance transformé en bombardier en 1916.

15 French Caudron GIII
Early tractor-engined bomber, also used by British and Italians. Later very successful trainer.

Früher Bomber mit Frontmotor, auch im britischen und italienischen Einsatz. Später sehr erfolgreich als Schulflugzeug.

Premier bombardier à hélice tractive. Employé aussi par les Britanniques et les Italiens. Plus tard, avion d'entraînement.

16 German Fokker DVII
With ace Ernst Udet. Delivered early 1918. Best German fighter of war. Inflicted 'Bloody April'.

Mit Fliegeras Ernst Udet. In Dienst gestellt Anfang 1918. Bester deutscher Kriegsjäger, verantwortlich für den »blutigen April«.

Ici avec Ernst Udet. Mis en service au début 1918. Le meilleur chasseur de la guerre. Participa à l'« Avril sanglant ».

17 German Gotha GVb
Delivered 1916. Variant of main Gotha bomber used against Paris and London.

In Dienst gestellt 1916. Eine Variante des Gotha-Bombers, mit dem die Einsätze gegen Paris und London geflogen wurden.

Mis en service en 1916. Variante du grand bombardier Gotha utilisé contre Paris et Londres.

18 Russian *Ilya Mourometz*
Built by Igor Sikorsky (on right) as first four-engined passenger plane. Delivered as bomber late 1914.

Von Igor Sikorsky (rechts) als erstes viermotoriges Passagierflugzeug konstruiert. Seit Ende 1914 im Bombereinsatz.

Premier quadrimoteur construit par Igor Sikorsky (à droite) pour le transport de passagers. Bombardier fin 1914.

No. 1 Squadron, RAF

This classic photograph, taken at Claremarais, France, in April 1918, represents almost the entire history of military aviation. In continuous operation since 1912 when it was an airship formation in the new Royal Flying Corps, No. 1 Squadron was formed in 1878 as No. 1 Balloon Company, Royal Engineers. It flew Hurricanes in the 1940 Battle of Britain and now flies Harrier jump jets. The squadron periodically strikes exactly the same pose for posterity, including the Warrant Officer with his stick (3rd from right) and the pilot with his beagle hound. Dogs were popular on World War I airfields, giving rise to the Snoopy cartoon character. The 'white scarf' image of combat pilots never quite faded.

Das 1. Geschwader der Royal Air Force

Aus dieser klassischen Aufnahme, entstanden im französischen Claremarais im April 1918, läßt sich fast die gesamte Geschichte der Militärluftfahrt ablesen. Das 1. Geschwader entstand 1878 als 1. Ballonkompanie der Royal Engineers (Pioniertruppe), und seit 1912 war es, zunächst als Luftschiffeinheit im neugegründeten Royal Flying Corps, ständig im Einsatz. 1940 zogen die Männer mit Hurricanes in die Luftschlacht um England, heute fliegen sie Harrier-Senkrechtstarter. Von Zeit zu Zeit nimmt das Geschwader in exakt derselben Pose Aufstellung und läßt sich erneut für die Nachwelt festhalten, bis hin zum Stabsoffizier mit seinem Stock (dritter von rechts) und dem Piloten mit dem Beagle. Hunde nahm man gern mit auf die Flugfelder des Ersten Weltkriegs – der Ursprung des Cartoonhundes Snoopy. Bis heute sind Militärpiloten die galanten Kämpfer mit den weißen Schals geblieben.

L'Escadrille N° 1 de la RAF

Cette photographie, prise à Claremarais (France) en avril 1918, illustre presque toute l'histoire de l'aviation militaire. Le N° 1 Squadron, créé en 1878 sous le nom de N° 1 Balloon Company, Royal Engineers, fut en opération à partir de 1912 une fois devenu une formation de dirigeables du nouveau Royal Flying Corps. Ils disposaient de Hawker Hurricane lors de la Bataille d'Angleterre de 1940 et volent aujourd'hui sur Harrier. L'ensemble de l'escadrille pose périodiquement pour la même photographie devant des appareils différents mais toujours avec l'adjudant au stick (3e à partir de la droite) et le pilote tenant le beagle mascotte. Le personnage de Snoopy s'inspire de ces chiens souvent présents sur les terrains d'aviation de la Première Guerre mondiale. L'écharpe blanche du pilote demeure un des attributs légendaires des pilotes de combat.

Exposed

Bombing missions were usually long, uncomfortable and very cold. The Handley Page 0/400 (**1**) had a maximum speed of only 97 mph and its four-man crew had to spend up to seven hours sitting in an open cockpit.

Bitter kalt

Bomberflüge waren meist lang, unbequem und bitter kalt. Die Handley Page 0/400 (**1**) flog maximal 156 Stundenkilometer, und die vierköpfige Besatzung mußte bis zu sieben Stunden im offenen Cockpit durchhalten.

Mission de plein air

Les missions de bombardement étaient généralement longues, inconfortables et frigorifiantes. Le Handley Page 0/400 (**1**), avec une vitesse maximum de 156 km/h seulement, obligeait son équipage de quatre membres à passer jusqu'à sept heures assis dans un cockpit ouvert.

Safety in numbers

Bomber and fighter pilots learned that formation flying (**3**) not only provided a concentrated force to strike targets and deter attack but also allowed gunners to cover each other. A flight of SE5s from No. 1 Squadron at St Omer, France (**2**), had good command of the air by June 1918.

Gemeinsam geht es besser

Bomber- und Jagdpiloten lernten bald, daß Flüge im Verband (**3**) nicht nur einen konzentrierteren Angriff auf das Ziel ermöglichten, sondern auch den Gegenangriff besser abwehrten, denn die Kanoniere konnten sich gegenseitig decken. Eine SE5-Staffel des britischen 1. Geschwaders hat im Juni 1918 den Luftraum über St.-Omer, Frankreich, ganz für sich (**2**).

Le nombre pour la sécurité

Les pilotes de bombardiers et de chasseurs se rendirent vite compte que le vol en formation (**3**) améliorait non seulement leur force de frappe et la prévention des attaques surprises mais permettait aussi aux mitrailleurs de se protéger mutuellement. En volant ainsi en juin 1918, ces SE5 britanniques du N° 1 Squadron de Saint-Omer (France) (**2**) s'assurent la maîtrise du ciel.

War at sea

On 2 August 1917, Squadron Commander H. Dunning made the first landing on a ship under way, HMS *Furious*, the world's first aircraft carrier (**1**). Against a strong headwind, his Sopwith Pup was almost hovering when crewmen pulled it on to the deck. Dunning was killed five days later trying to repeat the feat. In a new offensive role in July 1918, *Furious* approached the German coast and launched seven Sopwith Camels to destroy two Zeppelins in their sheds at Tondern, Germany (**2**).

Krieg auf See

Am 2. August 1917 gelang dem Staffelkommandeur H. Dunning die erste Landung auf einem Schiff auf See – der HMS *Furious*, die auch der erste Flugzeugträger der Welt war (**1**). Der Gegenwind war so stark, daß seine Sopwith Pup beinahe in der Luft hing und Besatzungsmitglieder sie herunterziehen mußten. Fünf Tage später kam Dunning bei einem zweiten Versuch ums Leben. Später wurde die *Furious* offensiver eingesetzt, und im Juli 1918 nähert sie sich der deutschen Küste mit sieben Sopwith Camels (**2**), die einen Angriff gegen die Zeppelinhallen in Tondern flogen und zwei Luftschiffe zerstörten.

La guerre en mer

C'est le 2 août 1917 que le Squadron Commander H. Dunning réalise le premier appontage sur un navire en mouvement, le HMS *Furious*, premier porte-avions du monde (**1**). Ayant un fort vent de face, son Sopwith Pup a une vitesse presque nulle qui permet aux matelots de le saisir. Dunning se tua cinq jours plus tard en essayant de renouveler son exploit. Affecté à un rôle offensif en juillet 1918, le *Furious* approcha des côtes allemandes et lança sept Sopwith Camel pour détruire deux zeppelins dans leurs hangars de Tondern (**2**).

Watch on the Rhine

In May 1919, an RAF Handley Page 0/400 bomber of 48 Squadron flew along the Rhine and over the small town of Bonn as part of Britain's new occupation duties in Germany. The lessons of big, strategic-capable bombers would largely be missed by Berlin, which avoided being bombed by new V/1500 bombers, able to fly 2,600 miles or with a 7,500lb bomb load, only by the ending of the war the previous November. Britain was already using its aircraft in new ways around the world. Within a month of this photo this aircraft was patrolling India's North-West Territories.

Die Wacht am Rhein

Ein Handley Page 0/400-Bomber des 48. Geschwaders bei einem Patrouillen-flug über dem Rhein und dem Städtchen Bonn im Mai 1919. Solche Flüge gehörten zu den Aufgaben der Royal Air Force während der Besetzung des Rheinlandes. Nur das Kriegsende im November 1918 hatte Berlin davor bewahrt, die neuen strategischen V/1500-Bomber kennenzulernen, die mit über 4.000 Kilometern Reichweite 3.400 Kilogramm Bombenlast tragen konnten. 1919 waren britische Kriegsmaschinen bereits überall auf dem Erdball wieder in friedlicherem Einsatz: Einen Monat später patrouillierte diese Maschine schon über den indischen Nordwestteritorien.

Surveillance du Rhin

Berlin n'évitera d'être attaquée par les nouveaux bombardiers stratégiques V/1500, capables de voler sur 4 000 km ou avec un chargement de 3 400 kg de bombes, que grâce à la cessation des hostilités, en novembre 1918. En mai 1919, ce bombardier Handley Page 0/400 du 48 Squadron de la RAF patrouille au-dessus du Rhin et de la petite ville de Bonn dans le cadre des missions d'occupation de la Grande-Bretagne en Allemagne. Les Anglais employaient déjà ces nouveaux appareils dans leur colonies, notamment dans les Territoires du Nord-Ouest de l'Inde.

6
The World Shrinks: Aviation's Second Age

The end of World War I saw an increase in the world's aircraft from a few hundred to scores of thousands. France had built 68,000 planes since August 1914, Britain 55,000, Germany 48,000, Italy 20,000, America 15,000. From the fragile contraptions made by amateurs and craftsmen four years earlier, aircraft had become strong, sophisticated machines built with industrial efficiency. The British aircraft industry alone employed 350,000 people and another 300,000 were in the RAF.

Then it came to a stop. Thousands of new fighters and bombers headed for the scrapheap, and massive demobilization took aircrew, skilled riggers, fitters and manufacturers out of aviation.

For those remaining there was really only one way to go: passenger airlines and air freight. Somehow, money had to be made out of Breguet 14 reconnaissance bombers, De Havilland DH-4As, Friedrichshafen GIIIA bombers and Curtiss flying-boats. The RAF modified several DH-4As with enclosed passenger cabins to establish the first regular post-war international passenger and mail run – between London and Paris, mainly for the benefit of the Versailles peace conference.

France, still considering itself the leader in aviation, encouraged its first airline, the Lignes Aériennes Latécoère, to open its first service with Breguet 14s from Toulouse to Barcelona on Christmas Day 1918. But it was the restoration of civil flying in Germany in January 1919 that gave the first big break to a new civilian airline company on internal routes. In February, Deutsche Luft-Reederei, using AEG and LVG single-engined biplanes, began regular passenger-carrying operations between Berlin and Weimar, new site of the National Assembly of the German Republic. A month later the Junkers company started a route between Berlin and Weimar with a modified J10 bomber, the first air service by an all-metal aeroplane.

Stung by this fresh challenge from a constrained enemy, a consortium of famous French aviation pioneers formed the Compagnie des Messageries Aériennes (CMA). They included Louis Blériot, Henry Farman, René Caudron, Louis Renault, Robert Morane and Louis Breguet, who ensured prompt provision of Breguet 14s. Cargo routes and a regular passenger service between Paris and Brussels were established.

But these converted warplanes were not really suitable for passengers; they were cold and uncomfortable and risked weather delays and even crashes. Flights were often expensive and barely quicker than boats and trains. In America trains were so efficient there was hardly a market for passenger-carrying aircraft at all. More importantly, after four years of war the old promise of publicly beneficial aviation was tarnished: too many people still thought of aeroplanes as machines of war.

A new spirit of adventure was needed. In England, someone remembered that Lord Northcliffe's 1913 offer of £10,000 to be the first to fly directly across the Atlantic was still open. It seemed tailor-made to show the passenger potential of two of Britain's biggest bombers, the four-engined Handley Page V1500 and Vickers Vimy, both of which were developed just too late for the war.

On 18 May 1919, the first of four planes, a Sopwith flown by Harry Hawker and Lieutenant-Commander Kenneth McKenzie-Grieve, set off for Ireland from Newfoundland. They were immediately followed by two others in a heavier Martinsyde which crashed on take-off. Tension grew on both sides of the Atlantic as, first, the Sopwith disappeared, and then three US Navy Curtiss NC flying-boats, flying in hops to be the first to cross the Atlantic by air (they were not in the race), stopped at the Azores. By the time Captain John Alcock and Lieutenant Arthur Whitten Brown were ready to take off on 14 June, public excitement was running high, particularly when Hawker and McKenzie-Grieve showed up on board a ship after being lost for a week, and one of the US Navy Curtiss's finally arrived in Portugal.

The overloaded Vimy took off from a hastily prepared grass airstrip, just missed a stone wall and trees and, after 11 hours of difficult navigation, crossed the Irish coast and crash-landed in a bog in County Galway. In a reception comparable to that for Blériot's crossing of the Channel ten years earlier, they were greeted as heroes, their train to London escorted by aircraft, with crowds at every station. The next morning King George V knighted them both. Travel between continents had suddenly shrunk from weeks to hours. Three weeks later the first airship crossing of the Atlantic – 108 hours from Scotland to New York by the British airship R34 – proved that nothing could beat a heavier-than-air plane for speed and control.

Fired by the excitement, the Australian Prime Minister William Hughes offered £10,000 for the first to fly from London to Australia, a challenge met in November by ex-RAF Australian brothers Keith and Ross Smith, again in a Vimy. After an eventful, 28-day journey of 11,130 miles across lands that had never seen an aeroplane, they arrived in Darwin on 10 December to great applause; they too were knighted. That same month another route was blazed in three Vimys and a DH-9 by the South Africans Lieutenant-Colonel Pierre van Ryneveld and Christopher Q. Brand from London to Cape Town.

But such trail-blazing could still only point to the possibilities. Shorter routes were more practicable, and in this second age of aviation it was Germany's turn to lead the way. Germany was forbidden by the Versailles Treaty to build military aircraft, but towns and states offered subsidies for industry to build civil ones. Seven civil airlines were started in 1919, and another six in 1920. Subsidies helped the French, too. In 1920 each of the eight French airlines worked its own sphere of influence without competition: CFRNA east from Paris, eventually to Constantinople, for instance; Latécoère from Marseilles to French North Africa. By 1924 France was linked by air to 12 foreign countries, with the policy of national subsidy firmly established.

Airlines in Britain, however, almost disappeared. Without subsidy, Air Transport and Travel, Handley Page and Instone Airlines stopped flying by February 1921. Forced into action, the government provided subsidies and began to appreciate the political importance of flagship airlines. In 1924 it compelled the independent airlines to merge into Imperial Airways, to serve the British Empire by air.

The RAF had built military airfields, but surveying routes for civil passengers was different. Imperial found Alan Cobham, an enthusiastic, outgoing pilot who made three major trips around the empire and stimulated fresh interest in aviation. Thousands applauded his seaplane when it landed on the Thames after a return trip to Australia in October 1926. He was awarded a knighthood.

Civil airlines were developing in other imperial nations. KLM of the Netherlands was formed in 1919; so was SNETA, predecessor of the Belgian flagship airline Sabena. And France's Latécoère airline – simply 'The Line' to its devoted pilots – began an airmail service between France and South America that was to become synonymous with daring and adventure. This was the world of Antoine de Saint-Exupéry, Didier Daurat and Jean Mermoz, of pilots lost in the desert and of murderous, extortionist tribesmen.

There were other great feats of long-distance flying. In May 1923, US Army Lieutenants Kelly and MacReady made the first

non-stop crossing of America in a Fokker T-2, flying 2,516 miles in 26 hours 50 minutes; from April to September 1924, two US Army Douglas World Cruiser biplanes made the first round-the-world flight – 27,500 miles in 15½ days' flying time; from July to September 1926, two Junkers G25 airliners flew from Berlin to Peking and back.

And then there was the North Pole, a magnet for aviation adventurers since three Swedes had tried to reach it in a balloon from Svalbard in 1897. The Norwegian explorer Roald Amundsen missed landing at the North Pole by 180 miles in 1925 and returned the next year to try with the Italian airship *Norge*. This time, however, he had competition from US Lieutenant-Commander Richard Byrd in a prototype, American-designed Fokker F.VIIa-3m. Byrd flew over the Pole on 9 May 1926, followed by Amundsen in the *Norge* two days later.

It was America's turn to wave the flag. Aeroplanes designed in Europe had led the way almost since the start of aviation, but in 1927 the land that produced the Wright brothers reasserted itself with a vengeance, largely because of one quiet-spoken, unassuming man – Charles Lindbergh.

Zu Anfang des Ersten Weltkriegs gab es weltweit nur einige Hundert Flugzeuge; am Ende waren es Tausende. In Frankreich waren seit August 1914 68.000 Maschinen, in England 55.000, in Deutschland 48.000, in Italien 20.000 und in Amerika 15.000 gebaut worden. Aus den zerbrechlichen Geräten, die vier Jahre zuvor Amateure und Handwerker gebastelt hatten, waren stabile, ausgeklügelte Maschinen geworden, die aus hochmodernen Fabriken kamen. Allein die britische Luftfahrtindustrie beschäftigte 350.000 Menschen, und hinzu kamen die 300.000 Angehörigen der Royal Air Force (RAF).

Doch mit einem Mal war alles vorüber. Auf Tausende von neuen Bombern und Jagdflugzeugen wartete der Schrotthändler, und die Demobilisierung machte Flugmannschaften, Bodenpersonal, Monteure und Unternehmer arbeitslos.

Denen, die im Geschäft blieben, stand nur eine einzige Möglichkeit offen: der Passagier- und Frachtverkehr. Es mußte Wege geben, einen Breguet 14-Aufklärungsbomber, eine De Havilland DH4A, einen Friedrichshafen GIIIA-Bomber oder ein Curtiss-Flugboot zu verwerten. Die Royal Air Force baute einige DH4A-Maschinen zu Passagierflugzeugen um und betrieb die erste regelmäßige Nachkriegs-Fluglinie – Passagier- und Postverkehr zwischen London und Paris, vor allem für die Vertreter der Versailler Friedenskonferenz.

Frankreich, das sich nach wie vor als die führende Fliegernation verstand, gab der ersten Fluglinie Starthilfe, und die Lignes Aériennes Latécoère nahmen am Weihnachtstag 1918 mit Breguet 14-Maschinen und einem Flug von Toulouse nach Barcelona ihren Betrieb auf. Doch der erste große Schritt in Richtung einer neuen Zivilluftfahrt wurde im Januar 1919 in Deutschland mit inländischen Flugrouten getan. Im Februar begründete die Deutsche Luft-Reederei mit einmotorigen AEG- und LVG-Doppeldeckern einen regelmäßigen Passagierverkehr zwischen Berlin und Weimar, dem Sitz der Nationalversammlung der jungen deutschen Demokratie. Im Monat darauf nahm auch Junkers mit einem modifizierten J10-Bomber den Linienverkehr zwischen Berlin und Weimar auf, der erste Flugdienst mit einem Ganzmetallflugzeug.

Die Erfolge des gerade erst bezwungenen Gegners ließen eine Reihe berühmter französischer Flugpioniere nicht ruhen, und sie gründeten die Compagnie des Messageries Aériennes (CMA). Zu den Gründern zählten Louis Blériot, Henry Farman, René Caudron, Louis Renault, Robert Morane und Louis Breguet, der sofort Breguet 14-Maschinen zur Verfügung

stellte. Der Frachtverkehr und ein Linien-Passagierdienst zwischen Paris und Brüssel wurden aufgenommen.

Doch die umgebauten Kriegsflugzeuge waren nicht gerade das, was man sich für den Passagierverkehr vorstellte; sie waren kalt und unbequem, und man riskierte wetterbedingte Verspätungen oder sogar Abstürze. Die Flüge waren meist teuer, und kaum schneller als Schiff oder Zug. In Amerika war das Eisenbahnwesen so gut entwickelt, daß ein Markt für Passagierflugzeuge kaum bestand. Und was noch schwerer ins Gewicht fiel: Vier Jahre Krieg hatten die alte Vorstellung vom Fliegen zum Wohle der Menschheit in den Schmutz gezogen – für zu viele Menschen war ein Flugzeug nach wie vor ein Kriegsgerät.

Es fehlte etwas, das die Begeisterung wieder anfachte. Man erinnerte sich, daß Lord Northcliffe 1913 einen Preis von £ 10.000 für den ersten Direktflug über den Atlantik ausgesetzt hatte. Das schien genau die richtige Gelegenheit zu zeigen, daß die beiden größten britischen Bomber, die viermotorige Handley Page V1500 und die Vickers Vimy, die zu spät für den Kriegseinsatz fertig geworden waren, Maschinen für den Zivilverkehr sein konnten.

Am 18. Mai 1919 startete der erste von vier Kandidaten, eine von Harry Hawker und Lieutenant-Commander Kenneth McKenzie-Grieve geflogene Sopwith, von Neufundland aus in Richtung Irland. Zwei weitere Flieger in einer schweren Martinsyde folgten unmittelbar darauf, stürzten jedoch schon beim Start ab. Die Spannung stieg beiderseits des Atlantiks, als zuerst die Sopwith spurlos verschwand und dann drei Curtiss NC-Flugboote der U.S.-Marine, die in Etappen flogen und ebenfalls die Ehre der ersten Atlantiküberquerung erringen wollten (wenn auch nicht nach den Bedingungen des Wettbewerbs), auf den Azoren anlangten. Bis Captain John Alcock und Lieutenant Arthur Whitten Brown am 14. Juni für den Start bereit waren, war die Spannung überall auf dem Höhepunkt, zumal Hawker und McKenzie-Grieve, nachdem sie eine ganze Woche lang verschollen gewesen waren, an Bord eines Schiffes wieder auftauchten und eine der drei Curtiss-Maschinen der U.S.-Navy tatsächlich in Portugal anlangte.

Die viel zu schwer beladene Vimy hob von einer notdürftig hergerichteten Graspiste ab, kam knapp über eine Mauer und eine Baumreihe hinweg und erreichte nach elf Stunden schwierigen Flugs die irische Küste, wo sie in einem Sumpf in der Grafschaft Galway notlandete. Die Begrüßung der beiden Flieger ließ sich mit derjenigen Blériots nach seiner Kanal-

Lieutenant John MacReady dressed for his altitude flying record. In May 1923 he made the first US non-stop transcontinental flight.

Lieutenant John MacReady in der Kluft für seinen Höhen-Rekordflug. Im Mai 1923 gelang ihm der erste Nonstopflug quer über den amerikanischen Kontinent.

Le lieutenant John MacReady, portant ici sa combinaison du record d'altitude, réalisa la première traversée non-stop des États-Unis en mai 1923.

überquerung zehn Jahre zuvor vergleichen; sie wurden als Helden empfangen, Flugzeuge begleiteten ihre Zugfahrt nach London, und an jedem Bahnhof jubelten ihnen die Menschen zu. Am nächsten Morgen erhob König Georg V. sie beide in den Adelsstand. Mit einem Male dauerte die Reise zwischen zwei Kontinenten nur noch Stunden statt vormals Wochen. Drei Wochen darauf überquerte das erste Luftschiff den Atlantik – die britische R34, die in 108 Stunden von Schottland nach New York flog –, doch damit war nur bewiesen, daß in puncto Schnelligkeit und Steuerbarkeit nichts das Motorflugzeug überbot.

Von der Publicity dieses Rennens angefeuert, setzte der australische Premierminister Willim Hughes £ 10.000 für den ersten aus, der von London nach Australien flog – eine Herausforderung, die im November die australischen Brüder Keith und Ross Smith, ehemalige Piloten der RAF, wiederum in einer Vimy annahmen. Nach einem schwierigen Flug – 17.900 Kilometer über Gegenden, die noch nie ein Flugzeug erblickt hatten – erreichten sie am 10. Dezember unter großem Beifall Darwin; auch diese beiden wurden geadelt. Im selben Monat eröffneten der südafrikanische Oberstleutnant Pierre van Ryneveld und Christopher Q. Brand mit drei Vimys und einer DH-9 eine weitere neue Route, von London nach Kapstadt.

Die Fernflüge steckten zunächst nur Möglichkeiten für die Zukunft ab. Kürzere Routen waren praktikabler, und in diesem neuen Kapitel der Luftfahrt sollten die Deutschen den Kurs bestimmen. Der Versailler Vertrag verbot ihnen den Bau von Kriegsflugzeugen, doch Länder und Städte boten Prämien für Firmen, die Zivilmaschinen entwickelten. Sieben Flugzeuge für die Zivilluftfahrt starteten 1919, weitere sechs 1920. Auch in Frankreich gab es Unterstützung. Jede der acht Luftlinien, die 1920 aktiv waren, hatte ihren eigenen Flugbereich, in dem sie konkurrenzlos war: CFRNA etwa war für die Gegenden östlich von Paris zuständig, bis nach Konstantinopel; Latécoère flog von Marseille nach Französisch-Nordafrika. 1924 hatte Frankreich bereits Flugverbindungen zu zwölf Ländern, und das Konzept der staatlichen Luftlinien hatte sich bewährt.

In Großbritannien hingegen verschwanden die Fluglinien fast ganz. Ohne staatliche Unterstützung mußten Air Transport and Travel, Handley Page und Instone Airlines bis Februar 1921 ihren Betrieb einstellen. Die Regierung begann jedoch bald, den nationalen Fluglinien entsprechende Unterstützungen zu gewähren. 1924 brachte sie die unabhängigen Fluglinien dazu, sich zu den Imperial Airlines zusammenzuschließen, dem Luftfahrtdienst des Britischen Empires.

Die Royal Air Force hatte zwar vielerorts Flugfelder angelegt, doch neue Routen für den Zivilverkehr einzurichten war doch etwas anderes. Imperial fand dafür Alan Cobham, einen enthusiastischen, risikofreudigen Piloten, der drei große Reisen durch das britische Weltreich unternahm und, wohin er kam, Interesse an der Luftfahrt weckte. Tausende applaudierten, als er nach einem Hin- und Rückflug nach Australien im Oktober 1926 mit seinem Wasserflugzeug wieder auf der Themse landete. Auch er erhielt Prämie und Adelstitel.

Auch in anderen Kolonialreichen entstanden Fluglinien. Die holländische KLM wurde 1919 gegründet, ebenso SNETA, die Vorläuferin der belgischen Nationallinie Sabena. Und in Frankreich nahm Latécoère – »die Linie«, wie ihre ergebenen Piloten sie schlicht und einfach nannten – eine Luftpostlinie nach Südamerika auf, die geradezu zum Inbegriff von Wagemut und Abenteuerlust werden sollte. Das war die Welt von Antoine de Saint-Exupéry, Didier Daurat und Jean Mermoz, den Fliegern, die flogen, bis sie in der Wüste oder im Dschungel unter mörderischen Eingeborenen verschollen blieben.

Auch andere große Leistungen des Langstreckenflugs fallen in diese Zeit. Im Mai 1923 unternahmen Kelly und MacReady, Lieutnants der U.S. Armee, in einer Fokker T-2 den ersten Nonstopflug quer über den amerikanischen Kontinent, 4.048 Kilometer in 26 Stunden und 50 Minuten; zwischen April und September 1924 gelang zwei Douglas-World-Cruiser-Doppeldecker der U.S.-Armee die erste Weltumrundung – 44.200 km in 15½ Tagen –, und von Juli bis September 1926 flogen zwei Junkers G25 von Berlin nach Peking und zurück.

Der Nordpol war der reinste Magnet für Flugabenteurer, seit drei Schweden 1897 den ersten Versuch unternommen hatten, ihn von Spitzbergen aus mit einem Ballon zu erreichen. Der norwegische Polarforscher Roald Amundsen verfehlte ihn 1925 um 290 km und unternahm im folgenden Jahr einen zweiten Anlauf mit dem italienischen Luftschiff *Norge*. Diesmal hatte er allerdings Konkurrenz, den amerikanischen Lieutenant-Commander Richard Byrd in einem amerikanischen Fokker-Prototypen, der F.VIIa-3m. Byrd überflog den Pol am 9. Mai 1926, zwei Tage bevor Amundsen mit der *Norge* eintraf.

Die nächsten Zeichen sollte Amerika setzen. Fast seit den Anfangstagen der Luftfahrt hatten europäische Flugzeuge den Weg gewiesen, doch 1927 trat das Land, das die Gebrüder Wright hervorgebracht hatte, wieder mit Macht auf den Plan, und es verdankte seinen neuen Triumph zum guten Teil einem einzigen stillen, bescheidenen Mann – Charles Lindbergh.

Dutchman Anthony Fokker not only provided aircraft vital to Germany in peace and war, but also designs for America's incomparable DC-2.

Der Holländer Anthony Fokker versorgte nicht nur die Deutschen mit hervorragenden Flugzeugen in Kriegs- wie Friedenszeiten, sondern entwarf auch die unvergleichliche amerikanische DC-2.

Le Néerlandais Anthony Fokker ne fournit pas seulement d'extraordinaires avions à l'Allemagne, il conçut également l'incomparable DC-2 américain.

À la fin de la Première Guerre mondiale, le nombre d'avions dans le monde est passé de quelques centaines à plusieurs milliers d'appareils. Depuis août 1914, la France a construit 68000 avions, la Grande-Bretagne 55000, l'Allemagne 48000, l'Italie 20000 et les États-Unis 15000. Loin des fragiles engins assemblés par des bricoleurs et des artisans quatre ans plus tôt, l'avion est désormais une machine robuste et sophistiquée, fabriquée selon des normes industrielles. La construction aéronautique britannique emploie alors à elle seule 350000 personnes, tandis que 300000 hommes travaillent pour la RAF.

Puis tout s'arrête, la guerre finie. Des milliers de chasseurs et de bombardiers neufs sont expédiés à la ferraille en même temps que la démobilisation envoie massivement au chômage équipages, mécaniciens, ouvriers et constructeurs.

Ceux qui sont restés dans l'aviation n'ont qu'un moyen pour continuer à voler: se reconvertir dans le transport de passagers ou de fret. Il devient d'ailleurs impératif de rentabiliser les bombardiers de reconnaissance Breguet 14 ou De Havilland DH-4A, les Friedrichshafen GIIIA ou les hydravions Curtiss. La RAF entreprend de transformer plusieurs de ses DH-4A en avions civils et d'y aménager une cabine fermée afin d'ouvrir, notamment à l'occasion de la conférence de la Paix à Versailles, la première ligne aérienne commerciale – passager et poste – régulière de l'après-guerre entre Londres et Paris.

La France, qui entend conserver son premier rang dans l'aviation, autorise les Lignes Aériennes Latécoère, première compagnie aérienne française, à ouvrir, le 25 décembre 1918, la route Toulouse-Barcelone sur Breguet 14. C'est cependant la restauration de l'aviation civile en Allemagne, en janvier 1919, qui permet le développement d'une nouvelle compagnie aérienne sur les lignes européennes. En effet, en février, la Deutsche Luft-Reederei, utilisant des biplans monomoteur AEG et LVG, inaugure un service régulier de transport de passagers entre Berlin et Weimar, siège de l'Assemblée nationale de la nouvelle République allemande. Un mois plus tard, la société Junkers ouvre la ligne Berlin-Weimar avec un bombardier J10 modifié, consacrant la première exploitation régulière d'un avion entièrement métallique.

Aiguillonnés par ce nouveau défi de l'ancien ennemi, les célèbres pionniers de l'aviation que sont Louis Blériot, Henry Farman, René Caudron, Louis Renault, Robert Morane et Louis Breguet – qui fournit des Breguet 14 – s'associent pour

créer la Compagnie des Messageries Aériennes (CMA), qui assurera un service régulier fret et passagers entre Paris et Bruxelles.

Ces anciens avions militaires reconvertis ne conviennent pas tout à fait à la clientèle qui peut les emprunter; ils manquent de confort, il y fait froid et ils sont trop souvent tributaires de la météo et des accidents. De plus, les tarifs sont souvent élevés et la durée du voyage à peine moindre que par bateau ou en train. Aux États-Unis, le chemin de fer est alors si efficace qu'il n'y a pratiquement pas de marché pour le transport aérien de passagers. À cela s'ajoute que, après ces quatre années de combats, l'image ancienne de l'avion bienfaiteur de l'humanité est devenue celle d'une machine de guerre moderne.

Il faut redonner à l'aviation le souffle de l'aventure. En Angleterre, on se souvient alors que la proposition faite par lord Northcliffe en 1913 d'offrir 10000£ au premier homme à franchir l'Atlantique tient toujours. Le défi semble parfaitement convenir pour démontrer le potentiel sur long-courrier de deux des plus gros bombardiers britanniques, le quadrimoteur Handley Page V1500 et le Vickers Vimy, appareils développés trop tard pour avoir combattu.

Le 18 mai 1919, le premier de quatre avions, un Sopwith Atlantic piloté par Harry Hawker et le capitaine de corvette Kenneth, s'envole de Terre-Neuve en direction de l'Irlande. Ils sont immédiatement suivis par un Martinsyde qui, trop lourd, s'écrase au décollage. La tension monte des deux côtés de l'Atlantique après l'annonce de l'arrêt aux Açores des trois hydravions Curtiss NC lancés par la US Navy (mais sans participer à la course) dans cette première traversée de l'Atlantique. Lorsque le capitaine John Alcock et le lieutenant Arthur Whitten Brown s'apprêtent à décoller, le 14 juin, l'excitation du public est à son comble, d'autant que l'on apprend que Hawker et McKenzie-Grieve, portés disparus depuis une semaine, ont été recueillis à bord d'un navire et que l'un des Curtiss américains est finalement arrivé au Portugal.

Le Vimy, très alourdi, s'élève péniblement depuis une piste en herbe préparée à la hâte, manque de heurter un muret de pierre, frôle quelques arbres et, au bout de 11 heures d'une navigation difficile, aborde les côtes irlandaises avant de se mettre en pylône dans une tourbière du comté de Galway. La durée du voyage entre l'ancien et le nouveau continent est subitement tombée de plusieurs semaines à quelques heures. Accueillis en héros, à l'instar de Blériot dix ans plus tôt lors de sa traversée de la Manche, escortés par des avions et acclamés

General Umberto Nobile's ill-fated airship *Italia* in June 1928, moored at Svalbard before an attempt to reach the North Pole.

General Umberto Nobiles glückloses Luftschiff *Italia* wartet im Juni 1928 auf Spitzbergen auf seinen Nordpolflug.

Le malheureux dirigeable *Italia* du général Umberto Nobile, amarré en juin 1928 à Svalbard avant sa tentative d'atteindre le pôle Nord.

par la foule à chaque gare dans le train qui les emmène à Londres, les deux hommes sont anoblis le lendemain matin par le roi George V. Trois semaines plus tard, le R34 britannique, premier dirigeable à traverser l'Atlantique – 108 h de l'Écosse à New York – prouve que rien ne peut désormais égaler un plus lourd que l'air en maniabilité et en vitesse.

Pris par le «jeu», le Premier ministre australien William Hughes offre 10 000 £ pour le premier vol Londres-Australie. Le défi est relevé en novembre par deux anciens pilotes australiens de la RAF, les frères Keith et Ross Smith, à nouveau sur Vickers Vimy. Après un périple mouvementé de 28 jours et 17 900 km au-dessus de terres qu'aucun avion n'a jamais survolées, ils atterrissent triomphalement à Darwin le 10 décembre avant d'être également anoblis par le roi d'Angleterre. Le même mois, les Sud-Africains Pierre van Ryneveld, lieutenant-colonel et Christopher Q. Brand, capitaine inaugurent la ligne entre Londres et Le Cap (Afrique du Sud) en pilotant successivement trois Vimy et un DH-9.

Si ces raids permettent de démontrer le potentiel ultime de l'avion, il reste des routes plus «faciles» à ouvrir. Les débuts de cette deuxième ère de l'aviation sont tout d'abord marqués par l'Allemagne. Le Traité de Versailles lui ayant interdit de construire des avions militaires, plusieurs villes et États étrangers accordent des subventions à son industrie aéronautique pour la construction d'appareils civils, permettant ainsi la création de sept compagnies aériennes civiles allemandes en 1919, et de six autres en 1920. En 1920, également aidées par l'État, chacune des huit compagnies aériennes françaises dispose, sans concurrence, de son propre «terrain de manœuvres»: à titre d'exemple, la CFRNA (Compagnie Franco-Roumaine de Navigation Aérienne) organise les liaisons vers l'Orient, jusqu'à Constantinople, tandis que Latécoère dessert l'Afrique du Nord au départ de Marseille. En 1924, la France entretient – et subventionne tout naturellement – des liaisons aériennes avec 12 pays étrangers.

Les compagnies aériennes britanniques, en revanche, ont pratiquement disparu. Privées de tout financement public, au contraire des Français, Air Transport and Travel, Handley Page et Instone Airline doivent cesser leurs vols en février 1921. Contraint d'agir, et comprenant l'intérêt d'une politique aérienne nationale, le gouvernement accorde finalement son aide puis incite les compagnies indépendants à fusionner en 1924 pour former les Imperial Airways, dont la vocation est désormais de desservir l'Empire britannique.

Les lignes commerciales sont à créer, même si les aérodromes militaires construits par la RAF peuvent servir. Imperial Airways trouve dans Alan Cobham un pilote enthousiaste qui, effectuant trois importants voyages dans tout l'Empire britannique, stimule l'intérêt des Anglais pour l'aviation. En octobre 1926, à son retour d'Australie, des milliers de personnes applaudiront son «amerrissage» sur la Tamise, à Londres, avant qu'il ne soit anobli.

D'autres compagnies aériennes civiles naissent et se développent: KLM, aux Pays-Bas, est créée en 1919, ainsi que la SNETA, ancêtre de la compagnie belge Sabena. En France, les Lignes Aériennes Latécoère inaugurent une liaison postale régulière entre la France et l'Amérique du Sud. «La Ligne», comme disent ses pilotes – Antoine de Saint-Exupéry, Didier Daurat ou Jean Mermoz – devient rapidement synonyme de risque et d'aventure, de naufrages dans le désert et de lutte contre des tribus sanguinaires et agressives.

Les vols long-courriers sont l'occasion de nombreux autres grands exploits. En mai 1923, les lieutenants américains Kelly et MacReady effectuent la première traversée non-stop des États-Unis à bord d'un Fokker T-2, ayant parcouru 4 048 km en 26 h 50; entre avril et septembre 1924, deux biplans Douglas World Cruiser de l'armée américaine font le premier tour du monde – 44 200 km en 15½ jours de vol, tandis que deux avions de ligne Junkers G25 effectuent le trajet Berlin-Pékin et retour de juillet à septembre 1926.

Il reste la tentation du Pôle Nord, fabuleuse gageure pour tout aventurier depuis que trois Suédois ont tenté de l'atteindre en ballon depuis le Spitzberg, en 1897. Après avoir manqué le Pôle Nord de 290 km en 1925, l'explorateur norvégien Roald Amundsen y retourne l'année suivante avec le dirigeable italien *Norge*. Cette fois, il est en concurrence avec le capitaine de corvette américain Richard Byrd, qui pilote le Fokker F.VIIa-3m, un prototype de conception américaine. Byrd survole le pôle le 9 mai 1926, précédant de deux jours Amundsen à bord du *Norge*.

C'est désormais aux États-Unis de porter le flambeau de l'aviation. Si les aéroplanes conçus en Europe ont ouvert la voie depuis les débuts de l'aviation, en 1927, la nation des frères Wright relève la tête pour affirmer sa prééminence. Elle le doit en grande partie à un homme modeste et réservé: Charles Lindbergh.

A monument erected at Svalbard to mark Roald Amundsen's 1925 attempt to reach the North Pole. He missed by 180 miles.

Ein Denkmal auf Spitzbergen, das an Roald Amundsens Versuch des Jahres 1925 erinnert, den Nordpol zu erreichen. Er verfehlte ihn um 290 Kilometer.

Ce monument de Svalbard fut érigé en l'honneur de la tentative de 1925 de Roald Amundsen d'atteindre le Pôle Nord, qu'il manqua de 290 km.

Liners of the sky

Count von Zeppelin died in 1917, but construction of 'Zeppelins' continued. At the Short Brothers balloon shop, England, in 1919, women stuck together panels of goldbeater's skin, made from cattle intestines – the same procedure as for making gold leaf – then glued them onto linen panels to make a gas-tight, flexible covering (**1**).

Leichter als Luft

Graf von Zeppelin war 1917 gestorben, doch »Zeppeline« wurden weiter gebaut. In der Ballonwerkstatt der Gebrüder Short, England 1919, fügen die Frauen Bahnen aus Goldschlägerhaut zusammen – Rindsdarmhäute, wie sie auch beim Hämmern von Blattgold verwendet werden –, die sie dann auf Leinen kleben, so daß eine flexible, gasdichte Hülle entsteht (**1**).

Les paquebots du ciel

Le comte von Zeppelin disparaît en 1917 mais la construction de ses «zeppelins» se poursuit. Dans l'atelier de l'usine anglaise Short Brothers, en 1919, les femmes cousent d'abord ensemble les panneaux de baudruche, une pellicule fabriquée avec des intestins de bovins, puis les encollent sur des panneaux en lin afin d'obtenir un tissu souple et imperméable au gaz (**1**).

Stomach for heights

Light, strong, aluminium frames (**2**) were covered by goldbeater's skin and then filled with millions of cubic feet of dangerous hydrogen. These skins, which could not rip or give off sparks when rubbed, used about 50,000 cow stomach linings for each gas cell; each airship had up to 20 gas cells (**3**).

Auf hohlen Magen

Leichte, doch kräftige Aluminiumrahmen (**2**) wurden mit Goldschlägerhaut bezogen und mit Tausenden von Kubikmetern des gefährlichen Wasserstoffgases gefüllt. Diese Hüllen, die sehr rißfest waren und keine Funken abgaben, wenn etwas sie streifte, brauchten etwa 50.000 Rindsmagenhäute pro Gaszelle, und die Luftschiffe hatten bis zu 20 Zellen (**3**).

Des boyaux pour «saucisses»

Le dirigeable est une structure en aluminium légère et solide (**2**), recouverte d'une enveloppe de baudruche que l'on remplit de plusieurs millions de mètres cube d'hydrogène très inflammable. Cette pellicule, qui ne se déchire pas et ne provoque pas d'étincelle par frottement, nécessite le tannage de près de 50 000 boyaux de bœuf pour chacun des 20 compartiments à gaz composant le dirigeable (**3**).

Labour-intensive airships

Hundreds of women worked on Shorts' delicate balloons:
rolling up the finished gas cell cover once the panels were
stitched together (**1**), scraping the goldbeater's skins clean,
moistening each frequently in brine solution (**2**), joining up the
girder frames (**3**), completing the gondola (**4**) and patching
tiny holes inside a gas cell (**5**).

Arbeitsintensive Luftschiffe

Hunderte von Frauen arbeiteten bei Short an den empfind-
lichen Ballons. Hier rollen sie die fertig zusammengenähte
Hülle einer Gaszelle auf (**1**), schaben Goldschlägerhaut, die
stets in Salzlake flexibel gehalten wird (**2**), montieren den
Gitterrahmen (**3**), legen letzte Hand an die Gondel (**4**) und
stopfen winzige Löcher im Inneren einer Gaszelle (**5**).

Une main-d'œuvre importante

Des centaines d'ouvrières étaient employées à la confection
des ballons Short: elles devaient rouler les laizes des compartiments de gaz une fois les panneaux cousus ensemble (**1**),
nettoyer la baudruche en l'humidifiant fréquemment par une
solution saline (**2**), assembler les poutrelles de la structure (**3**),
effectuer les finitions de la nacelle (**4**) et rapiécer les petits
trous de l'enveloppe (**5**).

Transatlantic race

In May 1919, twelve aircraft competed to be first across the Atlantic. A Sopwith flown by Harry Hawker and Lt-Commander McKenzie-Grieve (**3**) left Newfoundland, but was lost at sea for a week. A US Navy Curtiss NC-4 (**1**), one of a team of three, made it by hopping via the Azores to Lisbon, but as the journey took 15 days and was not a direct flight it did not officially count.

Das Transatlantik-Rennen

Im Mai 1919 traten zwölf Maschinen zum Wettkampf um die erste Atlantiküberquerung an. Eine Sopwith mit Harry Hawker und Lieutenant-Commander McKenzie-Grieve (**3**) startete in Neufundland und war eine ganze Woche lang über dem Meer verschollen. Die Curtiss NC-4 der U.S.-Marine (**1**) – eine von dreien – kam über die Azoren nach Lissabon, doch da sie 15 Tage unterwegs war und es kein Direktflug war, galt es nicht als Sieg.

Course transatlantique

Douze avions concourent en mai 1919 pour être le premier à traverser l'Atlantique. Un Sopwith piloté par Harry Hawker et le capitaine de corvette McKenzie-Grieve (**3**) quitte Terre-Neuve mais disparaît en mer pendant une semaine. Un des trois Navy Curtiss NC-4 américains (**1**) réussit en revanche la traversée mais doit se poser aux Açores et à Lisbonne avant d'arriver à Plymouth ; le vol ayant duré 15 jours et avec escale ne fut pas officiellement homologué.

2

SHAMROCK

3

Unlucky *shamrock*
A hefty crank of the propeller did not help this Shorts' machine at Eastchurch, England, cross the Atlantic. The *Shamrock* (**2**), with a huge extra fuel tank, was one of six aircraft which dropped out of the race in 1919.

Kein Glück für das »Kleeblatt«
Auch der kräftige Ruck am Propeller half dieser Maschine von Short, die im englischen Eastchurch startete, nicht über den Atlantik. Die *Shamrock* (»Kleeblatt«, **2**) mit ihrem gewaltigen Zusatztank war eine von sechs Maschinen, die beim Rennen von 1919 aufgeben mußten.

La malchance du *Shamrock*
Malgré un puissant moteur, apparemment difficile à lancer, le Short (ici à Eastchurch, Angleterre) ne parviendra pas à franchir l'Atlantique. Le *Shamrock* (**2**), avec son gros réservoir supplémentaire, fut l'un des six appareils qui abandonnèrent la course de 1919.

1

First across the Atlantic

On 14 June 1919, an overloaded British Vickers Vimy bomber flown by Captain John Alcock and Lieutenant Arthur Whitten Brown climbed out of Newfoundland (**1**) and was soon swallowed up by fog and cloud. Unable to orientate themselves, and with a faulty airspeed indicator, they stalled – Alcock managed to pull out just 100 feet above the waves. Battling snow, hail and sleet they crossed the Irish coast near Clifden, Co. Galway, and landed nose-first in a bog (**2**). They had been 16 hours 28 minutes in the air and flown 1,890 miles.

Die ersten Atlantikflieger

Am 14. Juni 1919 erhob sich ein viel zu schwer beladener britischer Vickers-Vimy-Bomber mit Captain John Alcock und Lieutenant Arthur Whitten Brown in den Himmel über Neufundland (**1**) und war bald in Wolken und Nebel verschwunden. Außerstande, sich zu orientieren, mit schadhaftem Geschwindigkeitsmesser, gingen sie bald in den Sinkflug, und Alcock konnte die Maschine gerade noch dreißig Meter über den Wellen wieder abfangen. In Schnee, Graupel und Hagel überflogen sie die irische Küste bei Clifden in der Grafschaft Galway und landeten mit der Nase in einem Sumpf (**2**). Sie waren 16 Stunden und 28 Minuten unterwegs gewesen und hatten 3.041 Kilometer zurückgelegt.

Le premier à traverser l'Atlantique

Le 14 juin 1919, le bombardier britannique, Vickers Vimy piloté par le capitaine John Alcock et le lieutenant Arthur Whitten Brown, décolle lourdement de Terre-Neuve (**1**) avant d'être bientôt environné d'un épais brouillard et de nuages. Incapables de s'orienter correctement, et disposant d'un indicateur de vitesse défectueux, ils manquent décrocher mais Alcock parvient à rester à 30 m au-dessus des vagues. Luttant contre la neige et la grêle, ils finissent par aborder la côte irlandaise près de Clifden (comté de Galway) pour atterrir en se plantant en pylône dans la tourbe (**2**). Ils ont passé 16 h 28 dans les airs et parcouru 3 041 km.

240

The new Blériots

Exhaustion lined the faces of Captain Alcock and Lieutenant Whitten Brown (2) as they ate breakfast on the morning after their historic transatlantic flight. They left their Vickers Vimy in an Irish field (1) for knighthoods and a hero's welcome in London (3). It had been ten years since Louis Blériot's famous Channel crossing.

Die Blériots ihrer Zeit

Die Erschöpfung ist Captain Alcock und Lieutenant Whitten Brown noch anzumerken, als sie am Morgen nach dem historischen Atlantikflug beim Frühstück sitzen (2). Die Vickers Vimy ließen sie auf einer irischen Wiese zurück (1) und tauschten sie gegen Adelstitel und einen triumphalen Empfang in London (3). Gerade zehn Jahre waren seit Blériots historischer Kanalüberquerung vergangen.

Les nouveaux Blériot

La fatigue creuse encore les visages du capitaine Alcock et du lieutenant Whitten Brown (2), photographiés au cours du petit déjeuner au lendemain de leur vol transatlantique historique. Ils abandonnèrent leur Vickers Vimy, planté dans un champ irlandais (1), pour recevoir un accueil de héros à Londres où ils furent anoblis (3). Dix ans auparavant, Louis Blériot traversait la Manche.

Transatlantic ease

A month after Alcock and Brown, Britain's R34 proved that airships were slower but just as good at long-distance travel. On 13 July 1919, the R34 arrived at Pulham, England (**3**), after a two-way crossing of the Atlantic via Mineola, New York (**1**). Flown under Major G.H. Scott (**2**), it had a crew of 31 and one stowaway.

Gemächlich geht es auch

Einen Monat nach Alcock und Brown bewies die britische R34, daß Luftschiffe zwar langsamer flogen, doch ebenso gut für den Langstreckenverkehr geeignet waren. Am 13. Juli 1919 trifft die R34 nach Überquerung des Atlantiks in beiden Richtungen mit Landung in Mineola, New York (**1**) wieder im englischen Pulham ein (**3**). Das Schiff, das unter dem Kommando von Major G.H. Scott stand (**2**), flog mit 31 Mann Besatzung und einem blinden Passagier.

Facilité transatlantique

Un mois après Alcock et Brown, le R34 britannique démontra que les dirigeables, certes plus lents que les avions, pouvaient aussi franchir de longues distances. Le R34 arrive à Pulham (Angleterre) le 13 juillet 1919 (**3**) après une traversée de l'Atlantique dans les deux sens via Mineola, dans l'État de New York (**1**). Piloté par le major G.H. Scott (**2**), il avait emmené un équipage de 31 membres… et un passager clandestin.

By air to Australia

Aussies Lieutenant Keith Smith, his brother Captain Ross Smith, and Sergeants W. Shiers and J. Bennett flew a Vickers Vimy (2) 11,294 miles from London to Darwin in 28 days in November–December 1919, collecting a £10,000 prize from the Australian government. Ross Smith (1, on left) and Keith Smith (on right) were later fêted with Quentin Brandon (centre), who opened a London to Cape Town route at about the same time. They were all knighted.

Der Luftweg nach Australien

Der australische Lieutenant Keith Smith, sein Bruder Captain Ross Smith und die Sergeants W. Shiers und J. Bennett flogen im November 1919 mit einer Vickers Vimy (2) in 28 Tagen die 19.186 Kilometer von London nach Darwin und erhielten dafür den Preis von £ 10.000, den die australische Regierung ausgesetzt hatte. Ross Smith (1, links) und Keith Smith (rechts) wurden später zusammen mit Quentin Brandon (Mitte) gefeiert, der etwa zur gleichen Zeit erstmals die Route von London nach Kapstadt geflogen war. Alle erhielten Adelstitel.

En Australie par avion

En novembre 1919, le lieutenant australien Keith Smith, son frère le capitaine Ross Smith et les sergents W. Shiers et J. Bennett, à bord d'un Vickers Vimy (2), effectuèrent les 19 186 km entre Londres et Darwin en 28 jours, remportant le prix de 10 000 £ offert par le gouvernement australien. Ross Smith (1, à gauche) et Keith Smith (à droite) furent ensuite fêtés avec Quentin Brandon (au centre), qui avait ouvert la route Londres-Le Cap à peu près à la même époque. Tous furent anoblis par le roi d'Angleterre.

Exploring Africa

Africa proved an immense challenge to the pioneers, with many early routes established by the mail-carrying Société des Lignes Aériennes Latécoère, founded by Pierre-Georges Latécoère. In August 1919 the six-man crew of a French Farman Goliath, piloted by Lucien Bossoutrot (**2**), was rescued after six gruelling days wrecked on the coast of Mauretania. Like Bossoutrot, who in 1920 flew a record 24 hours 19 minutes, Sadi Lecointe (**1**) combined aviation records with long-distance flying. Attempting a record 3,500-mile flight from Paris to the Persian Gulf in 1925 (**4**), pilot Thiérry was killed when he crashed in Germany. Pilot Koenneck made it to Hinaidi airfield, Baghdad, in his *Germania* (**3**).

Afrikaforscher

Afrika war für die Flugpioniere eine besondere Herausforderung, und schon früh legten die Postflugzeuge der von Pierre-Georges Latécoère begründeten Société des Lignes Aériennes Latécoère eine Reihe von Routen fest. Im August 1919 wurde die sechsköpfige Besatzung einer französischen Farman Goliath mit ihrem Piloten Lucien Bossoutrot (**2**) nach sechs bangen Tagen vor der mauretanischen Küste gerettet, wo sie notgelandet waren. Wie Bossoutrot (der 1920 einen Langstreckenrekord von 24 Stunden 19 Minuten aufstellte) war auch Sadi Lecointe (**1**) ein Rekord- und Langstreckenflieger. Der Pilot Thiéry stürzte 1925 beim Versuch eines 5.600-Kilometer-Rekordflugs von Paris zum Persischen Golf (**4**) in Deutschland ab und kam ums Leben. Der Flieger Koenneck hingegen erreichte mit seiner *Germania* das Hinaidi-Flugfeld in Bagdad (**3**).

Explorer l'Afrique

Immense défi pour les pionniers de l'aviation, l'Afrique fut sillonnée par les avions de la postale de la Société des Lignes Aériennes Latécoère, fondée par Pierre-Georges Latécoère. En août 1919, les six hommes d'équipage du *Farman Goliath* piloté par le Français Lucien Bossoutrot (**2**) sont recueillis après avoir passé six épouvantables jours, naufragés sur les côtes de Mauritanie. À l'instar de Bossoutrot, qui réalise en 1920 le record de durée de vol (24 h 19), Sadi Lecointe (**1**) remporte le record de distance et de durée. Au cours de sa tentative de 1925, parcourir 5 600 km entre Paris et le Golfe persique (**4**), le pilote Thiéry se tue en s'écrasant en Allemagne. Le pilote Koenneck parvient en revanche à l'aérodrome d'Hinaidi, près de Bagdad, à bord de son *Germania* (**3**).

Spectacle and tragedy

Alan Cobham (**2**), who had earlier flown from London to Cape Town and back, returned from a 26,703-mile round trip to Australia, landing his DH-50 seaplane in the Thames opposite the House of Commons (**1**, **3**) on 1 October 1926. He was without his friend and engineer Arthur Elliott, who was shot and killed by a Bedouin tribesman as they flew over Iraq.

Trauriger Triumph

Alan Cobham (**2**), der zuvor schon mit einem Hin- und Rückflug von London nach Kapstadt Aufsehen erregt hatte, trifft nach seinem 42.965-Kilometer-Flug nach Australien und zurück am 1. Oktober 1926 wieder in London ein und wassert mit seiner DH-50 auf der Themse gegenüber dem Parlamentsgebäude (**1**, **3**). Doch er kehrt ohne seinen Freund und Kopiloten Arthur Elliott zurück, den beim Flug über den Irak ein Beduine erschossen hatte.

Spectacle et tragédie

Alan Cobham (**2**), qui avait précédemment effectué le trajet Londres-Le Cap et retour, pose son hydravion DH-50 sur la Tamise en face de la Chambre des Communes (**1**, **3**) le 1er octobre 1926, après un parcours de 42 965 km depuis l'Australie. Il est seul, son ami et mécanicien Arthur Elliott ayant été tué par un Bédouin lors du survol de l'Irak.

Race for the North Pole

The Norwegian Arctic explorer Roald Amundsen, first to reach the South Pole in 1911, failed to reach the North Pole by air in 1925 when engine failure forced his Dornier-Wal seaplane (2) down 150 miles short. He was back next year with the airship *Norge* (1), piloted by the Italian Umberto Nobile. But on 7 May 1926, US Navy Commander Richard E. Byrd got there first in a Fokker tri-motor (3) named after the daughter of his backer Henry Ford. The *Norge* crossed the Pole to Alaska two days later.

Wettlauf zum Nordpol

Der norwegische Polarforscher Roald Amundsen, der 1911 als erster den Südpol erreicht hatte, scheiterte 1925 mit dem Versuch, aus der Luft zum Nordpol vorzustoßen; ein Maschinenschaden seines Dornier-Wal-Flugboots zwang ihn 290 Kilometer vor dem Ziel zur Aufgabe (2). Im folgenden Jahr unternahm er einen neuen Anlauf mit dem Luftschiff *Norge* (1), gesteuert von dem Italiener Umberto Nobile. Doch Richard E. Byrd, Commander der U.S.-Navy, kam ihm zuvor. Am 7. Mai 1926 überflog er als erster den Pol, in einer dreimotorigen Fokker-Maschine, die er nach der Tochter seines Geldgebers Henry Ford benannt hatte (3). Zwei Tage darauf langte die *Norge* auf ihrem Weg nach Alaska am Pol an.

La course au pôle Nord

Le grand explorateur de l'Arctique et le premier homme à avoir atteint le Pôle Sud en 1911, le Norvégien Roald Amundsen, ne réussit pas à atteindre le Pôle Nord par la voie des airs en 1925, contraint par une panne de moteur à poser son hydravion Dornier-Wal (2) à 290 km du but. Il recommença l'année suivante avec le dirigeable *Norge* (1), piloté par l'Italien Umberto Nobile mais est devancé, le 7 mai 1926, par le commandant Richard E. Byrd, de l'US Navy, à bord d'un trimoteur Fokker (3), baptisé du nom de la fille de son sponsor, Henry Ford. Le *Norge* reliera le pôle à l'Alaska deux jours plus tard.

Byrd and compass

Commander Byrd's claim that he had crossed the North Pole was widely disputed. However, he took numerous observations, including use of this sundial compass (4).

Byrd mit Kompaß

Commander Byrds Anspruch auf den ersten Nordpolflug wurde vielfach bestritten. Fest steht jedoch, daß er zahlreiche wissenschaftliche Studien anstellte, unter anderem mit diesem Sonnenuhr-Kompaß (4).

Byrd et la boussole

La réalité de la traversée du Pôle Nord par le commandant Byrd fut l'objet de controverses malgré les nombreuses observations qu'il avait faites, grâce notamment à un compas solaire (4).

London to Paris luxury

The Handley Page Pullman (**1**) of December 1919 was one of the first British attempts to compete against the luxurious London to Paris Pullman boat-train services. The 14 seats (**3**) had cushions, curtains, candlesticks, and on the London–Brussels route the first airline meals – lunch baskets at three shillings each. However, publicity efforts, such as this travelling French rowing team (**2**), failed to make the flights competitive without subsidy.

London-Paris im Luxus

Die im Dezember 1919 vorgestellte Handley Page Pullman (**1**) war der erste britische Versuch, mit einem Flugzeug gegen den luxuriösen Pullmanzug London-Paris anzutreten. Die 14 Sitze (**3**) hatten Kissen, Vorhänge und Kerzenhalter, und auf der Strecke London-Brüssel gab es sogar erstmals Bordverpflegung – Lunchkörbchen zu drei Shilling. Doch trotz Werbeaufwand, hier etwa mit einer französischen Rudermannschaft (**2**), waren die Flüge nie profitabel.

Le luxe du Londres-Paris

Le Handley Page Pullman (**1**) représente, en décembre 1919, l'une des grandes tentatives britanniques pour concurrencer les luxueux services offerts par le train et le bateau entre Londres et Paris. Les 14 passagers de la cabine (**3**), agrémentée de panneaux matelassés, de rideaux, de chandeliers, y bénéficiaient du premier service de repas à bord – des paniers-repas à trois shillings – sur la ligne Londres-Bruxelles. Cependant, les opérations de promotion, par exemple pour cette équipe de rameurs français (**2**), ne furent pas suffisants pour rendre ces vols compétitifs sans subventions.

Airline specials

With expensive tickets, the earliest British airlines advertised themselves as something special. Because of small planes and high overheads, the mass market would not develop until much later. International flying from Hounslow Aerodrome, London, was inaugurated on 25 August 1919, when a custom officer gave a clearance certificate to the pilot of a 'Special' to Paris (1). American students came from Paris to London by struggling Instone Airlines in August 1922 (2).

Etwas ganz Besonderes

Die ersten britischen Passagierflüge waren teuer, und die Werbung präsentierte sie als ein ganz besonderes Erlebnis. Die Betriebskosten der kleinen Maschinen waren zu hoch, ein Massenmarkt sollte sich erst Jahre später entwickeln. Der Londoner Flugplatz Hounslow nahm am 25. August 1919 seinen internationalen Betrieb auf, nachdem ein Zollbeamter dem Piloten die Flugerlaubnis für den Sonderflug nach Paris (1) überreicht hat. Im August 1922 kommen amerikanische Studentinnen mit der kleinen Instone Airlines von Paris nach London (2).

Lignes spéciales

Les premières compagnies aériennes britanniques utilisèrent l'argument de la cherté du billet pour d'offrir un « service spécial ». Les petits appareils et les frais de fonctionnement élevés empêcheront pendant le développement du marché de masse. Les vols internationaux au départ de l'aérodrome de Hounslow, près de Londres, seront inaugurés le 25 août 1919, après que l'officier des Douanes a visé le congé de navigation du pilote de ce vol « Spécial » vers Paris (1), et ces étudiantes américaines feront en août 1922 le Paris–Londres sur la petite Instone Airlines (2).

Commercial appeal
Efforts to attract business use included delivery of the first cargo of Russian gold to Croydon, London, in August 1926 (**3**). That year the Tellus Super Vacuum Cleaner Company demonstrated its marvellous invention (**4, 5**).

Wirtschaftlicher Nutzen
Im August 1926 trifft die erste Lieferung russischen Goldes in Croydon bei London ein (**3**) – ein Versuch, die Wirtschaft für die Möglichkeiten der Luftfracht zu interessieren. Im selben Jahr führt die Tellus Super Vacuum Cleaner Company ihre fabelhaften Staubsauger an Flugzeugen vor (**4, 5**).

Promouvoir l'air
Le transport du premier chargement d'or russe vers Croydon (Londres), en août 1926 (**3**), faisait partie des efforts entrepris pour attirer la clientèle d'affaires. Cette année-là, la société Tellus Super Vacuum Cleaner fait la démonstration de sa merveilleuse invention (**4, 5**).

Highest German standards

German airlines were the envy of Europe in the 1920s, providing the first in-flight movies in April 1925 (**1**). These films were single-reel shorts and, of course, silent – useful since engine noise was too great to hear anything anyway. Meals and steward service on Lufthansa's Berlin–Vienna Air Express were second to none (**3**). The Junkers all-metal F13 four-seater was by far the most significant German post-war passenger plane, serviced like a hotel (**2**).

Deutsche Qualität

In den zwanziger Jahren blickten alle europäischen Luftlinien neidisch nach Deutschland. In deutschen Maschinen gab es erstmals im April 1925 Filmvorführungen an Bord (**1**). Es waren nur Kurzfilme, und natürlich waren sie stumm – was nur gut war, denn der Motorenlärm hätte jeden anderen Ton erstickt. Mahlzeiten und Bedienung auf dem Lufthansa-Flugexpreß von Berlin nach Wien waren unerreicht (**3**). Der Ganzmetall-Viersitzer F13 von Junkers war die mit Abstand wichtigste deutsche Passagier-maschine der Zeit nach dem Ersten Weltkrieg und wurde gepflegt wie ein Hotel (**2**).

Un service de grande classe

Les compagnies aériennes allemandes firent l'envie de l'Europe en offrant à leurs passagers, au mois d'avril 1925, la première projection cinémato-graphique en vol (**1**). Ces courts métrages d'une seule bobine étaient naturellement des films muets – le bruit des moteurs était d'ailleurs trop fort pour qu'on puisse entendre quoi que ce soit. La qualité des repas et du service de bord sur l'Air Express Berlin-Vienne de la Lufthansa était sans égal (**3**). Le Junkers F13, appareil entièrement métallique à quatre places passager, était de loin, grâce à un service digne d'un hôtel, l'avion de ligne le plus représentatif de l'Allemagne de l'après-guerre (**2**).

Departures and arrivals

Airlines began to reorganize themselves in the mid-1920s. Sir Samuel Instone (**1**, in centre) wound up Instone Airlines in March 1924, when it was rolled into the new Imperial Airways. Aero Lloyd and Junkers merged to become Deutsche Lufthansa, with this Dornier Komet III inaugurating scheduled services from Berlin to Zurich in April 1926 (**3**). A Russian 'air sleeping carriage' (**2**) was a rarity. While the Italian Gianni Caproni did not get this airliner quite right (**4**) the future of airlines was, indeed, with bigger planes.

Manche kommen, manche gehen

Mitte der zwanziger Jahre begannen die Fluglinien sich neu zu organisieren. Sir Samuel Instone (**1**, Mitte) brachte im März 1924 seine Instone Airlines in die neuen Imperial Airways ein. Aero Lloyd und Junkers schlossen sich zur Deutschen Lufthansa zusammen, und im April 1926 begann mit dieser Dornier Komet III der Linienverkehr von Berlin nach Zürich (**3**). Die russische Maschine mit Schlafabteil (**2**) blieb eine Kuriosität. Die Konstruktion des Italieners Gianni Caproni (**4**) war noch nicht ganz ausgereift, doch mit der Grundidee eines größeren Passagierflugzeugs war sie ein Schritt in die Zukunft.

Départs et arrivées

Au milieu des années 1920, on assiste à la réorganisation des compagnies aériennes. La nouvelle Imperial Airways britannique absorbe ainsi, en mars 1924, Instone Air Lines, fondée par Sir Samuel Instone (**1**, au centre). Aero Lloyd et Junkers se regroupent pour former la Deutsche Lufthansa, dont le Dornier Komet III inaugure un service régulier Berlin-Zurich en avril 1926 (**3**). L'«avion-couchettes» russe (**2**) demeure une exception de même que l'appareil géant de l'Italien Gianni Caproni (**4**), qui comprit – trop tôt pour l'époque – que l'avenir des compagnies aériennes dépendait d'avions plus grands.

261

Linking Europe and Asia
Germany, after 1918, was restricted by treaty, sentiment and lack of colonies from expanding overseas like the British and French. Nevertheless, the newly formed Lufthansa blazed a trail from Berlin to Peking via Moscow and Omsk in August 1926. One of two new all-metal Junkers G24s was warmly received in Harbin, Manchuria (**1**).

Europa und Asien wachsen zusammen
Die Bestimmungen des Versailler Friedensvertrags, die öffentliche Meinung und der Verlust der Kolonien hinderten die Deutschen nach 1918 daran, in dem Maße über die Grenzen ihres Landes hinauszugehen, wie Engländer und Franzosen es taten. Trotzdem eröffnete die neugegründete Lufthansa im August 1926 eine Flugroute von Berlin über Moskau und Omsk nach Peking. Hier wird eine der beiden brandneuen Junkers G24 freundlich in Harbin in der Mandschurei begrüßt (**1**).

Relier l'Europe à l'Asie
Après 1918, l'Allemagne fut empêchée par le traité de Versailles, l'opinion publique et la perte de ses colonies, de s'étendre à l'étranger à l'exemple des Britanniques et des Français. La nouvelle Lufthansa ouvrit néanmoins la ligne Berlin-Pékin via Moscou et Omsk en août 1926 avec ce nouveau Junkers G24 à carlingue métallique, chaleureusement reçu à Harbin, en Mandchourie (**1**).

Opposite directions

In the mid-1920s, as the Dutch KLM airline was establishing a route to the Dutch East Indies by way of Dum Dum, Calcutta (**2**), Japanese airmen Abe and Kawachi landed in Berlin on the first flight from Tokyo to London (**3**). Japan, aware of developments in aviation, launched its first purpose-built aircraft carrier, the *Hosho*, in December 1922.

Auch in die andere Richtung

Mitte der zwanziger Jahre, als die holländische KLM ihre Route nach Niederländisch-Ostindien über Dum Dum bei Kalkutta begründete (**2**), machen die beiden japanischen Flieger Abe und Kawachi auf dem ersten Flug von Tokio nach London in Berlin Station (**3**). In Japan verfolgte man die Entwicklung der Luftfahrt aufmerksam, und im Dezember 1922 lief der erste dafür entworfene japanische Flugzeugträger vom Stapel, die *Hosho*.

Des directions opposées

Au milieu des années 1920, pendant que la compagnie néerlandaise KLM inaugure une route vers les Indes orientales via Dum Dum, près de Calcutta (**2**), les aviateurs japonais Abe et Kawachi atterrissent à Berlin après avoir effectué le premier vol Tokyo-Londres (**3**). Le Japon, conscient de l'avenir de l'aviation, lança son premier porte-avions, le *Hosho*, en décembre 1922.

3

—7—
Air Comes into its Own

America's late entry into World War I meant it had an immature aviation industry compared with the Europeans in the early 1920s, with few heavy bombers and little on which to build a passenger-carrying airline business. The only real value of aeroplanes seemed to be the long-distance carrying of mail. Allan and Malcolm Loughead (Lockheed), who had designed their first plane in 1913, disbanded their company in 1921 because of a glut of surplus military planes on the civilian market.

Privatization of the mail routes in 1925 finally encouraged businesses, and names that would dominate aviation for generations began to appear. William Boeing not only formed Boeing Air Transport – eventually to become United Air Lines – but produced the significantly all-American Type 40 two-seat passenger plane. In 1926, the Lougheads came back with a streamlined, high-wing monoplane designed by John K. Northrop, the Lockheed Vega (see below). Then one of America's most famous post-war planes, the Ford Motor Company's tri-motor 'Tin Goose', made its first appearance.

Conditions were ripe for an explosive increase in American aviation. The fuse was lit in 1926 with a determined take-up of the $25,000 Orteig Prize, offered in 1920 for the first direct flight between New York and Paris. It was twice the distance of Alcock and Brown's 1919 transatlantic flight.

The first to try was René Fonck, the top-scoring World War I French fighter ace. His overloaded three-engined Sikorsky crashed on take-off at New York in September 1926, and two of his crew were killed. But that only heightened interest in the prize. Next came Richard Byrd, America's North Pole champion, but his Fokker tri-motor crashed in April 1927. Two days later another US Navy competitor and his co-pilot were killed on a test flight. By 8 May, when Charles Nungesser, the third-ranked French air ace of the war, took off from Paris for New York, excitement on both sides of the Atlantic was at fever pitch, not lessened when this hero was never seen again.

On 19 May 1927, 25-year-old Charles Lindbergh, backed by St Louis businessmen, took off from New York in a specially built Ryan high-winged monoplane. Thousands watched him go and millions more listened with bated breath as the radio reported him flying over St John's, Newfoundland, and out over the Atlantic. Battling fatigue, ice and storms, he finally crossed the coast of Ireland, then the English Channel, and as his second night of flying approached he found Le Bourget air-field in France. It was ablaze with car headlights as thousands of people willed him to land safely.

International Lindbergh fever did not abate for months. He was the perfect star: handsome, unassuming, courteous – he even paid a visit to Nungesser's distraught mother. Everyone, from the man in the street to the President of France and the King of England, wanted to see him. When he flew the *Spirit of St Louis* from Le Bourget to Croydon, even more people waited for him than in Paris. President Coolidge sent the warship USS *Memphis* to bring him home to an American welcome rarely, if ever, exceeded. He was showered with honours and used by US diplomats to ease relations with Mexico, equally rapturous at being visited by him.

Money and talent poured into aircraft production and airlines. From 12 airmail companies in 1926 there were 25 in 1928. Within days of Lindbergh's flight a new company was formed, Transcontinental Air Transport (predecessor of TWA), to which he was appointed chairman of the technical committee, charged with route-surveying. By 1930, air traffic in America was twice that of the whole of Europe with just four big airlines: TWA, United, Eastern and American.

By then, too, most of the world's major air routes had been established. A year after Lindbergh's flight, a German Junkers W33 made the first east–west crossing of the north Atlantic, a Lockheed Vega flown by the Australians Hubert Wilkins and Carl Ben Eilson went west to east across the Arctic and then crossed the Antarctic. Only one major prize, the Pacific, remained, and that was claimed on 9 June 1928 by the Australians Charles Kingsford Smith and Charles Ulm flying from San Francisco to Brisbane via Honolulu and Fiji in their Fokker *Southern Cross*. Kingsford Smith, who at one stage held 11 world records, was knighted.

Significantly, most of these pioneering aircraft were monoplanes, whose low drag capabilities outweighed the stability of biplanes as aircraft went ever faster. Almost entirely due to the cantilever wing policy of the German Hugo Junkers, whose first F13 low-wing passenger plane was produced in 1915, aircraft designers around the world increasingly found low wings useful for retractable undercarriages, and Junkers's all-metal structures provided a stressed skin for structural support. Anthony Fokker's high-winged monoplanes were particularly appealing to designers because almost any engine could be fitted to them. The standard was set in the late 1920s by the Lockheed Vega, developed from a Fokker, with a 425hp radial engine cruising with pilot and six passengers at about 120mph over a range of up to 900 miles.

Most passengers wanted speed *and* comfort, and for some airlines that meant sticking with slower biplanes in order to focus on the passenger cabin. An improvement on the 1929 Imperial Airways route from London to Karachi, for instance, was desirable: it was hardly convenient. Passengers paid £130 and flew from Croydon to Basle in a 20-seat Armstrong-Whitworth Argosy with a toilet and baggage space at the rear. Then, to avoid a dispute with Italy, they took a train to Genoa, embarked on a Shorts' Calcutta flying-boat to Alexandria, and changed to a seven-seater De Havilland 66 Hercules biplane in which two seats had been removed to make room for a bar. They probably needed it: their flight took them across Arabia, stopping at night at desert camps fortified against local tribes-men, then taking a southern route away from the Persian coast, where locals sometimes took potshots at aircraft.

Airlines still had to keep a close eye on their more comfortable competitors, the airships. Indeed, it is no coincidence that Imperial Airways' Handley Page Heracles biplane – specifically designed to minimize noise and vibration in the passenger cabin – was ordered in 1929 just after the remarkable *Graf Zeppelin* airship's inaugural flight to New York. The 775-foot-long Zeppelin, the only really successful airship ever built, came with a luxury lounge, bar, beautiful kitchen and individual cabins.

But at the other end of the scale, performance did matter. Thousands of young World War I fighter pilots, with dull futures ahead of them, hankered after the sheer thrill of flying. They struggled to pursue it by giving joyrides and barnstorming shows, particularly in America. Stunt flying in war-surplus Curtiss Jennies was common, and even, occasionally, practical. Barnstormers introduced low-level crop-dusting, and when Wesley May carried a two-gallon can of fuel from one biplane to another by stepping from wing-tip to wing-tip in mid-air he incidentally pioneered air-to-air refuelling. In Europe, stunt flyers in Avro 504s provided the public with their *baptême de l'air*, or first flip.

Joyrides and barnstorming engendered private flying clubs and a whole industry of ever smaller, lighter and more manoeuvrable craft. It was in such planes as the Dutch Koolhoven, American Globe Swift and De Havilland Moth – in which Amy Johnson flew alone from Britain to Australia in 1931 – that most people learned to fly.

There was still a shortage of suitable airfields around the world. For many years one answer remained the seaplane. Pan American Airways had the big, passenger-carrying champion Sikorsky S40 and S41 flying-boats, which in 1930 started to weave routes into South America to compete with the Dornier-Wals of expanding German airlines.

For smaller seaplanes, the Schneider Trophy, first offered in 1911 for technical progress, by the late 1920s had become the world's most prestigious speed prize, with designers and engineers vying to produce ever-faster race machines. National pride was at stake, and the French, American, Italian and British governments committed resources to winning the trophy. The climax came in 1931 when a British Supermarine S6 – the future Spitfire fighter – secured it for Britain.

While no other aviation trophy again commanded such government involvement, the National Air Races and Thompson Trophy in the US, and Coupe Deutsch de la Meurthe in France, continued the link between racing and combat aircraft that would be vindicated ten years later, as war once again gripped the world

The Blériot stand at the 1930 Paris Air Show reveals fascinating designs: the passenger-carrying catamarans of the new 125 with the famous Blériot XII nestling underneath. A SPAD 91 monoplane is seen in the foreground.

Der Stand von Blériot auf der Pariser Luftfahrtschau von 1930 wartet mit faszinierenden Maschinen auf, darunter dem neuen Passagier-Katamaran-flugzeug 125, unter dessen Flügel die berühmte Blériot XII Unter-schlupf gefunden hat. Im Vorder-grund ein SPAD 91-Eindecker.

Des projets fascinants sont exposés sur le stand Blériot du Salon de l'Aviation de Paris de 1930 : notamment le Blériot 125, un « catamaran » pour passagers, abritant sous son aile le fameux Blériot XII, et, visible au premier plan, un monoplan SPAD 91.

Da die Amerikaner erst spät in den Ersten Weltkrieg eingetreten waren, war auch ihre Luftfahrtindustrie in den frühen zwanziger Jahren wenig entwickelt; es gab nur einige schwere Bombermodelle und wenig, was als Basis für den Passagierflug hätte dienen können. Der einzige Verwendungszweck für Flugzeuge schien der Langstrecken-Postverkehr. Allan und Malcolm Loughead (Lockheed), die 1913 ihr erstes Flugzeug gebaut hatten, lösten ihre Firma 1921 auf, da der Markt mit Maschinen aus Militärbeständen überschwemmt war.

Die Geschäfte gingen besser, als die Postrouten 1925 privatisiert wurden, und Namen, die in der Flugzeugindustrie Generationen lang vorherrschen sollten, erschienen nun. William Boeing gründete die Boeing Air Transport – aus der die United Air Lines entstanden – und baute die uramerikanische Zweisitzermaschine Typ 40. 1926 meldeten sich die Lougheads mit einem von John K. Northrop entworfenen stromlinienförmigen Hochdecker zurück, der Lockheed Vega (siehe unten). Und schließlich erschien eines der berühmtesten Flugzeuge der amerikanischen Nachkriegszeit, die dreimotorige »Tin Goose« (Blechgans) der Ford Motor Company.

Die Zeichen standen günstig für einen großen Aufschwung der amerikanischen Luftfahrt. Die Zündschnur brannte, als 1926 der Orteig-Preis in Angriff genommen wurde – ein schon 1920 ausgesetzter Preis von $ 25.000 für den ersten Nonstopflug zwischen New York und Paris, doppelt so weit wie der Atlantikflug von Alcock und Brown im Jahre 1919.

Den ersten Anlauf nahm René Fonck, der erfolgreichste französische Flieger des Ersten Weltkriegs. Seine zu schwer beladene dreimotorige Sikorsky stürzte im September 1926 beim Start in New York ab; zwei Besatzungsmitglieder kamen um. Der Nächste war Richard Byrd, der amerikanische Nordpolchampion im April 1927, doch auch seine dreimotorige Fokker stürzte ab. Zwei Tage darauf verunglückten ein weiterer Mitstreiter aus der U.S.-Navy und sein Kopilot bei einem Probeflug tödlich. Als Charles Nungesser, auf dem dritten Rang der französischen Kriegs-Fliegerhelden, am 8. Mai in Paris aufstieg, war die Erregung beiderseits des Atlantiks auf dem Höhepunkt, und sie ließ auch nicht nach, als Nungesser auf seinem Flug für immer spurlos verschwand.

Am 19. Mai 1927 machte sich, finanziert von Geschäftsleuten aus St. Louis, der 25jährige Charles Lindbergh mit einem eigens dafür gebauten Ryan-Hochdecker in New York auf den Weg. Tausende winkten ihm zum Abschied zu, und Millionen saßen gebannt an den Radiogeräten und lauschten den Berichten aus St. John's, Neufundland, wie er hinaus aufs offene Meer flog. Er bezwang Müdigkeit, Eis und Unwetter und gelangte schließlich an die irische Küste, von wo er den Ärmelkanal überquerte und bei Einbruch seiner zweiten Nacht in den Lüften das französische Flugfeld Le Bourget erreichte. Es war von Automobilscheinwerfern hell erleuchtet, denn Tausende sehnten seine sichere Landung herbei.

Das weltweite Lindbergh-Fieber ließ erst Monate später wieder nach. Er war ein Held wie aus dem Bilderbuch: gutaussehend, bescheiden, höflich – er besuchte sogar die verzweifelte Mutter Nungessers. Jeder, vom Mann auf der Straße bis hin zum französischen Präsidenten und dem König von England, wollte ihn sehen. Als er mit der *Spirit of St. Louis* von Le Bourget nach Croydon kam, warteten noch mehr Leute auf ihn als in Paris. Präsident Coolidge entsandte das Kriegsschiff USS *Memphis*, um ihn nach Hause zu holen, und selten wurde jemandem ein größerer Empfang bereitet. Er wurde mit Ehren überhäuft, und die U.S.-Diplomatie konnte mit seiner Hilfe die Spannungen mit Mexiko entschärfen, denn auch dort begrüßten ihn die begeisterten Mengen.

Geld und Talent flossen nun in den Flugzeugbau und die Fluglinien. 1926 hatte es zwölf Luftpostlinien gegeben, 1928 waren es bereits 25. Nur Tage nach Lindberghs Flug wurde eine neue Gesellschaft gegründet, Transcontinental Air Transport (Vorläuferin der TWA), und er wurde Vorsitzender des technischen Ausschusses, verantwortlich für das Einrichten neuer Routen. 1930 unternahmen in Amerika die vier größten Fluglinien – TWA, United, Eastern und American – bereits doppelt so viele Flüge wie in ganz Europa.

Inzwischen waren die meisten Hauptflugrouten weltweit festgelegt. Ein Jahr nach Lindberghs Flug gelang mit einer deutschen Junkers W33 die erste Ost-West-Überquerung des Nordatlantiks, und eine Lockheed Vega mit den Australiern Hubert Wilkins und Carl Ben Eilson überquerte die Arktis und dann die Antarktis ostwärts. Nur den Pazifik galt es noch zu erobern, und diese Trophäe errangen die Australier Charles Kingsford Smith und Charles Ulm am 9. Juni 1928, als sie mit ihrer Fokker *Southern Cross* von San Francisco über Honolulu und Fidschi nach Brisbane flogen. Kingsford Smith wurde für seine 11 Weltrekorde in den Adelsstand erhoben.

Bemerkenswert ist, daß fast alle Maschinen, mit denen diese Erfolge errungen wurden, Eindecker waren, deren niedrigerer Luftwiderstand bei zunehmender Geschwindigkeit den

The *Graf Zeppelin*, the world's most successful airship, flies over the Brandenburg Gate, Berlin, in October 1928.

Die *Graf Zeppelin*, das erfolgreichste Luftschiff der Welt, im Oktober 1928 über dem Brandenburger Tor in Berlin.

Le *Graf Zeppelin*, le dirigeable le plus célèbre du monde, survolant la porte de Brandebourg à Berlin, en octobre 1928.

Stabilitätsvorteil der Zweidecker überwog. Die freitragenden Tragflächen, die der Deutsche Hugo Junkers 1913 mit seinem ersten Passagierflugzeug, dem Tiefdecker F13, eingeführt hatte, setzten sich weltweit durch, denn sie ermöglichten einziehbare Fahrgestelle, und der Ganzmetallrumpf übernahm tragende Funktionen. Attraktiv fanden die Konstrukteure auch Anthony Fokkers Hochdecker, denn in diese Maschinen ließ sich beinahe jeder Motor einsetzen. Ende der zwanziger Jahre setzte die Lockheed Vega, die auf Fokker-Basis entwickelt war, den neuen Standard – der 425-PS-Sternmotor erlaubte dem Piloten und sechs Passagieren bei einer Reisegeschwindigkeit von 190 km/h eine Reichweite von bis zu 1.450 km.

Die meisten Reisenden wollten Geschwindigkeit *und* Komfort, und manche Fluggesellschaften blieben lieber bei den langsameren Zweideckern und konzentrierten sich auf die Passagierkabine. So ließ sich der Flug, den die Imperial Airways 1929 von London nach Karatschi boten, durchaus noch verbessern – bequem konnte man ihn nicht gerade nennen. Die Passagiere zahlten £ 130 und flogen dafür zunächst mit einer 20sitzigen Armstrong-Whitworth Argosy mit Bordtoilette und Gepäckraum von Croydon nach Basel. Von dort ging es, um Auseinandersetzungen mit Italien zu vermeiden, per Zug weiter nach Genua, von wo die Reisenden mit einem Short Calcutta-Flugboot nach Alexandria übersetzten; dort stiegen sie in einen 7sitzigen De Havilland 66 Hercules Doppeldecker um, dessen zwei weitere Sitze einer Bar gewichen waren. Der Flug führte sie über Arabien, wobei sie in Wüstenlagern nächtigten, die gegen Angriffe einheimischer Stämme befestigt waren, und dann nach Süden fort von der persischen Küste (denn es war bekannt, daß die dortigen Einheimischen bisweilen auf Flugzeuge schossen).

Die Fluglinien mußten auch ihre komfortableren Konkurrenten im Auge behalten, die Luftschiffe. Es war kein Zufall, daß die Imperial Airways den Handley Page Heracles-Doppeldecker – speziell auf minimales Geräusch und Vibrationsarmut in der Passagierzelle konstruiert – 1929 in Auftrag gaben, kurz nachdem das sensationelle Luftschiff *Graf Zeppelin* seinen Jungfernflug nach New York absolviert hatte. Der 236 Meter lange Zeppelin, der einzige erfolgreiche, der je gebaut wurde, konnte mit luxuriösem Aufenthaltsraum, Bar, einer wunderschönen Küche und Kabinen aufwarten.

Am unteren Ende der Erfolgsleiter kam es auf Schnelligkeit an. Tausende junger Kampfpiloten des Ersten Weltkriegs, die in eine ungewisse Zukunft blickten, sehnten sich nach dem Abenteuer des Fliegens, und taten alles, damit sie weiterfliegen konnten, gerade in den Vereinigten Staaten; sie machten Rundflüge oder traten auf Jahrmärkten als Flugakrobaten auf. Flugkunststücke in ausgemusterten Curtiss Jennies sah man überall, und manchmal waren sie sogar noch praktisch. Es waren Kunstflieger, die das Besprühen von Feldern mit Insektenmittel aufbrachten, und als Wesley May im Flug einen Benzinkanister von einem Doppeldecker zum anderen brachte, indem er einfach einen großen Schritt von einer Tragfläche zur anderen tat, da hatte er die Luftbetankung erfunden. In Europa boten die Kunstflieger in ihren Avro 504-Maschinen dem Publikum Rundflüge an, und viele kamen so zu ihrer Lufttaufe.

Solche Vergnügungen riefen die privaten Fliegerclubs ins Leben, und eine ganze neue Industrie entstand, die kleinere, leichtere und noch besser beherrschbare Flugzeuge baute. In Maschinen wie der Koolhoven aus Holland, der Globe Swift aus Amerika und der britischen De Havilland Moth – mit der Amy Johnson 1931 ihren Alleinflug von England nach Australien unternahm – lernten die meisten neuen Piloten das Fliegen.

Brauchbare Flugfelder waren weltweit nach wie vor knapp, und ein guter Ausweg blieb lange Jahre das Wasserflugzeug. Pan American Airways flog seit 1930 mit den großen, leistungsstarken Sikorsky-S40- und S-41-Flugbooten und wetteiferte auf den Südamerikarouten mit den deutschen Linien, die ihre Erfolge den Wal-Flugbooten von Dornier verdankten.

Für kleinere Wasserflugzeuge war der Schneider-Pokal, der 1911 zunächst für technische Fortschritte ausgesetzt worden war, in den späten zwanziger Jahren zum angesehensten Hochleistungspreis geworden, und Konstrukteure und Mechaniker wetteiferten um die schnellste Maschine. Es war eine Frage des Nationalstolzes, und die Regierungen in Frankreich, Amerika, Italien und Großbritannien gaben Geld für neue Maschinen, die den begehrten Preis in ihr Land bringen sollten. Der Höhepunkt kam im Jahr 1931, als eine britische Supermarine S6 – die Vorläuferin des Spitfire-Jägers – die Trophäe nach England holte.

Für keinen anderen Pokal setzten sich je wieder die amtlichen Stellen so ein, doch die National Air Races und die Thompson Trophy in den Vereinigten Staaten und der Coupe Deutsch de la Meurthe in Frankreich hielten auch weiterhin die Verbindung zwischen Rennsport und Kampfflugzeugen aufrecht. Zehn Jahre später sollte sich zeigen, daß es weise Voraussicht gewesen war, denn wiederum erschütterte die Welt ein Krieg.

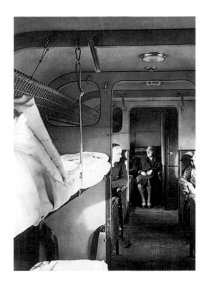

Passengers on long hauls in the early 1930s sometimes had the extra comfort of a sleeping cabin, as in this German Junkers.

Für die Passagiere der Langstreckenflüge in den frühen dreißiger Jahren gab es bisweilen sogar den Luxus einer Schlafkabine, wie hier in einer deutschen Junkers.

Les passagers des vols long-courrier du début des années 1930 bénéficiaient parfois du confort d'une couchette, comme dans ce Junkers allemand.

Disastrous beginnings

The great New York–Paris race started badly in September 1926. Despite being christened by the Mayor of New York (**1**). Captain René Fonck's three-engined Sikorsky S-35 crashed on take-off at Roosevelt Field, New York (**3**). Fonck and his co-pilot escaped but two other crew were killed. Igor Sikorsky had wanted a thorough test, but Fonck was anxious to go before winter set in over the Atlantic.

Auftakt mit Katastrophen

Das große Wettfliegen New York – Paris nahm im September 1926 einen schlechten Anfang. Auch die Taufe durch den New Yorker Bürgermeister (**1**) brachte Capitaine René Foncks dreimotoriger Sikorsky S-35 kein Glück; sie stürzte beim Start auf dem New Yorker Roosevelt Field ab (**3**). Fonck und sein Kopilot überlebten, doch zwei Besatzungsmitglieder kamen um. Igor Sikorsky hatte die Maschine zuerst gründlich erproben wollen, doch Fonck wollte fliegen, bevor auf dem Atlantik der Winter begann.

Des débuts difficiles

La grande «course» New York-Paris commence mal puisque, malgré un baptème par le Maire de New York (**1**), le trimoteur Sikorsky S-35 du capitaine René Fonck s'écrase au décollage de Roosevelt Field (New York) en septembre 1926 (**3**). Fonck et son copilote en sortent indemnes, les deux autres membres de l'équipage sont tués. Igor Sikorsky avait voulu effectuer des essais approfondis mais Fonck était trop pressé de partir sur l'Atlantique avant l'hiver.

And more tragedy

Worse came on 8 May 1927, when French war hero Charles Nungesser and co-pilot François Coli (2) set off for New York from Le Bourget, Paris (4). Millions waited by radios for news, and crowds waited on the New York waterfront. But they were never seen again.

Und noch eine Tragödie

Noch schlimmer kam es am 8. Mai 1927, als der französische Kriegsheld Charles Nungesser und sein Kopilot François Coli (2) vom Flughafen Le Bourget bei Paris aufbrachen (4). Millionen saßen an den Radiogeräten, und in New York hatten sich Menschenmengen am Hafen versammelt, um Nungesser zu begrüßen, doch die beiden blieben für immer verschollen.

La tragédie continue

Le pire se produit le 8 mai 1927, lorsque l'as français Charles Nungesser et son copilote François Coli (2) décollent du Bourget pour New York (4). Des millions de gens écoutent alors la radio pour avoir des nouvelles des deux aviateurs tandis qu'une foule immense les attend sur les quais de New York. On ne les reverra jamais plus.

Unassuming competitor

Charles A. Lindbergh (**1**) was the ideal American hero: tall, clean-cut, good-looking and quiet. Raised in Minnesota, the 25-year-old barnstormer, airmail runner and Army Air Corps reserve pilot used business contacts in St Louis to finance his San Diego-built Ryan, whose fuel tank was so large it blocked all forward vision. His transatlantic flight on 19 May 1927 immediately followed a record-breaking transcontinental trip.

Der stille Konkurrent

Charles A. Lindbergh (**1**) war das Ideal des amerikanischen Helden: groß, gepflegt, gutaussehend und wortkarg. Der 25jährige, in Minnesota großgeworden, war als Kunstflieger aufgetreten, hatte Luftpostflugzeuge geflogen und war Reservepilot des Army Air Corps. Er hatte Geschäftsleute aus St. Louis dazu gebracht, seine in San Diego gebaute Ryan-Maschine zu finanzieren, deren Kraftstofftank so groß war, daß er ihm alle Sicht nach vorn nahm. Unmittelbar vor seinem Atlantikflug vom 19. Mai 1927 hatte er einen Rekordflug über den amerikanischen Kontinent unternommen.

Un concurrent modeste

Charles A. Lindbergh (**1**) a les qualités du héros américain idéal: grand, soigné, de belle prestance et laconique. Élevé dans le Minnesota, ce pilote d'aéropostale et réserviste de l'Armée de l'Air de 25 ans utilise ses contacts dans le milieu des affaires de St Louis pour financer son Ryan construit à San Diego, dont le réservoir d'essence occupait tout l'avant. Il venait d'effectuer une traversée «coast to coast» des États-Unis avant son vol transatlantique du 19 mai 1927.

Hero worship

Rarely before or since has America given so much
adulation to one person as to Charles Lindbergh. The
ticker-tape welcome to New York (**2**) after his epic flight
was unprecedented. Within weeks he was stirring aviation
fever on tours across America. He went on to be a
consultant to three airlines, advised Transcontinental Air
Transport (later TWA), became an unofficial US
ambassador and made headlines again when his child was
kidnapped and murdered. He quit America in disgust in
1935; returning in 1941, he was reviled as a fascist and
isolationist.

Heldenverehrung

Kaum je zuvor oder je wieder hat Amerika einen Mann
so gefeiert wie Charles Lindbergh. Eine Begrüßung mit
einem Menschenauflauf und Konfettiwirbel wie diesem
bei seiner Rückkehr vom heroischen Ozeanflug hatte New
York noch nicht gesehen (**2**). Wochenlang war er auf dem
Kontinent unterwegs und schürte das Flugfieber, wohin er
kam. Er wurde Berater bei drei Luftfahrtgesellschaften,
darunter dem Transcontinental Air Service (der späteren
TWA), und war inoffizieller amerikanischer Botschafter;
später machte er von neuem Schlagzeilen, als sein Sohn
entführt und ermordet wurde. 1935 kehrte er Amerika
enttäuscht den Rücken, und als er 1941 zuruckkehrte,
wurde er als Faschist und Defätist beschimpft.

L'adoration du héros

L'Amérique a rarement adulé quelqu'un autant que
Charles Lindbergh, et son accueil à New York (**2**) est
sans précédent. En quelques semaines, la tournée qu'il
effectue aux États-Unis enfiévra l'aviation. Il fut engagé
comme consultant de trois compagnies aériennes,
conseilla la Transcontinental Air Transport (future TWA),
devint un ambassadeur officieux des États-Unis et fent
les gros titres des journaux du monde entier lors de
l'enlèvement et du meurtre de son fils. Dégoûté, il quitte
les États-Unis en 1935 ; lorsqu'il y reviendra en 1941, il
sera vilipendé comme fasciste et isolationniste.

2

Atlantic conqueror

Charles Lindbergh was, in fact, the 92nd person to cross the Atlantic by air, but the first to do it alone, direct, and over a record 3,590 miles. He battled storms, ice and exhaustion in the 33-hour 39-minute flight in his Ryan (**1**). His reception at Le Bourget, where he met Louis Blériot, conqueror of the channel 18 years earlier, was tumultuous (**2**). The adulation grew: thousands waited for him at Croydon Aerodrome (**3**) when he flew from Paris to London on 29 May 1927.

Der Bezwinger des Atlantiks

Genau genommen war Charles Lindbergh schon der 92., der den Atlantik mit einem Luftfahrzeug überquerte, doch er war der erste, dem es im Alleinflug ohne Zwischen-landung und über die Rekorddistanz von 5.780 Kilometern gelang. Mit seiner Ryan-Maschine widerstand er Stürmen, Eis und Müdigkeit und war 33 Stunden, 39 Minuten in der Luft (**1**). In Le Bourget wurde er enthusiastisch gefeiert, unter anderem von Louis Blériot, der 18 Jahre zuvor den Ärmelkanal bezwungen hatte (**2**). Mit jeder Station wurde die Begrüßung stürmischer: Tausende warteten auf dem Flugfeld von Croydon (**3**), als er am 29. Mai 1927 von Paris nach London kam.

Le conquérant de l'Atlantique

Si Charles Lindbergh est en réalité le 92e pilote à traverser l'Atlantique par la voie des airs, il est le premier à le faire en solo, sans escale et sur la distance record de 5 780 km. Ayant passé 33 h 39 dans son Ryan (**1**), il dut lutter contre les orages, le froid et la fatigue. Sa réception à l'aérodrome du Bourget, où il rencontre Louis Blériot (**2**), vain-queur de la Manche 18 ans plus tôt, fut pour le moins tumultueuse. Des milliers de personnes l'attendaient également sur l'aérodrome de Croydon (**3**) lorsqu'il se rendit à Londres depuis Paris, le 29 mai 1927.

New York to Berlin
Transatlantic competitors Clarence
Chamberlin and Charles Levine
finally crossed the Atlantic on 6
June 1927 in the Wright/Bellanca
plane Lindbergh had wanted to
buy. Their record 3,911-mile flight
ended 100 miles short of Berlin.
But they eventually reached the
capital (1), where Chamberlin was
carried aloft (2).

Von New York nach Berlin
Clarence Chamberlin und Charles
Levine, die ebenfalls zum
Transatlantik-Wettflug angetreten
waren, gelang die Überquerung am
6. Juni 1927 mit der Wright/Bel-
lanca-Maschine, die Lindbergh
ursprünglich kaufen wollte. Mit
6.300 Kilometern stellten sie einen
neuen Rekord auf, auch wenn sie
160 Kilometer vor Berlin zwischen-
landen mußten. Die Berliner hoben
Chamberlin auf die Schultern (2),
als sie am Ende doch noch in der
Hauptstadt eintrafen (1).

De New York à Berlin
Clarence Chamberlin et Charles
Levine traversèrent finalement
l'Atlantique le 6 juin 1927 à
bord d'un Wright/Bellanca, que
Lindbergh avait d'ailleurs voulu
acheter. Leur vol de 6 300 km, une
distance record, s'acheva à 160 km
de Berlin. Ils parvinrent toutefois
à rejoindre la capitale allemande
(1) où Chamberlin fut porté en
triomphe (2).

Record-breaking Australian

Over 18 years of flying, World War I pilot Charles Kingsford Smith (**3**, centre left) held 11 aviation records. His epic 1928 California–Australia flight in his Fokker FVIIB *Southern Cross* was perhaps the best known, but he and co-pilot Charles Ulm (**3**, centre right) broke many other long-distance records, including Australia to London in July 1929, and the first global flight. Modest and meticulous, 'Smithy' was knighted, but was lost off Burma in 1933.

Der australische Rekordhalter

In 18 Flugjahren stellte Charles Kingsford Smith (**3**, Mitte links), Veteran des Ersten Weltkriegs, 11 Weltrekorde auf. Sein größter Erfolg war wohl der Flug von Kalifornien nach Australien, den er 1928 mit seiner Fokker FVIIB *Southern Cross* unternahm, doch er und Kopilot Charles Ulm (**3**, Mitte rechts) brachen auch viele andere Langstreckenrekorde, darunter mit einem Flug von Australien nach London im Juli 1929, und unternahmen den ersten Flug rund um die Welt. »Smithy«, ein gewissenhafter, bescheidener Mann, der für seine Leistungen geadelt wurde, ist 1933 vor der Küste von Birma verschollen.

Un record australien

Ayant volé plus de 18 années, notamment pendant la guerre, Charles Kingsford-Smith (**3**, au centre à gauche) détenait 11 records d'aviation. Si son vol épique entre la Californie et l'Australie à bord de son Fokker FVIIB *Southern Cross* est sans doute le plus célèbre, il était titulaire de bien d'autres records de vol long-courrier avec son copilote Charles Ulm (**3**, au centre à droite), dont Australie-Londres en juillet 1929 et le premier vol autour du monde. Modeste et consciencieux, «Smithy» fut anobli avant de disparaître en Birmanie en 1933.

3

Front-rank women

Women flyers were increasingly acceptable by the late 1920s. Mrs Keith Miller (**1**), wife of an Australian journalist, flew from London to Australia with Captain William Lancaster in October 1927. The Dutch airline KLM hired the long-distance aviator Lady Heath as its first woman pilot in 1928 (**2**). The German Christel Schulthes demonstrated her mechanical knowledge (**3**).

Prominente Frauen

Ende der zwanziger Jahre hatten Fliegerinnen keine Schwierigkeiten mehr, sich durchzusetzen. Mrs. Keith Miller (**1**), die Frau eines australischen Journalisten, flog mit Captain William Lancaster im Oktober 1927 von London nach Australien. Die holländische Fluglinie KLM stellte 1928 die Langstreckenfliegerin Lady Heath als ersten weiblichen Piloten an (**2**). Christel Schulthes aus Deutschland (**3**) zeigt, daß sie auch etwas von Motoren versteht.

Des femmes de premier plan

Vers la fin des années 1920, les femmes sont de mieux en mieux acceptées dans le milieu de l'aviation. Keith Miller (**1**), épouse d'un journaliste australien, vola de Londres en Australie avec le capitaine William Lancaster en octobre 1927. Un an plus tard, la compagnie néerlandaise KLM engageait la première femme pilote de ligne, l'aviatrice Lady Heath (**2**). L'Allemande Christel Schulthes fait ici la preuve de ses compétences techniques (**3**).

Star quality

Pilot Ruth Elder angered women's groups for attracting more attention to herself than to aviation. In October 1927 – her hairstyle prompting a vogue for 'Ruth ribbons' (4) – she admitted that her flight instructor would do most of the flying on her transatlantic flight that was aborted in the Azores. Shown signing autographs at Le Bourget (5), she married six times and developed a movie career.

Der Star der Flugplätze

Die Pilotin Ruth Elder war den Frauengruppen ein Dorn im Auge, weil sie stets sich selbst und nicht das Fliegen in den Vordergrund stellte. Im Oktober 1927 – als »Ruth ribbons«, ihre Frisur mit dem Stirnband, überall große Mode waren (4) – gab sie zu, daß bei ihrem Atlantikflug, den sie auf den Azoren aufgab, ihr Fluglehrer die meiste Arbeit getan hatte. Elder, die hier (5) Autogramme auf dem Flughafen Le Bourget gibt, war sechsmal verheiratet und machte auch Karriere beim Film.

Une star

Ruth Elder, qui signe ici des autographes au Bourget (5), irrita certaines aviatrices en attirant plus l'attention sur elle que sur l'aviation. En octobre 1927, lançant la mode de la coiffure au «ruban» (4), elle admit que son instructeur de vol avait piloté la plus grande partie du temps lors de son vol transatlantique qui se termina aux Açores. Elle se maria six fois et fit une carrière cinématographique.

First flight to India

India, the 'Jewel' of the British Empire, demanded a lot of effort for aviation. The first aircraft there from England was an RAF Vickers 0/400, which departed on 28 July 1918 and arrived at Delhi (**1**) via Cairo and Baghdad on 12 December. A second flight begun that month by a four-engined V/1500 was so perilous that it was ten years before passenger flights to India became regular and more comfortable.

Der erste Indienflug

Nach Indien, dem »Kronjuwel« des Britischen Empire, zu fliegen, war nicht leicht. Die erste Maschine, die es von England aus versuchte, war eine Vickers 0/400 der Royal Air Force, die am 28. Juli 1918 aufbrach und nach einem Flug über Kairo und Bagdad am 12. Dezember in Delhi eintraf (**1**). Eine zweite Mannschaft brach im selben Monat mit einer viermotorigen V/1500 auf, doch der Flug erwies sich als so gefährlich, daß erst zehn Jahre später regelmäßigere und bequemere Passagierflüge nach Indien aufgenommen wurden.

Premier vol aux Indes

La desserte de l'Inde, «joyau» de l'Empire britannique, obligea l'aviation britannique à faire beaucoup d'efforts. Le premier avion à y parvenir depuis l'Angleterre était un Vickers 0/400 de la RAF qui, parti le 28 juillet 1918, arriva à Delhi (**1**) via Le Caire et Bagdad le 12 décembre. La seconde tentative, entreprise le même mois par un quadrimoteur V/1500, fut si périlleuse qu'il fallut attendre dix ans avant que la ligne pour passagers soit sûre et assurée avec régularité.

Imperial standards

Britain's Imperial Airways started in 1927 with the new Armstrong Whitworth Argosy (**1**), offering 20 passengers a first-class buffet, silver service, waiter and hot soup on the London to Paris route. It also carried mail (**2**). The De Havilland Hercules (**3**) carried seven passengers and mailbags over harsh routes to the Middle East and India.

Eines Weltreichs würdig

Die britischen Imperial Airways stellten 1927 die neue Armstrong Whitworth Argosy in Dienst (**1**), die auf der Strecke London – Paris 20 Passagieren ein erstklassiges Buffet mit Silberbesteck, Steward und sogar warmer Suppe bot. Sie beförderte auch Post (**2**). Die De Havilland Hercules (**3**) flog sieben Passagiere sowie Postsäcke über schwierige Routen im Nahen Osten und in Indien.

La classe impériale

Les Imperial Airways, compagnie aérienne britannique, ouvrit ses premières lignes en 1927 avec le nouvel Armstrong Whitworth Argosy (**1**), offrant aux 20 passagers de Londres-Paris un buffet luxueux, un service haut-de-gamme avec maître d'hôtel et des plats chauds. L'avion transportait aussi le courrier (**2**). Le De Havilland Hercules (**3**) transportait sept passagers et des sacs postaux sur la difficile ligne du Moyen-Orient et des Indes.

Anniversary celebrations

In 1929 the French Air Union's Golden Ray fleet celebrated the tenth anniversary of the London–Paris passenger service. Passengers boarded Breguet and Blériot planes at Le Bourget (**1**), and champagne was poured on a flight to Croydon (**2**). Three years later London chorus girls helped to inaugurate a new Golden Ray service to Le Touquet (**3**). The design of cockpits evolved slowly, hampered by inadequate atmospheric sensors.

Ein Grund zum Feiern

1929 feierte die Golden Ray-Flotte der French Air Union das zehnjährige Bestehen des Passagierdienstes London – Paris. Die Gäste gingen in Le Bourget an Bord der Breguet- und Blériot-Maschinen (**1**), und während des Flugs nach Croydon wurde Champagner ausgeschenkt (**2**). Drei Jahre darauf legen Londoner Tänzerinnen bei der Einführung einer neuen Golden Ray-Linie nach Le Touquet Hand mit an (**3**). Cockpits entwickelten sich nur langsam, denn es gab nach wie vor keine verläßlichen Druckmesser.

Anniversaires

En 1929, le service Le Rayon d'Or « Golden Ray » de la compagnie française Air Union célébrait le dixième anniversaire de sa ligne Paris-Londres. Les passagers embarquaient au Bourget à bord des Breguet ou des Blériot (**1**), où du champagne leur était servi avant d'arriver à Croydon (**2**). Trois ans plus tard, les girls de Londres participaient à l'inauguration d'un nouveau service Le Rayon d'Or au départ du Touquet (**3**). Les problèmes de pressurisation freinèrent longtemps l'évolution des cockpits.

Golden age of flying boats

Long sea transits and a shortage of Third World airfields encouraged development of flying boats. A three-engined, 15-seat Shorts' Calcutta was inspected by Members of Parliament in London in 1928 (**1**). Less commercially successful was Germany's 12-engined Dornier DO-X, seen in New York on a round-the-world trip in 1931 (**2**). In October 1929 it carried a record 150 passengers, a crew of ten and nine stowaways.

Die Goldene Zeit der Flugboote

Lange Flugzeiten über dem Meer und der Mangel an Flugfeldern in der dritten Welt legten die Entwicklung von Flugbooten nahe. 1928 inspizieren englische Parlamentarier in London die dreimotorige, 15sitzige Calcutta von Short (**1**). Kommerziell weniger erfolgreich war die deutsche Dornier DO-X mit ihren zwölf Motoren, die hier 1931 bei einer Weltumrundung in New York Station macht (**2**). Im Oktober 1929 beförderte sie die Rekordzahl von 150 Reisenden, zehn Besatzungsmitgliedern und neun blinden Passagieren.

L'âge d'or des hydravions

La longueur des vols transocéaniques et le manque d'aérodromes dans le tiers monde encouragèrent le développement des hydravions, comme ce trimoteur Short Calcutta de 15 places, posé sur la Tamise devant le Parlement de Londres en 1928 (**1**). Le Dornier DO-X allemand, à douze moteurs, que l'on voit ici à New York lors de son tour du monde en 1931 (**2**), eut un succès commercial moindre. En octobre 1929, il transporta le nombre record de 150 passagers, dix membres d'équipage… et neuf clandestins.

Lure of the sea

Flying boats were advertised as just that – more boat and less aeroplane. Workers at the Short Brothers seaplane works at Rochester, England, in 1927 checked the ship-like 'port-holes' of a new Calcutta flying boat (**1**), while others worked on the spacious saloon (**2**). Unlike narrow-bodied land-based passenger planes, the Calcutta had room for 15 passengers and a 'refreshment buffet' at one end, presided over by a uniformed steward. The RAF, which found flying boats invaluable for empire duties, flew five of them at an air show in Hendon, London, in June 1930 (**3**).

Flugzeug ahoi

Die Werbung für Flugboote stellte den Bootscharakter heraus. Arbeiter im Wasserflugzeugwerk der Gebrüder Short in Rochester, England, überprüfen 1927 die »Bull-augen« eines neuen Calcutta-Flugboots (**1**), andere statten den geräumigen Salon aus (**2**). Anders als die schmalen Landflugzeuge bot die Calcutta nicht nur Platz für 15 Passagiere, sondern sogar für ein »Erfrischungsbuffet«, an dem ein uniformierter Steward die Reisenden bediente. Die Royal Air Force, der die Flugboote bei ihren Aufgaben rund um den Erdball eine unschätzbare Hilfe waren, zeigt eine Fünferformation bei der Luftfahrtschau in Hendon bei London, Juni 1930 (**3**).

Le charme du vol en mer

Les hydravions étaient considérés, et annoncés, comme des paquebots volants. En 1927, ces ouvriers de l'usine d'hydravions Short Brothers de Rochester (Angleterre) vérifient les hublots du nouvel hydravion Calcutta (**1**), tandis que d'autres aménagent le spacieux salon (**2**). Contrairement aux avions à fuselage étroit, le Calcutta offrait un espace suffisant pour 15 personnes et une « buvette », assurée par un steward en uniforme. La RAF, qui appréciait l'hydravion pour accomplir ses missions dans l'Empire, effectue ici un vol de démonstration lors d'un meeting aérien à Hendon en juin 1930 (**3**).

Zeppelin appeal

Germany's Zeppelins commanded enormous respect from the allies, and both America and France demanded at least one as war reparations. ZR-1 went to America and was rechristened *Shenandoah* at Lakehurst, New Jersey, in October 1923 (**1**). The next year the famed Zeppelin captain Hugo Eckener (**3**, centre) posed with his crew at Friedrichshafen before flying ZR-3 to America. Renamed the *Los Angeles*, it flew over Washington DC in late 1924 (**2**). The *Shenandoah* broke up over Ohio in September 1925, killing 14 of its crew. France's reparation airship, *Dixmunde*, crashed in December 1923, killing all 50 crew.

Zeppelin-Appeal

Vor den deutschen Zeppelinen hatten die Alliierten einen gewaltigen Respekt, und die Vereinigten Staaten und Frankreich forderten nach dem Ersten Weltkrieg Luftschiffe als Teil der Reparationsleistungen. Das ZR-1 ging nach Amerika und wurde im Oktober 1923 in Lakehurst, New Jersey, in *Shenandoah* umgetauft (**1**). Im folgenden Jahr nimmt der berühmte Luftschiffkapitän Hugo Eckener (**3**, Mitte) mit seiner Mannschaft in Friedrichshafen vor der ZR-3 Aufstellung, bevor er sie nach Amerika überführt. Das Schiff, nun *Los Angeles* genannt, ist Ende 1924 über Washington, D.C., zu sehen (**2**). Die *Shenandoah* zerbrach im September 1925 bei einem Flug über Ohio, und 14 der Besatzungsmitglieder kamen um. Beim Absturz des französischen Reparationsschiffs *Dixmunde* im Dezember 1923 fanden alle 50 Insassen den Tod.

L'attrait des zeppelins

Les zeppelins allemands s'étant attiré le respect des Alliés, la France et les États-Unis en réclamèrent chacun un au titre des réparations de guerre. Le ZR-1 partit aux États-Unis où il fut rebaptisé *Shenandoah* à Lakehurst (New Jersey) en octobre 1923 (**1**). L'année suivante, le célèbre capitaine de zeppelin Hugo Eckener (**3**, au centre) posait avec son équipage à Friedrichshafen avant de convoyer le ZR-3 en Amérique. Rebaptisé le *Los Angeles*, il survola Washington à la fin de l'année 1924 (**2**). Après le *Dixmunde*, le dirigeable attribué à la France qui s'écrasa en décembre 1923 en tuant la totalité du personnel de bord (50 personnes), le *Shenandoah* se disloqua dans l'Ohio en septembre 1925 avec ses 14 membres d'équipage.

British airship

The R 100 was British industry's attempt to compete in the long-range luxury airship business. The strong geodetic structure of the 709-foot airship, seen at Howden, Yorkshire, in 1927 (**1**), was designed by Barnes Wallis and later used for Wellington bombers. The R 100 was ready for its maiden flight at Cardington, Bedfordshire, in late 1929 (**3**). Its huge size was overshadowed by the new *Graf Zeppelin*, landing nearby in 1930 (**2**).

Das Luftschiff der Briten

Die R 100 war der Versuch der britischen Industrie, im Geschäft mit luxuriösen Langstrecken-Luftschiffen mitzubieten. Das kräftige geodätische Gerüst des 216 Meter langen Schiffes, hier 1927 beim Bau in Howden, Yorkshire (**1**), war von Barnes Wallis entworfen und bildete später die Grundlage des Wellington-Bombers. Ende 1929 war die R 100 in Cardington, Bedfordshire, zum Jungfernflug bereit (**3**). Bei aller Größe wird sie doch von dem neuen Luftschiff *Graf Zeppelin*, das 1930 gleich neben ihr landete, noch in den Schatten gestellt (**2**).

Les dirigeables britanniques

Le R 100 devait permettre aux Britanniques de pénétrer le marché des dirigeables long-courriers de luxe. La robuste structure géodésique de ce dirigeable de 216 m, ici à Howden (Yorkshire) en 1927 (**1**), avait été dessinée par Barnes Wallis et fut reprise ensuite pour les bombardiers Wellington. Le R 100 s'apprête à effectuer son vol inaugural à Cardington (Bedforshire) à la fin de 1929 (**3**). Ses vastes dimensions n'ont cependant rien de comparable avec le nouveau gigantesque *Graf Zeppelin* allemand, posé près de lui en 1930 (**2**).

1

Luxury unlimited

The R100 was built to compete with the great ocean liners. Its hugely successful maiden voyage in July 1930 took 79 hours to Montreal, carrying 44 passengers in luxury that included a verandah deck (**1**) and a grand dining room (**2**). A privately funded enterprise, it competed with the government-built airship, the ill-fated R101.

Luxus ohne Grenzen

Die R100 sollte es mit den großen Ozeanschiffen aufnehmen. Der ausgesprochen erfolgreiche Jungfernflug im Juli 1930 brachte 44 Passagiere in 79 Stunden nach Montreal, und das in einem Luxus, zu dem ein Verandadeck (**1**) und ein großer Speisesaal (**2**) gehörten. Dieses privat gebaute Schiff konkurrierte mit der staatlichen R101, der ein weniger günstiges Schicksal beschieden war.

Un luxe inouï

Le R100 fut construit pour concurrencer les grands paquebots de luxe, avec un pont promenade vitré (**1**) et une vaste salle à manger (**2**). En juillet 1930, son voyage inaugural, très réussi, lui permit de rallier Montreal en 79 h avec 44 passagers. Appartenant à une compagnie privée, il fut le concurrent direct du malheureux dirigeable R101 construit par le gouvernement.

The ultimate Zeppelin

No airship was ever better than the *Graf Zeppelin*, the biggest at 775 feet. Its gondola (**2**) contained a luxury lounge (**1**), well-equipped kitchens (**3**), and beautifully appointed cabins (**4**). Its captain, Hugo Eckener, returned to Germany a hero after a ticker-tape parade in New York marked its inaugural voyage in October 1928.

Das Nonplusultra

Kein Luftschiff konnte es mit der *Graf Zeppelin* aufnehmen, die mit 236 Metern das größte überhaupt war. In der Gondel (**2**) befanden sich ein luxuriöser Aufenthaltsraum (**1**), eine gut ausgestattete Küche (**3**) und liebevoll gestaltete Kabinen (**4**). Kapitän Hugo Eckener, dem bei der Jungfernfahrt im Oktober 1928 in New York ein triumphaler Empfang bereitet wurde, kehrte als Held nach Deutschland zurück.

Le dernier zeppelin

Aucun dirigeable ne surpassa jamais le *Graf Zeppelin*, le plus grand de tous avec 236 m de long. Sa nacelle (**2**) abritait un salon luxueux (**1**), des cuisines bien équipées (**3**) et de magnifiques cabines (**4**). Son capitaine, Hugo Eckener, revint en héros en Allemagne après la traditionnelle parade dans les rues de New York à l'issue de son voyage inaugural en octobre 1928.

Großer Aufenthaltsraum

Küche mit elektrischer Heizung

Fahrgast-Kabine für die Nacht gerichtet

Cup Final surprise

Arsenal was playing Huddersfield in the Cup Final at Wembley, London, in 1930, when the *Graf Zeppelin* created a tremendous distraction (**5**). The airship was the first to travel around the world. It flew until 1938, just after its sister ship, the *Hindenburg*, met its fiery death.

Ablenkung vom Fußball

1930 ist im Londoner Wembley-Stadion das Meisterschaftsendspiel Arsenal gegen Huddersfield in vollem Gange, als die *Graf Zeppelin* über dem Sportfeld auftaucht und für helle Aufregung sorgt (**5**). Das Luftschiff war das erste, das die Welt umrundete, und flog bis 1938; der Betrieb wurde eingestellt, nachdem das Schwesterschiff *Hindenburg* in Flammen aufgegangen war.

La surprise du championnat

En 1930, Arsenal jouait contre Huddersfield dans la finale de la Coupe à Wembley, lorsque l'arrivée du *Graf Zeppelin* créa une formidable surprise (**5**). Ce dirigeable était le premier à avoir effectué le tour du monde. Il resta en service jusqu'en 1938, juste après l'embrasement de son «jumeau», le *Hindenburg*

5

Lightest of the light

Flying as a sport became increasingly popular in the early 1930s, when private pilots often learned to fly in gliders. An Austin Seven car helped launch one lady at Hanworth aerodrome, London, in 1931 (**1**), while near Paris a glider 'pigeon' landed in a field (**2**). On the Sussex Downs, England, in 1931, foreign entrants to a British Gliding Association competition received directions over a tiny Scud glider (**3**). In 1934 skilled pilot Miss Joan Meakin arrived at Heston, London, after a towed flight from Frankfurt (**4**). Herr Hentzen's glider *Vampyr* was a world champion (**5**).

Leichter denn je

In den frühen dreißiger Jahren wurde Fliegen als Freizeitvergnügen immer beliebter, und Privatleute lernten es in Segelflugzeugen. Auf dem Flugfeld von Hanworth, London, hilft 1931 ein Austin Seven einer Dame in die Luft (**1**), und bei Paris ist eine »Taube« im Feld niedergegangen (**2**). Auf den Sussex Downs in England veranstaltete die British Gliding Association Wettbewerbe, und auswärtige Teilnehmer bekommen 1931 auf der Tragfläche eines winzigen Scud-Seglers die Topographie erklärt (**3**). 1934 ließ sich Miss Joan Meakin, eine geschickte Fliegerin, in einem Segler von Frankfurt nach London ziehen; das Bild zeigt sie bei der Ankunft auf dem Flugplatz Heston (**4**). Hentzen errang mit seinem *Vampyr* weltweit Preise (**5**).

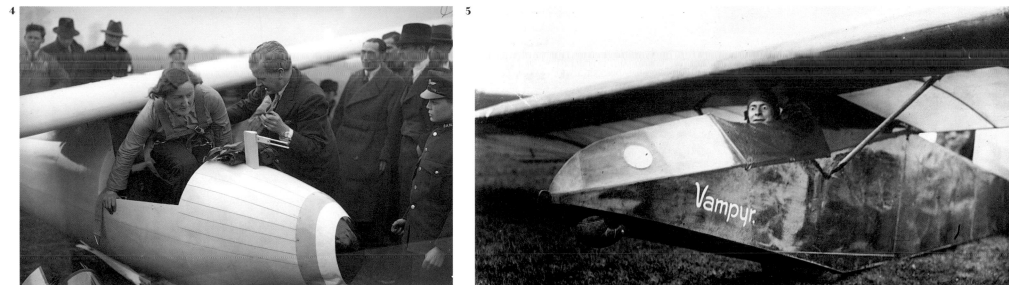

Les ultra-légers

L'aviation de loisirs avait gagné une certaine popularité au début des années 1930, et les pilotes privés se mirent au planeur. Cette Austin Seven tracte un Lady au décollage de l'aérodrome de Hanworth (Londres) en 1931 (**1**) tandis qu'un «Pigeon» atterrit dans un champ près de Paris (**2**). Dans les Sussex Downs (Angleterre), des concurrents étrangers sur un petit planeur Scud reçoivent leurs consignes lors de la compétition organisée en 1931 par la British Gliding Association (**3**). En 1934, Joan Meakin, une femme pilote d'expérience, arrive à Heston (Londres) après un vol tracté depuis Francfort (**4**). Le planeur *Vampyr* de Hentzen fut sacré champion du monde de vol à voile (**5**).

Fun and prizes

Owners of light aircraft loved to share their joy of flying in the 1920s. A group of British flyers 'nipped across' to France for the fun of a countryside picnic (**1**). At Lympne, Kent, in October 1924, light aeroplanes were lined up for the start of the Grosvenor Cup race (**2**). That year the British government helped to finance new flying clubs to encourage private flying. The long-term effect was to provide a pool of pilots who were desperately needed when war broke out in 1939.

Zum Spaß oder um die Trophäe

Wer in den zwanziger Jahren ein Leichtflugzeug hatte, flog gern mit anderen gemeinsam. Hier hat ein britisches Grüppchen einen »Ausflug« zum Picknick in Frankreich gemacht (**1**). In Lympne, Kent, sind im Oktober 1924 Leichtflugzeuge zum Wettflug um den Grosvenor-Pokal angetreten (**2**). Im selben Jahr begann die britische Regierung Fliegerclubs finanziell zu unterstützen, damit mehr Privatleute den Pilotenschein machten. Das Reservoir an Fliegern, das so entstand, hatte das Land 1939, als wieder der Krieg ausbrach, bitter nötig.

Aviation de loisirs et de compétition
Les possesseurs d'avions légers des années 1920 aimaient à faire partager leur plaisir de voler.
Ce groupe de Britanniques est venu en France pour le plaisir d'un pique-nique (**1**). Des
aéroplanes légers s'alignent à Lympne (Kent) au départ de la Grosvenor Cup en octobre 1924 (**2**).
Cette année-là, le gouvernement participa au financement de nouveaux aéro-clubs pour
encourager l'aviation privée. Cette mesure permit, à long terme, de fournir le contingent
de pilotes nécessaire au moment de la déclaration de guerre en 1939.

Joyriders
Redundant young World War I pilots all over Europe and
America tried to keep in practice by offering joyrides to the
public. Camping at Canvey Island, England, offered something
extra with a trip in an Avro 504 in 1923 (**1**).

Ein Rundflug
Arbeitslose Weltkriegspiloten schlugen sich überall in Europa
und Amerika damit durch, daß sie Vergnügungsflüge veranstalteten. Der Campingplatz von Canvey Island, England, bot
1923 einen Rundflug mit einer Avro 504 als zusätzliche
Attraktion (**1**).

Baptêmes de l'air
Les jeunes pilotes européens et américains de la Première
Guerre mondiale continuèrent de pratiquer en proposant des
baptêmes de l'air au public. En 1923, au camping à Canvey
Island (Angleterre) s'ajoute le plaisir d'une promenade à bord
d'un Avro 504 (**1**).

Female interest

'Two of the fair sex' were reported to be interested in an engine at Lympne, Kent, in 1926 (**2**), while in 1931 Miss D. Spicer was photographed starting her plane at the first All Women's Flying Meeting in Northamptonshire (**3**). 'Ladies lunching' at a garden party of the London Aeroplane Club at Hatfield in 1929 attracted attention (**4**).

Das schöne Geschlecht

»Zwei Vertreterinnen des schönen Geschlechts« interessieren sich, wie es in der Unterschrift zu diesem Bild heißt, 1926 für einen Motor in Lympne, Kent (**2**), und Miss D. Spicer fotografiert, wie sie beim ersten Frauen-Flugtreffen in Northamptonshire ihren Propeller anwirft (**3**). Der »Damentisch« war eine Attraktion der Gartenparty des London Aeroplane Club in Hatfield, 1929 (**4**).

Les femmes aussi

Ces deux personnes du «sexe faible» semblent très intéressées par le moteur à Lympne (Kent) en 1926 (**2**). En 1931, Miss D. Spicer doit lancer seule le moteur de son avion lors du premier All Women's Flying Meeeting de Northamptonshire (**3**). Ces aviatrices se détendent en pique-nique lors d'une garden party du London Aeroplane Club de Hatfield, en 1929 (**4**).

The barnstormers

In the early 1920s, when war-surplus planes and pilots flooded America and Europe, barnstormers competed to thrill the public. The daredevil exploits of the American Lillian Boyer (**1**) could command up to $3,000 a day. Most, however, earned less in a year. As time went on, stormers took on ever more dangerous stunts to maintain interest and income. In 1924, Gladys Roy (**2**) of Los Angeles walked the wing of her plane blindfolded.

Die Flugartisten

In den frühen zwanziger Jahren, als es überall in Europa und Amerika überschüssige Kriegsmaschinen und arbeitslose Piloten gab, wetteiferten die Flugartisten um die Gunst des Publikums. Die Amerikanerin Lillian Boyer konnte für ihre waghalsigen Kunststücke (**1**) bis zu $ 3.000 pro Tag verlangen, doch die meisten verdienten weniger als das im ganzen Jahr. Im Laufe der Zeit ließen sich die Artisten immer gefährlichere Nummern einfallen, um die Aufmerksamkeit des Publikums und ihr Einkommen zu halten. 1924 spazierte Gladys Roy (**2**) aus Los Angeles mit verbundenen Augen über die Tragfläche ihrer Maschine.

Les cascadeurs

Le début des années 1920 voit affluer en Europe et aux États-Unis des avions provenant des surplus de guerre et des anciens pilotes, certains se reconvertissant en cascadeurs. Les exploits de l'acrobate américaine Lillian Boyer (**1**) pouvaient lui rapporter jusqu'à 3 000 $ par jour, soit plus que ce que gagnaient en un an la plupart des aviateurs. Les cascades durent se faire de plus en plus dangereuses pour conserver l'attention du public; ainsi Gladys Roy (**2**), de Los Angeles, qui marche les yeux bandés sur les ailes de son biplan en 1924.

Barely hanging on
Hanging by his heels, the French barnstormer Vassard (**4**) played with death. Stuntman Schindler (**3**) was not so lucky. As he climbed from one plane on to the ladder of another near Berlin, the planes became entangled and crashed. All the occupants were killed.

Mit einem Bein im Grabe
Der französische Flugartist Vassard (**4**) riskiert sein Leben, als er sich kopfunter an die Tragfläche hängt. Der Stuntman Schindler (**3**) hatte weniger Glück. Als er bei Berlin von einem Flugzeug auf die Leiter eines anderen steigen wollte, berührten sich die Maschinen, und beide stürzten ab. Alle Beteiligten kamen um.

Travail sans filet
Accroché par les talons, le cascadeur français Vassard (**4**) joue avec la mort. Schindler (**3**) ne fut pas si chanceux ; alors qu'il montait à l'échelle pour passer d'un avion à un autre, en plein vol, près de Berlin, les deux appareils se heurtèrent et s'écrasèrent, tuant tous leurs occupants.

'Amy, wonderful Amy'

A popular song of that name marked the tremendous excitement of the British public after 26-year-old Amy Johnson returned to Britain following a record-breaking 19-day solo flight to Australia in May 1930. She waved to a huge crowd in Australia (**2**) and her tiny De Havilland Gipsy Moth attracted much attention back at Croydon airport (**1**).

»Amy, wonderful Amy«

Daß sie in Music-Hall-Liedern besungen wurde, gibt einen Begriff davon, welche Begeisterung die 26jährige Amy Johnson im britischen Publikum weckte, als sie im Mai 1930 von ihrem 19tägigen Alleinflug nach Australien – ein neuer Rekord – zurückkehrte. In Australien winkt sie den Menschen-mengen zu (**2**), und bei der Ankunft in Croydon wird die winzige De Havilland Gipsy Moth begeistert begrüßt (**1**).

« Amy, wonderful Amy »

Cette chanson populaire témoigne de la passion du public britannique pour Amy Johnson, aviatrice de 26 ans que l'on voit ici saluer la foule australienne (**2**). Son petit De Havilland Gipsy Moth éveilla la curiosité du public de Croydon à son retour d'un périple en solitaire de 19 jours de l'Angleterre à l'Australie, en mai 1930 (**1**).

Quiet heroine

Much of Amy Johnson's appeal lay in her modest character but determined love of aviation (3). When she left Croydon for Australia only her father and a couple of friends were there to say goodbye. An engineer from Hull, she turned down scores of lucrative offers; she died in England in 1941 when her military plane crashed.

Die stille Heldin

Ein Geheimnis von Amy Johnsons Erfolg war ihre bescheidene Art, ganz von der Liebe zum Fliegen bestimmt (3). Beim Aufbruch zum Australienflug waren nur ihr Vater und ein paar Freunde in Croydon, um sie zu verabschieden. Nach ihrer Rückkehr schlug die Ingenieurin aus Hull Dutzende attraktiver Angebote aus; 1941 fand sie in England beim Absturz mit einer Militärmaschine den Tod.

Une héroïne bien tranquille

Le charme d'Amy Johnson devait autant à sa modestie qu'à sa passion de l'aviation (3). Lorsqu'elle quitte Croydon pour l'Australie, seuls son père et un couple d'amis sont là pour lui dire au revoir. Ingénieur diplômée de Hull, elle refusa nombre d'offres lucratives et mourut en Angleterre en 1941 dans l'accident de son avion.

3

Legendary Earhart
Amelia Earhart, probably the world's most famous woman pilot, was a well-established air adventurer when she crossed the Atlantic as a passenger in a two-seat plane in 1928 (**2**). She achieved hero status in 1932 when she became the first woman to fly solo across the Atlantic after a perilous journey in a Lockheed Vega (**1**). But her enduring legend began in 1937 when she disappeared without trace over the Pacific.

Earhart – eine Legende
Amelia Earhart, wohl die berühmteste Pilotin aller Zeiten, hatte sich als Abenteurerin der Lüfte schon einen Namen gemacht, als sie als Kopilotin einer zweisitzigen Maschine 1928 den Atlantik überquerte (**2**). 1932 flog sie in einer gefährlichen Unternehmung mit einer Lockheed Vega als erste Frau allein über den Atlantik und wurde als Heldin gefeiert (**1**). Doch wirklich Legende wurde sie 1937, als sie spurlos über dem Pazifik verschwand.

Une figure de légende
Amelia Earhart, probablement la femme pilote la plus célèbre au monde, était déjà une aventurière de l'air lorsqu'elle traversa l'Atlantique en 1928 comme passagère à bord d'un avion biplace (**2**). Elle fut saluée en héros en devenant, en 1932, la première femme à franchir l'Atlantique en solo dans son Lockheed Vega (**1**). Sa disparition au-dessus du Pacifique en 1937 entretint sa légende.

2

Speed merchants

The Schneider Cup seaplane speed
competition, begun in 1911, reached its peak
in the late 1920s. Thousands watched at the
Venice Lido (2) in 1927 as Captain Fernando
Guazzetti flew a Macchi Fiat M52 overhead.
However, he retired with mechanical trouble
on the sixth of seven 50km laps. The winner
was a specially built British Supermarine S5
at a record speed of 281mph (1).

Geschwindigkeit ist alles

Der Wasserflugzeug-Geschwindigkeits-
wettbewerb um den Schneider-Pokal, erstmals 1911 veranstaltet, erreichte seinen
Höhepunkt Ende der zwanziger Jahre.
Tausende waren 1927 am Lido von Venedig
zusammengekommen (2), als Capitano
Fernando Guazzetti in einer Macchi Fiat
M52 über ihre Köpfe hinwegzog. Er mußte
allerdings in der sechsten von sieben
50-Kilometer-Runden wegen technischer
Schwierigkeiten ausscheiden. Siegerin war
eine eigens dafür gebaute britische Supermarine S5, die mit 452 Stundenkilometern
einen neuen Weltrekord aufstellte (1).

Marchands de vitesse

La Coupe Schneider, compétition réservée
aux hydravions, fut créée en 1911 et atteignit
son apogée à la fin des années 1920. Les
milliers de personnes rassemblées en 1927 au
Lido à Venise (2) assistèrent ainsi au passage
du capitaine Fernando Guazzetti, sur son
Macchi Fiat M52, qui dut abandonner la
course à cause d'un problème mécanique au
sixième des sept tours de 50 km. Le vainqueur fut un Supermarine S5 britannique à
la vitesse record de 452 km/h (1).

1

Final victory

The Schneider Cup ended up as a battle of national prestige to produce the fastest, most efficient engine and plane. In 1929, against a determined challenge from Italy, Britain entered Billy Mitchell's Supermarine S6. While women watched the race at Southampton, England (**1**), mechanics held on as the Supermarine's massive 1900hp Rolls Royce engine was revved (**3**). It easily beat the Italian Macchi.

Verdienter Triumph

Das Rennen um den Schneider-Pokal hatte sich immer mehr zum Wettbewerb der Nationen um die schnellste, tüchtigste Maschine und den besten Motor entwickelt. 1929 traten die Engländer gegen erbitterte italienische Konkurrenz mit Billy Mitchells Supermarine S6 an. Frauen sehen dem Rennen, das im englischen Southampton stattfindet, vom Strand aus zu (**1**), und Mechaniker halten die Supermarine fest, als ihr 1900-PS-Rolls-Royce-Motor aufdreht (**3**). Sie schlug die italienische Macchi mühelos.

Victoire finale

La Coupe Schneider devint un enjeu pour le prestige national, chaque pays s'attachant à produire le moteur et l'avion les plus rapides et les plus efficaces. En 1929, sous les yeux de ces jeunes femmes à Southampton (**1**), la Grande-Bretagne remporta facilement la coupe sur le Macchi italien grâce au Supermarine S6 de Billy Mitchell, un appareil surpuissant doté d'un énorme moteur Rolls-Royce de 1900 ch que les mécaniciens tiennent ici (**3**).

2

3

The future Spitfire
Only one aircraft entered the 1931 Schneider Cup contest. After a test flight Flight-Lieutenant F. Long was brought ashore (**2**) from the Supermarine S6b in which Flight-Lieutenant Boothman carried off the cup for Britain. His aircraft, with a 2350hp Rolls Royce engine, later set a world speed record of 406mph.

Die zukünftige Spitfire
Nur eine Maschine bewarb sich 1931 um den Pokal. Flight-Lieutenant F. Long wird nach einem Testflug mit der Supermarine S6b an Land gebracht (**2**); Flight-Lieutenant Boothman holte mit dieser Maschine den Pokal für England. Dasselbe Flugzeug mit seinem 2350-PS-Rolls-Royce-Motor stellte später einen neuen Geschwindigkeits-Weltrekord von 655 Stundenkilometern auf.

Le futur Spitfire
Un seul avion fut inscrit dans la Coupe Schneider de 1931. Après un essai en vol, le capitaine F. Long est débarqué (**2**) du Supermarine S6b dans lequel le capitaine Boothman remporta la coupe pour la Grande-Bretagne. Cet appareil, disposant d'un moteur Rolls-Royce de 2350 ch, établit par la suite le record de vitesse à 655 km/h.

8

Air Power Reveals
its Promise

'In the air there are no streets, no channels, no point where one can say of an antagonist "If he wants to reach my capital he must come by here." In the air all directions lead everywhere'
— H.G. Wells, *The War in the Air*

When Wells wrote that in 1908 aeroplanes had barely been invented, Blériot had yet to fly the English Channel, and only a tiny number of people had even the vaguest vision of air power. Ten years later, as World War I abruptly came to an end, it seemed that Wells's vision had already come true: the capital cities of Europe had suffered air attack, and bombing of industrial targets was an established strategy. This wholly new phenomenon of war involved fighters, anti-aircraft guns and bombers in operations quite removed from the traditional battlefields.

But who, apart from a few visionaries like Wells, actually understood the enormous new power of aviation? Not the politicians and the war-weary public, who had millions of dead and crippled soldiers to mourn, and economies to rebuild. The 'War to end all Wars' was over, and within months the air forces of the combatant nations had been slashed by demobilization or proscribed by the Versailles Treaty, their budgets massively reduced. Air forces struggled against the argument that air power was simply a support for land or sea operations over which the traditional services had full control.

In America, General William 'Billy' Mitchell, hero of the Saint Mihiel Salient assault, was reduced to rage by cutbacks and by the US Navy's insistence that bombers did not pose a threat to warships. He proved his point in 1921 and 1923 when his fighter-bombers sank captured German ships and submarines in tests, but the navy still refused to change its mind. He was court-martialled for insubordination in 1925 and resigned, but he preached the gospel of air power until his death 11 years later. In 1941 Japan's attack on Pearl Harbor vindicated him. As America sent bombers to fight in Europe, Congress awarded him a posthumous Medal of Honor.

Even the most impressive arguments for air power struggled for acceptance in the 1920s. In 1921, after the ideological 'father' of independent air power, the Italian General Giulio Douhet, wrote in *Command of the Air* that bombing alone could win a future war, he was court-martialled and demoted for criticizing government policy. But he was more fortunate than Mitchell. When Mussolini came to power in 1923 Douhet was recalled to head the new, autonomous Italian Air Force, the Regia Aeronautica, which was to focus more on bombers than fighters. Future leaders of the German Luftwaffe, however, focused more on supporting the army in offensive operations at their secret training base at Lipetsk, Russia, and never developed strategic bombers akin to those of Britain and the United States – a failing, some have suggested, that ultimately lost Germany World War II. France, determined to regain its leading role in aviation, maintained Europe's largest air force, but hedged its bets on all fronts, achieving autonomy for its air force only in 1934, and permitting funding and development of both bombers and fighters to drop to inadequate levels.

The debate was crucial to the development of aviation in the inter-war years. Again came the fundamental question: what were aeroplanes *for*? Civilian aircraft were increasingly built for safety, comfort and cost-efficiency, greatly helped by improvements in air-cooled radial engines in the 1920s. But that did not help the cash-strapped military. Britain, strongly influenced by a national desire not to repeat the horrors of trench warfare, and with air-force funding of only £11 million in 1922 – 17 per cent of the total British defence budget – chose a bomber strategy, even though it had failed to stop Zeppelins and Gothas from bombing its cities and killing civilians. The use of air power to strike at the heart of the enemy was being firmly established.

The prospect of aerial bombardment horrified and fascinated people throughout Europe. Public debate grew in France and Italy. In Britain, which in 1932 had twice as many bombers as fighters, the former Prime Minister Stanley Baldwin told the House of Commons: 'I think it is well for the man in the street to realize that there is no power on earth that can protect him … the bomber will always get through.'

Baldwin spoke before the terror bombings of German Stukas at Guernica in 1936, but without bombers Britain would not have been able to police the empire and its mandated territories successfully. Air control of Mesopotamia following the collapse of the Ottoman Empire in 1918 not only saved the British Army from deploying thousands of troops, but gave the RAF a vital new role in defence and a rationale for its existence. From Kurdistan to Yemen – less successfully in north-west India and Afghanistan – small wars and insurgencies by local tribesmen were combated by DH-9s, Bristol F2bs and Fairey IIID float-planes dropping bombs, strafing, and

Royal Air Force armoured cars, troop carriers, bombers and fighters took over control of Mesopotamia (Iraq) in 1922.

1922 übernahmen Panzerwagen, Truppentransporter, Bomber und Jäger der Royal Air Force die Kontrolle in Mesopotamien (Irak).

Les véhicules blindés, les transports de troupe, les bombardiers et les chasseurs de la RAF prennent le contrôle de la Mésopotamie (Irak) en 1922.

spotting for ground troops. France, Italy and Belgium also used planes for policing their colonies.

Some aircraft were designed only for colonial operations and general work. Italy's tri-motor Caproni 101, for instance, was used both for bombing in the Abyssinia campaign and for maintaining supplies. The CA133 ferried Italian paratroops to invade Albania, and the British Vickers Victoria troop transport evacuated 586 civilians out of Kabul during the Afghanistan rebellion of 1928–29.

At sea, while still ignoring Billy Mitchell's strategic air-power warnings, the US Navy pressed ahead with its aircraft carrier programmes for fleet defence, commissioning the *Saratoga* and *Lexington* in late 1927 and developing catapult launches. Japan rapidly assembled a carrier force, commissioning its first carrier, the *Hosho*, in 1922 and dropping bombs on Chinese airfields from the carrier *Kaga* in 1932.

For the civil world, air power reached beyond big airliners flying regular routes. In Canada, Russia and Australia tough little monoplanes and float-planes opened up territory never seen before. In the latter, aeroplanes went one better when the Reverend Dr John Flynn established the first Flying Doctor base at Cloncurry, Queensland, in 1928. With the aid of pedal-generated radio sets at isolated farming stations and using a QANTAS DH50 biplane, the service made 50 flights in its first year, saw 250 patients and logged 20,000 flying miles.

Technical advances in aviation were made. Lawrence Sperry, who had demonstrated the first automatic pilot in 1912, the first remote-controlled aerial torpedo for the navy in 1917, perfected a gyro horizon and directional gyro which in 1929 saw Lieutenant James Doolittle take off in a Consolidated NY-2 biplane, fly a specific course and land again completely blind, without any reference to the earth. That year the American Edward Link sold his first Link trainer, the world's first electrical-mechanical flight simulator. New meteorological services ensured ever safer flights.

Fresh ideas of propulsion took shape. In 1924 France's Oehmichen No. 2 made the first helicopter flight of a one-kilometre circle, and in 1928 a Spanish-designed Cierva autogyro – a cross between a plane and a helicopter – flew across the English Channel. In Massachusetts in March 1926, Robert Goddard launched the first liquid fuel rocket, and the next year in Germany the Society for Space Flight (VIR) was established with young Werner von Braun as one of its founders.

The start of the 1930s saw the writing on the wall for the oldest form of aviation – the airship, mighty, luxurious and still practically the only way air travel could compete with ocean liners. Britain finally lost faith in lighter-than-air machines in October 1930, when the R101 crashed in France on its maiden voyage to India, killing 48 of the 54 on board, including the Secretary of State for Air and the Director of Civil Aviation. Only the United States and Germany remained in the airship business. Within four years America's *Macon* and *Akron* airships would be destroyed – and with them experiments to turn airships into airborne aircraft carriers – while in 1937, Germany's *Hindenburg* perished in flames as it landed in Lakehurst, New Jersey.

The future of aviation was to be with the descendents of Wright's little Flyer.

»In der Luft gibt es keine Straßen, keine Wasserwege, keinen Punkt, an dem man von einem Gegner sagen kann: ›Wenn er meine Hauptstadt erreichen will, muß er hier vorbeikommen.‹ In der Luft führen alle Richtungen überallhin.«
— H. G. Wells, Der Krieg in den Lüften

Als Wells diese Worte im Jahr 1908 schrieb, waren Flugzeuge gerade erst erfunden, Blériot hatte seinen Flug über den Ärmelkanal noch vor sich, und nur eine Handvoll Menschen hatte eine leise Vorstellung davon, daß Luftmacht einmal ein Faktor in zukünftigen Kriegen sein würde. Zehn Jahre darauf, als der Erste Weltkrieg zu Ende ging, da schien es, als habe sich Wells' Prophezeiung bereits erfüllt: Die Hauptstädte Europas hatten Luftangriffe kennengelernt, und das Bombardieren industrieller Anlagen war längst eine allgemein übliche Strategie. Bei dieser völlig neuen Form des Krieges waren Jäger, Flugabwehrwaffen und Bomber auf eine Weise im Einsatz, die kaum noch etwas mit dem traditionellen Krieg auf den Schlachtfeldern gemein hatte.

Doch wer, von ein paar Visionären wie Wells einmal abgesehen, verstand wirklich, welche Macht in der Luftfahrt schlummerte? Die Politiker gewiß nicht, und auch nicht die kriegsmüde Öffentlichkeit, die Millionen von Toten zu betrauern, Verstümmelte zu versorgen und die Wirtschaft ihrer Länder neu aufzubauen hatte. Der »Krieg, der alle Kriege beendet«, war vorüber, und binnen weniger Monate waren die Luftwaffen der beteiligten Staaten demobilisiert oder, im Falle Deutschlands, durch den Versailler Vertrag aufgelöst worden, und entsprechend schmal fielen die neuen Budgets aus. Gegen die Ansicht, daß Lufteinheiten lediglich den althergebrachten Heeres- und Marineeinheiten Schützenhilfe leisten, hatten sie einen schweren Stand.

In Amerika tobte General William »Billy« Mitchell, der Held von Saint-Mihiel, weil ihm die Mittel gestrichen wurden und die Navy behauptete, Bomber stellten keine Bedrohung für Kriegsschiffe dar. Zwar bewies er 1921 und 1923 seine Ansichten, indem er deutsche Schiffe und Unterseeboote mit Kampfbomben versenkte, doch die U.S.-Marine weigerte sich weiterhin. 1925 kam Mitchell wegen Insubordination vor ein Militärgericht und quittierte den Dienst, doch er predigte die Notwendigkeit einer Luftstreitmacht bis zu seinem Tod elf Jahre später. 1941 bewies der japanische Angriff auf Pearl Harbor auf tragische Weise, daß er recht gehabt hatte. Als Amerika seine Bomber in den Krieg nach Europa schickte, verlieh ihm der Kongreß postum eine Ehrenmedaille.

Selbst die schlagendsten Argumente für eine Luftstreitmacht ließen sich in den zwanziger Jahren nicht durchsetzen. 1921 schrieb der italienische General Giulio Douhet, der »Vater« des modernen Luftkriegs, sein Werk *Die Luftherrschaft*, in dem er darlegt, wie sich durch Bombardierung allein ein Krieg gewinnen ließe; er kam vor ein Militärgericht und wurde in den Ruhestand versetzt, weil er Regierungspolitik kritisiert hatte. Allerdings hatte er mehr Glück als Mitchell. Als Mussolini 1923 an die Macht kam, wurde Douhet rehabilitiert und zum Kommandanten der neugebildeten italienischen Luftwaffe ernannt, der Regia Aeronautica, die das Schwergewicht eher auf Bomber als auf Jagdflugzeuge legen sollte. Die zukünftigen Führer der deutschen Luftwaffe in ihrem geheimen Trainingslager im russischen Lipetsk hingegen verstanden Luftmacht eher als Unterstützung der offensiven Bodentruppe und entwickelten anders als die Engländer und Amerikaner keine strategischen Bomber – eine Fehleinschätzung, von der manche sagen, daß sie Deutschland den Sieg im Zweiten Weltkrieg kostete. Die Franzosen unterhielten in ihrem Bemühen, ihre Stellung als führende Luftfahrernation wiederzuerlangen, die größte Luftstreitmacht Europas, machten jedoch auf allen Seiten Kompromisse, organisierten ihr Fliegerkorps erst 1934 als eigenständige Truppe und stellten ungenügende Mittel für die Entwicklung von Bombern und Jägern zur Verfügung.

Die Entwicklung der Fliegerei zwischen den beiden Kriegen war ganz von dieser Debatte um den militärischen Nutzen geprägt. Wieder ging es um die Grundsatzfrage: Wozu sind Flugzeuge *gut*? Bei Zivilflugzeugen standen Sicherheit, Komfort und geringe Betriebskosten im Vordergrund, wobei die luftgekühlten Sternmotoren der zwanziger Jahre ein großer Fortschritt waren. Doch das waren keine Argumente für das finanziell knapp gehaltene Militär. In Großbritannien waren sich alle einig, daß es die Schrecken des Grabenkriegs kein zweites Mal geben durfte, und da 1922 nur elf Millionen Pfund für die Luftfahrt zur Verfügung standen – 17 Prozent des Budgets für das Kriegsministerium –, entschied man sich für eine Bomberstrategie, obwohl diese Strategie die Zeppelin- und Gotha-Bomber nicht hatte hindern können, britische Städte zu bombardieren und Menschenleben in der Bevölkerung zu fordern. Die Luftmacht als Mittel, den Feind in seinem Inneren zu treffen, wurde damit ausdrücklich anerkannt.

Die Vorstellung eines Bombardements aus der Luft faszi-

Italian leader General Benito Mussolini, seen here in 1935, had long been a fervent believer in air power.

Der Führer Italiens, General Benito Mussolini – hier in einer Aufnahme von 1935 –, war schon seit langem vom Nutzen einer Luftstreitmacht überzeugt.

Le général Benito Mussolini, ici en 1935, a longtemps été un fervent partisan de l'arme aérienne.

nierte und entsetzte ganz Europa. In Frankreich und Italien diskutierte man öffentlich darüber. In Großbritannien, wo es 1932 doppelt so viele Bomber wie Jäger gab, sagte der ehemalige Premierminister Stanley Baldwin im Parlament: »Der Mann auf der Straße muß wissen, daß es keine Macht auf Erden gibt, die ihn schützen kann... die Bomber werden immer durchkommen.«

Baldwin sprach, bevor deutsche Stukas 1936 ihr Terrorbombardement auf Guernica flogen, doch ohne Bomber wäre Großbritannien nicht in der Lage gewesen, Empire und Mandatsgebiete unter Kontrolle zu halten. Die Luftüberwachung Mesopotamiens nach dem Zusammenbruch des Osmanischen Reiches im Jahre 1918 ersparte es der britischen Armee, Tausende von Soldaten dort zu stationieren, und die Royal Air Force bekam damit eine wichtige Aufgabe, mit der sie ihre Existenz rechtfertigen konnte. Von Kurdistan bis zum Jemen – weniger erfolgreich auch in Nordwest-Indien und Afghanistan – wurden kleinere Kriege und Aufstände der Einheimischen von DH-9, Bristol F2b und Fairey IIID-Wasserflugzeugen aus bekämpft, die Bomben warfen, Terrains beharkten oder auf Erkundungsflug gingen. Auch Frankreich, Italien und Belgien setzten Flugzeuge zur Überwachung ihrer Kolonien ein.

Es entstanden sogar eigens Allzweckmaschinen für den Kolonialeinsatz. Die dreimotorige italienische Caproni 101 zum Beispiel diente im Abessinienkrieg als Bomber und zugleich als Transportmaschine. Die CA 133 brachte italienische Fallschirmspringer nach Albanien, und im Afghanistanaufstand von 1928/29 evakuierten die britischen Vickers Victoria-Truppentransporter 586 Zivilisten aus Kabul.

Zur See ignorierte die U.S.-Navy zwar nach wie vor Billy Mitchells Mahnung, eine strategische Luftmacht aufzubauen, doch der Bau von Flugzeugträgern für die Flottenverteidigung begann mit Macht – Ende 1927 wurden die *Saratoga* und die *Lexington* sowie die Entwicklung eines Startkatapultes in Auftrag gegeben. Japan baute in raschem Tempo seine Flugzeugträgerflotte aus; den ersten, die *Hosho*, gab es 1922 in Auftrag, und 1932 wurden mit Maschinen, die von der *Kaga* starteten, chinesische Flugfelder bombardiert.

Für die zivile Welt bedeutete Fliegen mehr als nur ein regelmäßiger Linienverkehr. In Kanada, Rußland und Australien machten stabile Eindecker und kleine Wasserflugzeuge Gegenden zugänglich, die noch nie ein Mensch zuvor gesehen hatte. In Australien wurden Flugzeuge unmittelbar zum Wohle der Menschheit eingesetzt; der Geistliche, Dr. John Flynn,

richtete 1928 in Cloncurry, Queensland, den ersten fliegenden Arzt-Notdienst ein, die »Flying Doctors«. Die Bewohner abgelegener Farmen sandten ihre Hilferufe mit dynamobetriebenen Funkgeräten, und schon im ersten Jahr unternahm der Service mit seinem QANTAS DH50-Doppeldecker 50 Flüge, behandelte 250 Patienten und legte 32.000 Flugkilometer zurück.

Im Laufe des Jahrzehnts gab es weitere technische Neuerungen. Lawrence Sperry, der den ersten automatischen Piloten schon 1912 und das erste automatische Torpedo für die Marine im Jahr 1917 vorgestellt hatte, erfand Kreiselhorizont und Kurskreisel, und Lieutenant James Doolittle unternahm mit Hilfe dieser beiden Geräte 1929 einen Start mit einem Consolidated NY-2-Doppeldecker, flog einen vorher festgelegten Kurs und landete wieder, alles im Blindflug, ohne daß er auch nur einmal zu Boden blickte. Im selben Jahr verkaufte der Amerikaner Edward Link seinen ersten »Link Trainer«, den weltweit ersten elektromechanischen Flugsimulator. Auch neue Wetterdienste leisteten ihren Beitrag zur Flugsicherheit.

Beim Antrieb von Flugzeugen nahmen Alternativen allmählich Formen an. 1924 flog der französische Hubschrauber Oehmichen Nr. 2 erstmals einen Kreis von einem Kilometer, und 1928 überquerte das in Spanien entstandene »Autogiro« von Cierva – ein Mittelding zwischen Flugzeug und Helikopter – den Ärmelkanal. Im März 1926 startete Robert Goddard die erste Rakete mit Flüssigtreibstoff, und im folgenden Jahr entstand in Deutschland der Verein für Raumschiffahrt (VfR), zu dessen Gründern der junge Wernher von Braun gehörte.

Zugleich war mit dem Beginn der dreißiger Jahre die Uhr für die älteste Form der Luftfahrt abgelaufen: die Luftschiffe – ehrfurchtgebietend, luxuriös, konnten den Ozeanriesen als einzige weiterhin Paroli bieten. In Großbritannien verlor man im Oktober 1930 endgültig den Glauben an Fluggeräte, die leichter waren als Luft, als die R101 auf ihrem Jungfernflug nach Indien in Frankreich abstürzte, wobei 48 der 54 Insassen umkamen, darunter der Luftfahrtminister und der Direktor des Zivilluftfahrtwesens. Nur die Vereinigten Staaten und Deutschland setzten nun noch auf Luftschiffe. Binnen der nächsten vier Jahre verunglückten die amerikanische *Macon* und die *Akron* – was zugleich auch das Ende der Experimente mit Luftschiffen als fliegende Flugzeugträger bedeutete –, und 1937 ging die deutsche *Hindenburg* bei der Landung in Lakehurst, New Jersey, in Flammen auf.

Die Zukunft der Luftfahrt lag bei den Nachfahren der zerbrechlichen Flyer der Brüder Wright.

Brigadier-General Billy Mitchell was America's most passionate supporter of air power, but lost his job in 1925.

Brigadier-General Billy Mitchell setzte sich in Amerika sehr für den Aufbau einer Luftstreitmacht ein, verlor jedoch 1925 seine Stellung.

Le général de brigade américain Billy Mitchell, l'un des plus chauds partisans de l'aviation, fut limogé en 1925.

*«Il n'y a ni rues, ni canaux, ni lieux dans le ciel qui permettent
de dire d'un adversaire ‹S'il veut atteindre ma capitale, il doit
passer par là›. Dans les airs, tous les chemins mènent à Rome»*
– H. G. Wells, *La Guerre du Ciel*

À l'époque où Wells écrit ces lignes, en 1908, l'aéroplane vient à peine d'être inventé, Blériot n'a pas
encore traversé la Manche et seul un petit nombre
de gens ont une vague idée de ce qu'est une force
aérienne. Dix ans plus tard, alors que la Première Guerre
mondiale s'achève brusquement, il semble que la vision de
Wells soi devenue réalité : les capitales de l'Europe ont subi
des attaques aériennes, et le bombardement de cibles industrielles a procédé d'une stratégie bien définie. Ce phénomène
totalement nouveau a vu mettre en œuvre des chasseurs, des
bombardiers et canons antiaériens dans des opérations assez
différentes de celles du champ de bataille traditionnel.

Mais qui, à l'exception de quelques visionnaires comme
Wells, a réellement compris l'énorme puissance de l'aviation ?
Ni les politiciens, qui devaient reconstruire toute l'économie,
ni les populations, qui avaient pleuré des millions de morts et
des soldats estropiés à vie. La «der' des der'» terminée, les
forces aériennes des nations combattantes, avec des budgets
réduits drastiquement, étaient soit décimées par la démobilisation soit interdites par le traité de Versailles, et devaient
lutter pour faire admettre qu'elles pouvaient avoir un tout autre rôle que le simple soutien des opérations terrestres et maritimes.

Aux États-Unis, le général William «Billy» Mitchell, héros
de l'assaut du saillant de Saint-Mihiel, rendu furieux par les
réductions budgétaires et par l'aveuglement de la Marine américaine, pour laquelle les bombardiers ne constituaient pas
une menace pour les navires, contre-attaqua en 1921 et 1923
en faisant couler plusieurs anciens navires et sous-marins allemands par ses chasseur-bombardiers devant un aréopage de
généraux. La Marine s'entêta et le fit traduire et dégrader en
cours martiale pour insubordination en 1925. Il mourut 11 ans
plus tard, n'ayant jamais cessé de prêcher l'évangile de l'arme
aérienne, vengé tragiquement par l'attaque japonaise sur Pearl
Harbour en 1941. Le Congrès américain lui décerna alors la
Médaille d'honneur à titre posthume, pendant que les États-
Unis envoyait ses bombardiers combattre en Europe.

Dans les années 1920, les arguments les plus persuasifs en
faveur de la force aérienne avaient du mal à être acceptés. En
1921, le général italien Giulio Douhet, «père» idéologique
d'une force aérienne indépendante, écrit dans *La Maîtrise de
l'air* que le seul bombardier peut gagner la guerre future ; traduit lui aussi en cours martiale, il sera dégradé pour avoir critiqué la politique du gouvernement. Il eut en revanche plus de
chance que Mitchell car, lorsqu'il prit le pouvoir en 1923, Mussolini rappela Douhet pour commander l'armée de l'air italienne récemment créée, la Regia Aeronautica, dans laquelle
les bombardiers allaient primer sur les chasseurs. Les futurs
chefs de la Luftwaffe allemande, installés dans leur base secrète de Lipetsk (Russie), préférèrent s'appuyer sur le soutien
aérien tactique des troupes offensives sans trop se soucier de
développer des bombardiers stratégiques, au contraire des Britanniques et des Américains. Cette erreur, selon certains, fit
perdre la Seconde Guerre mondiale à l'Allemagne. La France,
déterminée à reprendre un rôle dominant dans l'aviation, s'efforça de maintenir la plus importante armée de l'air d'Europe
mais en se dispersant sur trop de fronts ; elle n'accorda l'autonomie à sa force aérienne qu'en 1934, laissant le financement
et le développement de ses bombardiers et de ses chasseurs
tomber à des niveaux inacceptables.

Dans le débat crucial pour l'avenir de l'aviation dans l'entre-deux-guerres, se posait de nouveau la question fondamentale : à quoi servent les aéroplanes ? Si les appareils civils construits à l'époque offraient de plus en plus de sécurité, de confort et de rentabilité, grâce notamment à l'amélioration du moteur en étoile à refroidissement par air dans les années 1920,
cela ne résolvait en rien les problèmes financiers des militaires. La Grande-Bretagne, très influencée par la volonté nationale de ne pas voir se répéter les horreurs de la guerre de tranchées, et n'accordant au budget des forces aériennes que 11
millions de livres en 1922 – 17 pour cent du budget total de la
Défense –, se prononça en faveur des bombardiers. Même s'ils
n'avaient pu empêcher les Zeppelins et les Gotha de bombarder les villes et de tuer les civils, ils permettraient de frapper
le cœur de l'ennemi.

L'idée du bombardement aérien horrifiait et fascinait à la
fois les Européens. Des débats publics s'ouvrirent en France et
en Italie, tandis qu'en Grande-Bretagne, où on comptait deux
fois plus de bombardiers que de chasseurs en 1932, l'ancien
Premier ministre Stanley Baldwin déclarait à la Chambre des
Communes : «Je pense qu'il est bon que l'homme de la rue
comprenne qu'aucune puissance terrestre ne peut le protéger… les bombardiers passeront toujours à travers.»

Robert Goddard, here with an early
rocket in 1909, went on to become
America's foremost developer of
liquid-fuel rockets.

Robert Goddard, hier mit einem
Versuchsmodell von 1909, war
Amerikas führender Experte für
Flüssigtreibstoff-Raketen.

L'Américain Robert Goddard,
posant ici en 1909 avec une de
ses premières fusées, allait devenir
le principal concepteur des fusées
à carburant liquide.

En 1936, les bombardiers allemands Stuka anéantissaient Guernica! Sans ces bombardiers, la Grande-Bretagne n'aurait pu assumer avec autant de succès la police de l'Empire et de ses territoires sous mandat. Le contrôle des airs en Mésopotamie à la suite de l'effondrement de l'Empire ottoman en 1918 n'évita pas seulement à l'armée britannique de déployer des milliers de troupes mais fut l'occasion pour la RAF de démontrer son rôle vital de défense et d'avoir une raison supplémentaire d'exister. Du Kurdistan au Yémen – avec moins de réussite au nord-ouest de l'Inde et en Afghanistan – les guérillas et les insurrections des tribus rebelles furent ainsi réprimées grâce à l'action des hydravions DH-9, Bristol F2b et Fairey IIID, bombardant, mitraillant et repérant les troupes au sol. Suivant l'exemple de la Grande-Bretagne, la France, l'Italie et la Belgique se servirent également de l'aviation pour contrôler leurs colonies.

Certains appareils étaient conçus uniquement pour ces opérations de «police» et les missions utilitaires. Le trimoteur italien Caproni 101, par exemple, servit à la fois au bombardement et au ravitaillement lors de la campagne d'Abyssinie; le CA 133 transporta les parachutistes italiens dans l'invasion de l'Albanie; et les transports de troupe Vickers Victoria britanniques permirent d'évacuer 586 civils de Kaboul lors de la rébellion afghane de 1928–1929.

En mer, négligeant toujours les avertissements de Billy Mitchell, l'US Navy poursuivit son programme de construction de porte-avions avec la mise en service du *Saratoga* et du *Lexington* fin 1927 et en faisant améliorer le système de catapulte. Le Japon s'empressa également d'organiser ses transports, commanda en 1922 son premier porte-avions, le *Hosho*, et exerça ses pilotes dès 1932 en leur faisant bombarder les aérodromes chinois à partir du porte-avions *Kaga*.

Dans le domaine civil, l'aviation ne se contentait pas des gros avions de ligne volant sur des routes régulières mais se créait des activités nouvelles: au Canada, en Russie et en Australie, de robustes petits monoplans et des hydravions découvraient des territoires jusque-là inexplorés, tandis qu'en 1928, le révérend John Flynn, un médecin, inaugurait la première base des «Flying Doctors» à Cloncurry, au Queensland (Australie). Grâce à des radios à magnéto disséminées dans des fermes isolées, le «Médecin volant» et son biplan QANTAS DH50, totalisèrent dès la première année 50 vols pour 32 000 km parcourus et 250 patients visités.

L'aviation progressait également dans le domaine technique, ou améliorait d'anciennes inventions. Lawrence Sperry, qui avait présenté le premier pilote automatique en 1912 et la première torpille radio-commandée pour la marine en 1917, perfectionna les systèmes d'horizon gyroscopique artificiel et de gyroscope directionnel. En 1929, ces instruments permirent au lieutenant James Doolittle de décoller dans un biplan Consolidated NY-2, de suivre une route déterminée et d'atterrir sans visibilité et sans référence au sol. La même année, l'Américain Edward Link commercialisait le Link, premier simulateur de vol électromécanique du monde. La mise en place de nouveaux services météorologiques améliora aussi la sécurité des vols.

De nouveaux moyens de propulsion voyaient le jour. En 1924, le Français Oehmichen N° 2 est le premier à avoir parcouru un kilomètre sur son hélicoptère; en 1928, l'autogire – mi-avion mi-hélicoptère – de l'Espagnol Cierva traverse la Manche. Dans le Massachusetts, en mars 1926, Robert Goddard lance la première fusée à combustible liquide et, l'année suivante, en Allemagne, le jeune Werner von Braun et quelques autres créent la Société pour le Vol Spatial (VIR).

Au début des années 1930, on assiste à la fin d'un des plus anciens moyens de locomotion aérienne – le puissant et luxueux dirigeable, pratiquement le seul à avoir pu concurrencer les grands paquebots. La Grande-Bretagne renonce finalement aux «plus légers que l'air» en octobre 1930, lorsque le R101 s'écrase en France au début de son voyage inaugural en Inde; 48 de ses 54 passagers à bord, y compris le Secrétaire d'État pour l'Aviation et le directeur de l'Aviation civile britanniques, y trouveront la mort. Seuls les États-Unis et l'Allemagne vont conserver un temps des dirigeables. L'aventure s'achèvera en l'espace de quatre ans avec la disparition des dirigeables américains *Macon* et *Akron* – provoquant l'abandon des essais pour en faire des «porte-avions aériens» – et du dernier zeppelin géant, l'*Hindenburg* allemand, disparu dans les flammes à son atterrissage dans le Lakehurst, New Jersey, en 1937.

L'avenir de l'aviation allait désormais se construire avec les descendants du petit Flyer des Wright.

The end of an era in passenger-carrying airships came with the *Hindenburg* disaster in Lakehurst, New Jersey, in May 1937.

Das Ende eines Zeitalters der Passagierluftfahrt: Die *Hindenburg* geht im Mai 1937 in Lakehurst, New Jersey, in Flammen auf.

Le désastre du *Hindenburg* à Lakehurst, New Jersey, en mai 1937, marqua la fin de l'époque des dirigeables.

Air power

In 1919, a few British DH-9 bombers routed the 'Mad Mullah of Somaliland' in three weeks, an outcome not achieved by the British army in 20 years. It was a small demonstration of what the RAF was capable of. But the idea that it could control the newly mandated Mesopotamia was not enough in the face of traditionalists and budget cuts. To prove its point the RAF held its first public annual air show at Hendon, near London, in 1920, and the next year put on a spectacular bombing show at Hendon against a mocked-up village (**1**).

Luftmacht

Im Jahr 1919 schlug die britische Luftwaffe mit einigen wenigen DH-9-Bombern die somalischen Aufständischen (»Mad Mullah of Somaliland«) – etwas, was die Army zwanzig Jahre lang vergebens versucht hatte. Es war eine kleine Vorführung dessen, wozu die Royal Air Force in der Lage war. Doch nicht einmal die Tatsache, daß sie das neue Mandatsgebiet Mesopotamien unter Kontrolle halten konnte, hinderte die Traditionalisten daran, ihr weiter die Mittel zu kürzen. Um zu zeigen, worauf es ankam, veranstaltete die RAF 1920 die erste ihrer jährlichen Luftfahrtschauen in Hendon bei London, und im folgenden Jahr gab es einen spektakulären Bombenangriff auf eine eigens aufgebaute Dorfattrappe (**1**).

Force aérienne

En 1919, quelques bombardiers britanniques DH-9 mirent en déroute le «Mollah fou du Somaliland» en trois semaines, un résultat que l'armée britannique n'avait pas obtenu depuis 20 ans et qui démontra ce dont la RAF était capable. Cela ne suffit toutefois pas à obtenir des crédits et à convaincre le gouvernement et les militaires traditionalistes, qu'elle pouvait assurer seule le contrôle de la Mésopotamie, nouveau territoire sous mandat britannique. Pour tenter de démontrer sa puissance, la RAF organisa en 1920 sa première démonstration publique annuelle à Hendon (Londres) où, l'année suivante, elle mit en scène un spectaculaire exercice de bombardement sur un village de décor (**1**).

1

Parachutes finally acceptable

More than 6,000 British flyers were estimated to have died in World War I because they were not provided with parachutes, partly because it was thought they would not attempt to save their aircraft if allowed to jump. France felt similarly, Germany less so. By 1928 safe new parachutes were available and in that year all RAF aircrew were required to carry them. Training was done from the wing-tip of a Vickers Virginia bomber in 1934 (**1**), in groups at Henlow, Bedfordshire, in 1931 (**2**) and from a light plane using a seat chute (**3**).

Endlich Fallschirme

Man schätzt, daß über 6.000 britische Flieger im Ersten Weltkrieg umkamen, weil sie nicht mit Fallschirmen ausgerüstet waren – nicht zuletzt weil die Vorgesetzten davon ausgingen, daß sie nicht versuchen würden, die Maschinen zu retten, wenn sie springen durften. In Frankreich war die Lage ähnlich, in Deutschland hatte es teils Fallschirme gegeben. Inzwischen waren neue, sichere Modelle entwickelt, und 1928 wurde es für das fliegende Personal der RAF Vorschrift, Fallschirme zu tragen. Die Bilder zeigen die Ausbildung: 1934 auf der Flügelspitze eines Vickers Virginia-Bombers (**1**), 1931 in Henlow, Bedfordshire, in Gruppen (**2**) und von einem Leichtflugzeug aus dem Sitz heraus (**3**).

Enfin des parachutes

On estime que plus de 6 000 aviateurs britanniques furent tués pendant la Première Guerre mondiale parce qu'ils ne disposaient pas de parachute. Les militaires britanniques et français, ainsi que certains Allemands, pensaient que les pilotes ne chercheraient pas à sauver leur appareil s'ils pouvaient sauter. L'apparition de nouveaux parachutes plus sûrs en 1928 incita la RAF à en équiper tous ses hommes, que l'on voit sauter ici à l'exercice en 1931 au-dessus de Henlow (Bedfordshire) (**2**). En 1934, l'entraînement s'effectuait en sautant depuis l'extrémité de l'aile d'un bombardier Vickers Virginia (**1**) ou depuis un avion léger (**3**).

3

Popular military flying

By 1926 military air shows were appreciated by the British
public, and also served as a training goal for the RAF's ground
and air crews. Thousands watched 'evolution flying' at Hendon,
near London, that year (**2**), while on the ground a huge new
bomber was placed next to a tiny tailless craft (**1**).

Ein Publikumsmagnet

1926 waren Luftfahrtschauen in England längst eine beliebte
Freizeitattraktion, und Luft- und Bodenpersonal der RAF
trainierten dafür, um zu zeigen, was sie konnten. In jenem
Jahr verfolgten Tausende den Formationsflug in Hendon (**2**),
und am Boden ist ein mächtiger neuer Bomber gleich neben
einem winzigen leitwerklosen Modell zu sehen (**1**).

Spectacles militaires

Les shows aériens militaires, toujours appréciés du public
britannique, servent également à l'entraînement des équipes
au sol et des aviateurs de la RAF. En 1926, des milliers de
personnes assistent à leurs évolutions à Hendon (**2**), où étaient
présentés un nouveau grand bombardier et un petit appareil
sans empennage (**1**).

2

1

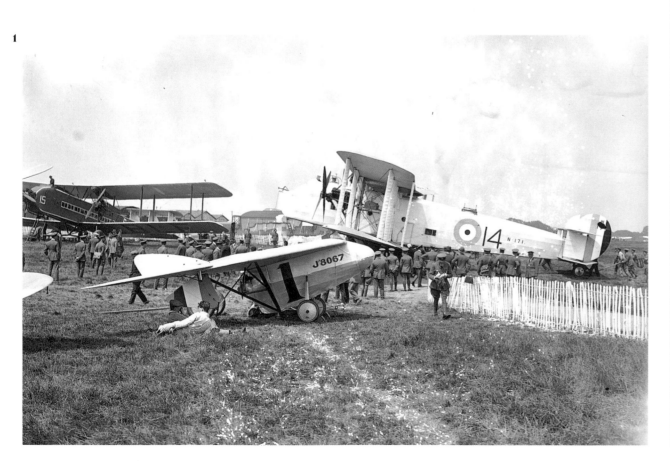

Bomber power

The French Armée de l'Air kept a balance between fighters and bombers, but British strategy gave considerably more importance to bombers in the inter-war years. With a third more aircraft, bomber crews had more of a public image than fighter pilots. The British were strapped for cash and equipment, however; the Vickers Virginia bomber (**2**, with scout planes) was outdated by 1928 compared with the French Farman. The Virginia could carry up to 3,000lb of bombs (**1**).

Bomberkraft

Die französische Armée de l'Air strebte ein Gleichgewicht zwischen Bombern und Jägern an, während die britische Strategie in den Jahren zwischen den Kriegen das Schwergewicht auf die Bomberflotte legte. Mit einem Drittel mehr an Maschinen genossen auch die Bomberpiloten in der Öffentlichkeit mehr Ansehen als die Jagdflieger. Allerdings waren in England Geld und Ausrüstung knapp; die Vickers Virginia-Bomber (**2**, mit Begleitflugzeugen) waren 1928 im Vergleich zu den französischen Farman veraltet. Die Virginia konnte bis zu 1.400 Kilogramm Bombenlast tragen (**1**).

Bombardiers

Dans l'entre-deux-guerres, l'Armée de l'Air française conserva une certaine parité entre chasseurs et bombardiers, alors que les stratèges britanniques accordaient une plus grande importance à ces derniers. Avec un tiers d'appareils en plus, leurs équipages étaient plus célèbres dans le public que les pilotes de chasse. Les Britanniques manquaient cependant d'argent et de matériel, comme en témoignent ces bombardiers Vickers Virginia (**2**, posés près d'avions de reconnaissance), déjà dépassés en 1928 comparés aux Farman français. Le Virginia pouvait emporter jusqu'à 1400 kg de bombes (**1**).

Pax Britannica Aeronautica

All imperial nations used aircraft in the war-weary 1920s and 30s to police their territories, but the British went further than any other. In Mesopotamia (Iraq) in 1922 they installed eight squadrons of planes to patrol and warn rebellious tribes, using armoured car squadrons to back them up. The RAF was less successful in India's North-West Territories. Some bombers also served as transports, such as the Vickers Valentias near Cairo in 1935 (**1**). Personnel served five-year tours without their families in many remote locations, and established a closeness not exceeded even in World War II.

Pax Britannica Aeronautica

Alle Kolonialmächte setzten in den kriegsmüden zwanziger und dreißiger Jahren Flugzeuge ein, um ihre Territorien zu kontrollieren, doch keine war dabei so konsequent wie Großbritannien. 1922 wurden acht Staffeln in Mesopotamien (dem heutigen Irak) stationiert, wo sie Patrouillenflüge unternahmen und aufrührerische Stämme in Schach hielten; dazu wurden sie von Bodentruppen in Panzerfahrzeugen unterstützt. Der Einsatz der RAF in den Nordwest-Territorien Indiens war weniger erfolgreich. Manche Bomber wurden auch als Transporter eingesetzt, wie hier 1935 die Vickers Valentia-Maschinen bei Kairo (**1**). Die Soldaten dienten fünf Jahre lang an oft sehr abgelegenen Orten, fern von ihren Familien, und die Kameradschaft, die sich dabei entwickelte, wurde nicht einmal im Zweiten Weltkrieg übertroffen.

Pax Britannica Aeronautica

Si toutes les nations coloniales se servirent de l'aviation dans les années 1920 et 1930 pour la surveillance de leurs territoires, la Grande-Bretagne l'utilisa plus que les autres. En 1922, elle installa huit escadrilles en Mésopotamie (Irak) pour des missions de patrouille et de prévention contre les tribus rebelles, soutenues par des escadrons blindés. La RAF eut moins de réussite dans les territoires du Nord-Ouest de l'Inde. Certains bombardiers servirent également au transport, comme ces Vickers Valentia au Caire en 1935 (**1**). Le service de cinq ans que devaient effectuer les aviateurs, sans leur famille et dans de nombreuses garnisons éloignées, instaura entre eux une intimité qui ne fut jamais retrouvée, même pendant la Seconde Guerre mondiale.

American air power

The United States, the sleeping giant of aviation, kept a low profile during the 1920s, its Army Air Corps essentially the handmaiden of army generals. The crews trained from these BT-7s at Randolph Field, Texas, in the early 1930s mostly went on to observation and 'pursuit' planes (1). At one point the USAAC had only one squadron of Martin bombers. The US Navy experimented with laying smoke from flying boats at Anacostia, Maryland (2).

Luftmacht Amerika

Der schlafende Riese der Fliegerei, die Vereinigten Staaten, regte sich in den zwanziger Jahren nur wenig, und das Army Air Corps war kaum mehr als eine Hilfstruppe der Armeegenerale. Die Piloten, die in den frühen dreißiger Jahren auf dem Flugfeld von Randolph, Texas, auf BT-7-Maschinen ausgebildet wurden, flogen später Aufklärungs- und Jagdflugzeuge (1). Zeitweise verfügte das USAAC über nur eine einzige Staffel Martin-Bomber. Die U.S.-Navy experimentierte in Anacostia, Maryland, mit künstlichem Nebel, der von Flugbooten gelegt wurde (2).

Forces aériennes américaines

Les États-Unis, géant endormi de l'aviation, conservent un profil bas pendant les années 1920, leur Armée de l'Air effectuant essentiellement des missions d'assistance des autres armes et l'USSAC ne disposant même, à un moment, que d'une seule escadrille de bombardiers Martin. Les équipages entraînés sur ces BT-7 à Randolph Field (Texas) au début des années 1930 étaient souvent affectés sur des avions d'observation et de «recherche» (1). La US Navy expérimenta la technique d'enfumage par hydravions à Anacostia, dans le Maryland (2).

Defiant air chief

Brigadier General William Mitchell (**2**), head of America's air service, fought vainly to prove the value of air power. A Martin bomber dropping a torpedo in 1920 (**4**), the sinking of the captured German battleship *Ostfriesland* by 2,000lb bombs in 1921 (**3**) and then destruction of the old USS *Alabama* (**1**) all failed to change navy minds. Court-martialled and dismissed in 1925, he was finally vindicated by Pearl Harbor, 1941.

Der trotzige Luftwaffenchef

Brigadegeneral William Mitchell (**2**), Kommandierender der amerikanischen Luftflotte, mühte sich vergebens, seine Vorgesetzten vom Nutzen einer Luftstreitmacht zu überzeugen. Weder der Martin-Bomber, der 1920 ein Torpedo abwarf (**4**), noch die Versenkung des gekaperten deutschen Schlachtschiffes *Ostfriesland* mit 900 Kilogramm Bomben (**3**) und anschließend die Zerstörung des ausgemusterten USS *Alabama* (**1**) brachte die Stellung der Navy ins Wanken. Mitchell kam 1925 vor ein Militärgericht und mußte seinen Abschied nehmen, doch Pearl Harbor gab ihm 1941 recht.

Le défi de Mitchell

Le général de brigade William Mitchell (**2**), chef de l'armée de l'air américaine, lutta en vain pour démontrer les qualités des forces aériennes. Ni ce bombardier Martin larguant une torpille en 1920 (**4**), ni le naufrage de l'*Ostfriesland*, un ancien navire allemand, coulé par des bombes de 900 kg (**3**), ni même la destruction du vieil USS *Alabama* (**1**) ne modifièrent l'état d'esprit de la Marine. Traduit en cours martiale et destitué en 1925, Mitchell fut tragiquement vengé par l'attaque japonaise sur Pearl Harbor en 1941.

Vertical hopes

Despite advances in all directions, vertical lift remained a mystery throughout the 1920s. Raoul Pescara's 16-bladed helicopter (2) was perhaps the best effort, flying half a mile at Issy-les-Moulineaux, Paris, in 1924, but it was not until Igor Sikorsky's VS-300 of the late 1930s that anti-torque rear rotors made helicopters a practical proposition. Meanwhile, Juan de la Cierva of Spain produced a good autogyro – half plane, half helicopter – which was tested at Farnborough, England, in 1925 (1). He flew it all over Europe in 1928 (3).

In die Vertikale?

In den zwanziger Jahren gab es Fortschritte an allen Fronten, doch die Probleme des vertikalen Fluges blieben ungelöst. Raoul Pescaras 16blättriger Helikopter war vielleicht der vielversprechendste Versuch und flog 1924 in Issy-les-Moulineaux bei Paris immerhin 800 Meter weit (2), doch erst Ende der dreißiger Jahre bekam Igor Sikorsky mit dem Heckrotor seines VS-300 die Drehung um die Mittelachse in den Griff und machte Hubschrauber praktikabel. Inzwischen stellte der Spanier Juan de la Cierva ein gutes Drehflügelflugzeug vor – den Autogiro, halb Flugzeug, halb Helikopter. Er testete es 1925 im englischen Farnborough (1) und war 1928 damit überall in Europa unterwegs (3).

Des sauts en l'air

Malgré les progrès réalisés dans divers domaines, le vol vertical resta inaccessible pendant les années 1920. L'hélicoptère à 16 pales de Raoul Pescara (2), qui parcourut 800 m à Issy-les-Moulineaux en 1924, marque une avancée certaine mais ce n'est pas avant le VS-300 d'Igor Sikorsky, à la fin des années 1930, et l'invention du rotor de queue que l'hélicoptère devint une réalité. Entre-temps, l'Espagnol Juan de la Cierva avait construit un autogiro – mi-avion, mi-hélicoptère –dont la viabilité fut testée à Farnborough en 1925 (1) avant qu'il ne parte effectuer une tournée de démonstration en Europe en 1928 (3).

2

3

Naval air power

The US Navy developed a naval air arm for fleet protection in the 1920s,
consisting largely of fighters and observation planes. A seaplane was
launched from the deck of the USS *Tennessee* off Los Angeles in 1926 (1),
two years after the navy's first aircraft carrier, the USS *Langley* (3), joined a
show of naval air strength off Baltimore. Britain tried out a small Parnall
seaplane launched from submarine M2 in 1931, but the submarine was lost
when the hangar door failed (2).

Luftmacht zur See

Die US-Navy baute in den zwanziger Jahren zum Schutz der Flotte eine
Luftstreitmacht hauptsächlich aus Jägern und Aufklärern auf. 1926 startete vor Los Angeles ein Wasserflugzeug vom Deck der USS *Tennessee* (1);
zwei Jahre zuvor hatte der erste amerikanische Flugzeugträger, die USS
Langley, bei einer Marineparade vor Baltimore Stärke gezeigt (3). In England versuchte man 1931, ein kleines Parnall-Wasserflugzeug vom U-Boot
M2 aus zu starten, doch das U-Boot ging verloren, als die Hangartür sich
nicht schloß (2).

L'aéronavale

C'est dans les années 1920 que la Marine américaine met en place une force
aéronavale, essentiellement représentée par des chasseurs et des avions
d'observation, pour la protection de la flotte. Cet hydravion est lancé au
large de Los Angeles depuis le pont de l'USS *Tennessee* en 1926 (1), deux
ans après que le premier porte-avions américain, l'USS *Langley* (3), a
participé à un défilé des forces aéronavales à Baltimore. En 1931, la Grande-
Bretagne fit des essais d'hydravion Parnall embarqué sur un sous-marin M2,
qui sombra à la suite d'une rupture de la porte du «hangar» (2).

Ill-fated airship

Unlike its privately-built sister airship the R100, Britain's R101 had a troubled history. Government-designed, built to link the empire in 1929, it was overweight and overbudget and its dining room did not compare to that of the R100 (**2**). In 1930 it was lengthened to 777 feet, two new gas cells installed and its heavy engines replaced. It was a magnificent sight in its shed at Cardington, Bedfordshire, on 3 October 1930 (**1**).

Das Unglücksschiff

Anders als sein privat gebautes Schwesterschiff R100 war dem britischen Luftschiff R101 kein glückliches Schicksal beschieden. Das 1929 von staatlichen Stellen gebaute Schiff sollte die Verkehrsverbindungen im Empire verbessern, doch es geriet zu schwer und zu teuer, und konnte sich trotzdem nicht mit dem Speisesaal des R100 messen (**2**). 1930 wurde es um zwei Gaszellen auf 237 Meter verlängert, und die schweren Motoren wurden ersetzt. Es ist ein prachtvoller Anblick, wie es am 3. Oktober 1930 in seiner Halle in Cardington, Bedfordshire, liegt (**1**).

Un dirigeable infortuné

Contrairement à son «jumeau» le R100, construit sur fonds privés, le R101 britannique eut une histoire troublée. Commandé par le gouvernement pour desservir l'Empire en 1929, ce magnifique dirigeable, que l'on voit ici le 3 octobre 1930 dans son hangar de Cardington (Bedfordshire) (**1**) se révéla trop lourd et trop cher, avec une salle à manger qui ne pouvait se comparer à celle du R100 (**2**). En 1930, sa longueur fut portée à 237 m par l'adjonction de deux nouveaux compartiments à gaz en même temps que l'on remplaçait ses trop gros moteurs.

Last of a breed

At 1.07am on 5 October 1930, on its maiden voyage to India, the R101 suddenly dived twice, the second time striking a low ridge at Beauvais, northern France. The engines were forced up into the gas bags and 5,000,000 cubic feet of hydrogen exploded. Only six of the 54 people on board survived the wreckage (**1**, **2**). Britain's airship programme was ended and the sister ship R100 scrapped.

Das letzte seiner Art

Um 1 Uhr 07 morgens am 5. Oktober 1930 verlor die R101 auf ihrem Jungfernflug nach Indien plötzlich zweimal an Höhe, und das zweite Mal schlug sie auf eine flache Hügelkette bei Beauvais in Nordfrankreich auf. Die Motoren wurden in die Gaszellen gedrückt, und 140.000 Kubikmeter Wasserstoff explodierten. Nur sechs der 54 Menschen an Bord überlebten den Absturz (**1**, **2**). Damit war die Epoche der Luftschiffahrt für Großbritannien zu Ende, und das Schwesterschiff R100 wurde abgewrackt.

La fin d'une époque

C'est à 1 h 07 du matin, le 5 octobre 1930, au début de son voyage inaugural aux Indes, que le R101 partit brutalement deux fois en piqué et heurta une colline basse près de Beauvais. Les moteurs crevèrent alors l'enveloppe en faisant exploser les 140 000 m³ d'hydrogène. Seuls six des 54 personnes à bord survécurent à l'accident (**1**, **2**). Le programme de dirigeables anglais fut interrompu et le R100 envoyé à la ferraille.

How to buy or license a picture from this book

The pictures in this book are drawn from the extensive archives of The Hulton Getty Picture Collection, originally formed in 1947 as the Hulton Press Library. The Collection contains approximately 15 million images, some of which date from the earliest days of photography. It includes original material from leading press agencies – Topical Press, Keystone, Central Press, Fox Photos and General Photographic Agency as well as from *Picture Post*, the *Daily Express* and the *Evening Standard*. Many of the photographs published in *Aviation: The Early Years* were rediscovered in the research for this book.

Picture Licensing Information
To license Hulton Getty pictures please call Getty Images + 44 171 544 3333 or email **info@getty-images.com** your picture selection with the page/reference numbers.

Getty Online
All of the pictures reproduced here and countless others are available via Getty Online at:
http://www.getty-images.com

Buying a print
For details of how to purchase exhibition-quality prints call The Hulton Getty Picture Gallery
+ 44 171 376 4525.